RACIAL EROTICS

RACIAL
EROTICS

GAY MEN OF COLOR, SEXUAL RACISM,
AND THE POLITICS OF DESIRE

C. Winter Han

UNIVERSITY OF WASHINGTON PRESS

Seattle

Design by Katrina Noble
Composed in Adobe Caslon Pro, typeface designed by Carol Twombly

25 24 23 22 21   5 4 3 2 1

Printed and bound in the United States of America

UNIVERSITY OF WASHINGTON PRESS
uwapress.uw.edu

LIBRARY OF CONGRESS CATALOGING-IN-PUBLICATION DATA
Names: Han, C. Winter, 1968– author.
Title: Racial erotics : gay men of color, sexual racism, and the politics of desire / C. Winter Han.
Description: Seattle : University of Washington Press, [2021] | Includes bibliographical references and index.
Identifiers: LCCN 2020053130 (print) | LCCN 2020053131 (ebook) | ISBN 9780295749082 (hardcover) | ISBN 9780295749099 (paperback) | ISBN 9780295749105 (ebook)
Subjects: LCSH: Gay men—Identity. | Whites—Race identity. | Blacks—Race identity. | Racism.
Classification: LCC HQ 76.25 .H346 2021 (print) | LCC HQ 76.25 (ebook) | DDC 306.76/62—dc23
LC record available at https://lccn.loc.gov/2020053130
LC ebook record available at https://lccn.loc.gov/2020053131

The paper used in this publication is acid free and meets the minimum requirements of American National Standard for Information Sciences—Permanence of Paper for Printed Library Materials, ANSI Z39.48–1984.∞

CONTENTS

ACKNOWLEDGMENTS

In the mid-2000s, while working on what later became my first book, *Geisha of a Different Kind: Race and Sexuality in Gaysian America*, I stumbled across a call for papers for a collected volume on intersectionality. It's been so long now that I forget the particulars of the call, but I remember being intrigued by it. Perhaps not so much at the call itself, but for the opportunity to take a break from the book while simultaneously addressing a nagging thought about a theme that didn't quite seem to fit the book but was evident throughout. As I was working on *Geisha of a Different Kind*, it was clear that whiteness was embedded in gay communities in deeply intimate ways. Yet writing a book about the experiences of gay Asian men, I was only able to touch briefly on the role that whiteness plays in gay life. So it was a relief to be able to write and submit a piece in response to the call I'd happened on because it gave me both an outlet to gather my thoughts on whiteness in gay communities and a short break from working on the book. But by the time I completed "They Don't Want to Cruise Your Type: Gay Men of Color and the Racial Politics of Exclusion," the deadline for the collection had long passed, and eager to share what I'd written, I started looking for a home for it.

To say that I had a difficult time finding such a home would be an understatement. Some of the comments I received from editors were encouraging. One editor "loved" the article but said that it just didn't fit the journal, a journal focusing on race. That was the way it sometimes was back then; journals that focused on race weren't particularly interested in queer topics, and journals that focused on sexuality often weren't interested in race. Other outlets were not as nice or encouraging. At one journal, the infamous Reviewer Two wrote, "This paper does not deserve to be published in this, or any other, journal." Ouch!

But eventually, the piece found its way to *Social Identities*. And it hit a chord. It soon became the most cited article in the journal and stayed the most cited article (based on a three-year moving average) for a decade. As of today, it is one of the most highly cited articles on racism in the gay community and has been reprinted in a widely read anthology. I guess it did deserve to be published "somewhere," and apparently, more than once. In a way, the article allowed me to close out *Geisha of a Different Kind* by giving me the outlet to write more specifically about whiteness in gay communities. At the same time, it opened up a whole new set of questions. Questions that then followed me and eventually led to this book. So it seems fitting now that I return to the article that closed my intellectual journey with *Geisha of a Different Kind* to start this new one.

That specific academic journey has been eventful. Like most such journeys, it has been filled with moments of frustration and happiness, some wins, some losses. This particular journey began at the University of Connecticut, and I want to start by thanking Nancy Naples, mentor and friend extraordinaire. Nancy's comments and suggestions were always thoughtfully and gracefully given, more encouragement than criticism, and her gentle prodding about its progress were much needed at different points of that journey. Needless to say, this project would not have been completed without her patient and steady support. I would also like to thank Marysol Ascencio and Debanuj DasGupa for their close reading and their gracious and generous comments. The book is much better because of them. I would also like to thank Mary Bernstein and Matthew Hughey who helped launch the project in its early stages. Much love to my UConn family, Christina Khan, Jordan McMillan and Kate Ragon. And while they all deserve significant praise for whatever readers might find good and useful about this book, I alone am responsible for any shortcoming readers might find.

At Middlebury College, I am lucky to have the support and friendship of many wonderful colleagues. I would like to thank the members of my department, Matt Lawrence, Jamie McCallum, Peggy Nelson, Linus Owens, Mari Price, and Rebecca Tiger. Working with them makes my life less stressful. Outside my department, I have been fortunate to find a network of support, for which I am immensely thankful. Enrique Garcia and Nikolina Dobreva, I am lucky to have found the two of you in rural Vermont. Mack Roark, a dear friend who proves that it is never too late to find everything you deserve. My friends and colleagues-in-arms, David Miranda Hardy, Jason Mittell, Natasha Ngaiza, Raquel Albarrán, Gloria Estela González Zenteno, Marcos Rohena-Madrazo, Daniel Silva, Laurie Essig, Tim Nguyen, Kevin Moss, Renee Wells, Sujata Moorti, Natasha Chang, Timothy Billings, Kemi Fuentes-George, Maggie Clinton, J. Finley, Carly Thomsen, Katrin Spencer, Will Nash, Erin Eggleston, Tara Affolter, Michael Warner, Marybeth Nevins, and many others that I am certain I am forgetting, thank you for your friendship and support. I've also had the great fortune to meet many exceptional students. Although there are too many to list, I would like to thank Christopher Boutelle and Margot Babington who served as my research assistants and helped collect craigslist casual encounters ads. During the process of writing this book, I've had the great privilege of acting as a mentor to ten of the most amazing students anyone could have asked for. Big love to Laurent Asiama, Brian Dulanto, Chellsa Ferdinand, Diego Garcia, Frank Gavilanez, Athena Haywood, Madison Jeanphilippe, Shenisis Kirkland, Shatavia Knight, and Miki Nakano. I would also like to thank Middlebury College for providing me with the academic leave needed to finish this book.

Outside of Middlebury, I have had the great fortune to meet and interact with incredible colleagues whose work and/or presence has enriched my life in numerous ways. While I won't even attempt to name all of them, I would like to thank Jesús Gregorio Smith, Kareem Khubchandani, Anthony Ocampo, Dana Berkowitz, Elroi Windsor, Ilene Kalish, Mike Killian, Nguyen Tan Hoang, Sony Coráñez, Michael Johnson Jr., Salvador Vidal-Ortiz, Joanie Mazelis, Shari Dworkin, Kimberley Goyette, Jason Orne, Shinsuke Eguchi, Rhacel Salazar Parrenas, Mary Stricker, Amy Steinbugler, Russell Leong, Oscar Martinez-Foyedo, Sylvia Chan-Malik, George Ayala, Robin Rodriguez, Michael Austin, Nolan Kline, Kristen

Barber, Tristen Bridges, Helen Kramer, Larry Icard, Denton Callander, Marcos Lopez, Helane Adams, Guy Mark Foster, Sulaimon Giwa, Martin Manalansan, Tawnya Pettiford-Wates, Michael Kimmel, and the many more that I am certain I will be embarrassed to have left unnamed as this list is far from complete. I would also like to thank my mentors and friends at the University of Washington, Ana Mari Cauce, Edwina Uhera, Rick Bonus, Johnella Butler, John Walter, and Connie So. Of course, I haven't forgotten Neha Vora, who came up with the wonderful title for this book!

Special gratitude goes out to the anonymous reviewers of this book. Their suggestions and comments greatly improved its focus and framing, and I thank them sincerely for their time and generous efforts. I would also like to thank Taylor & Francis Group, publishers of *Social Identities*, where parts of the introduction were originally published as "They Don't Want to Cruise Your Type," and *Sociological Spectrum*, where an earlier version of chapter 1 was published with my long-time mentor, Kyung-Hee Choi. Special thanks to Temple University Press, where a small section of chapter 3 will be published in *Q&A: Voices from Queer North America*, a follow-up to the groundbreaking anthology *Q&A: Queer in Asian America*.

I would also like to thank Larin McLaughlin and the wonderful team at the University of Washington Press for finding merit in this book. Many thanks to Julie Van Pelt and Margaret Sullivan for shepherding the book through the process, Jason Alley for keeping things on track, and Richard Feit for immaculate copyediting. Many thanks to Rye Gentleman for going above and beyond in creating the index. Although I grew up in San Francisco, I've always considered Seattle my home. The ten years I spent in Seattle as editor of *The International Examiner* and at the University of Washington where I received my doctorate have been the most rewarding of my life. It was in Seattle that I, to delve into a cliché, "found myself." The people I met and the experiences I had nurtured me through some of the most difficult times in my life and joined me in some of the best. Working with the press feels like a small bit of a homecoming, and it seems somehow fitting that this book brought me back home. I am grateful for the nostalgia it brought into my life, an added bonus that I could not have gotten anywhere else.

I would like to take a moment to thank my friends, those who have been with me through the experiences that have defined my life. Thank you, Kristopher Proctor, for being there when I needed a friend most. My friends Paul Shaw, Jerry Sladewski, Sevia Hui, Fernando Pineda, Tony Chung, Brian Anderson, Naomi Ishisaka, Aleks Martin, Yoosun Park, Carl Siebert, Darcy Siebert, Jill Chonody, Nila Kim, Charles Sasaki, Alan Lau, Anne Xuan Clark, Bennyroyce Royon, John Walston, Kieu-Anh King, Phi Nguyen, Mark Ellis, Bernadette Connor, Jane Liaw, Michael Byun, Nhan Tran, Nhan Thai, Cindy Domingo, Andy Mizuki, Ellen Suzuki, Elaine Ishihara, Hye-Kyung Kang, Antonio Perez, Gene Osias, David Nguyen, Collin Kwan, and Wilmer Galindo. It goes without saying that this list is far from complete. I am also fortunate to have an incredibly close and supportive family, particularly my siblings, Sophia, Helen, and Alex. Much love to my nephew Caleb and my niece Catelyn. Finally, to my partner Scott Rutledge, thank you for being my witness.

RACIAL EROTICS

Introduction

They Still Don't Want to Cruise Your Type

* discussion of if everyone can be racist *

THIRTY MINUTES AFTER THE POSTED STARTING TIME, MEN, AND a handful of women, continue to wander into the second-floor auditorium of an overlooked performance hall in the center of the city's gayborhood. Like many things gay, the scheduled forum on race, sponsored by one of the largest gay-identified organization in the city, begins on gay time. As the audible levels of side conversations begin to wane, organizers urge the audience to take their seats so we can all begin. Within minutes, a representative of the host agency lays out the ground rules of discussion, most notably that we will not, given the limited time, try to define racism, while quickly offering that "everyone is capable of racism," an assertion that many men of color in attendance would, if given the chance, vehemently dispute.

Perhaps it wouldn't have been such an issue if prominent gay men of color, who were invited to help plan the forum, hadn't spent weeks arguing for the need to discuss racism in the gay community and not to focus solely on race. Or perhaps it wouldn't have been such a slight if they were asked to provide an alternative definition of racism, particularly who is able, within the larger social structure, to practice it rather than being left with only one definition of it. In fact, the title Race Forum was specifically chosen, against the suggestions offered by gay men of color, so that the focus could be on race rather than the alleged trickier topic of racism.

"It's like they didn't hear a thing," one of the men told me immediately after the announcement. "Why did we go to the meetings? It's like we weren't even there. We might as well be invisible." Though flabbergasted, he also added that "it's no surprise." It seems that speaking up and being ignored has come to be a common occurrence. After all, being a gay man of color is to experience the unnerving feeling of being invited to a potluck while being told not to bring anything since nobody would be interested in what you bring, and then not being offered any food since you didn't bring anything anyway.

A sweeping glance across the audience makes two things immediately clear. First, the auditorium is noticeably emptier than usual given the tendency of other forums hosted by this agency to fill to capacity. More importantly, the faces are darker than those at other forums sponsored by this organization. One could conclude, if one were so inclined, that this forum on race was not as popular with many of the gay men who normally attend while bringing out other men who normally wouldn't. However, the composition of the audience reflects a larger picture of the broader "gay community" where issues of race and racism are often ignored and gay men of color are often not welcomed at the table to discuss allegedly gay issues.

Looking around any gayborhood, something becomes blatantly clear. Within the queer spaces that have sprung up in neighborhoods that were once thought to be neglected, inside the slick new storefronts and trendy restaurants, and on magazine covers—as well as between the covers, for that matter—gay America has given a whole new meaning to the term *whitewash.*

We, as a collective, have rehabilitated homes in allegedly neglected neighborhoods. We've planted flowers. We've painted the walls, fixed old roofs, and generally increased the value of areas that were once believed to be, albeit erroneously in some cases, in urban decline. Whitewash.

We've revived old storefronts, bringing a multitude of retail shops (and the accompanying tax base) to streets once reserved for activities outside of the law—not that everything we did within our own houses or behind the storefronts was within the comfortable boundaries of legally sanctioned activities. Whitewash.

We've fought hard to counter allegedly negative stereotypes that proliferate in mainstream culture and replace them with images that some find more respectable. Yet that respectable image has come to be overwhelmingly white.

whiteness in gay is common + desire (handwritten)

Whiteness in the gay community is everywhere, in what we see, what we experience, and more blatantly, what we desire. The power of whiteness, of course, derives from appearing to be nothing in particular.[1] Whiteness is powerful precisely because it is everywhere but nowhere in particular. When we see whiteness, we process it as if it doesn't exist or its existence is simply natural. Precisely because we see it constantly, we don't see it at all. It blends into the background and is then erased from scrutiny.

Contemporary media images of gay men promote a monolithic image of the gay community as being overwhelmingly upper middle class—if not simply rich—and white. Even the most perfunctory glance through gay publications exposes the paucity of non-white men. It's almost as if no gay men of color exist outside of fantasy cruises to Jamaica, Puerto Rico, or the "Orient." And even then, they exist only to fulfill the sexual fantasies of gay white men. Exotic vacations to faraway places are marketed to rich white men, and poor colored bodies are only another consumable product easily purchased with Western dollars. Gay men of color, whether found within Western borders or conveniently waiting for white arrival in the far-off corners of the globe, are nothing more than commodities. *(handwritten margin: white gay men are represented as rich always)*

It's not just the media; the gay community is no less to blame. Gay organizations themselves promote and reinforce the whiteness of gay life. The gay movement that once embodied the ideals of liberation, freedom, and social justice quickly turned to the causes of promoting gay pride through visibility and lobbying efforts that forced established institutions, particularly media institutions, to reexamine mainstream heterosexist bias against gay men and women. Yet promoting gay rights became synonymous with promoting gay assimilation rather than liberation, as evidence by the cause célèbre of gay marriage. To win acceptance, gay activists adapted various whitening practices to sell gay America to the heartland of America by *(handwritten margin: gay morals/ideals have changed recently)*

mirroring the whiteness of men who run powerful institutions
as a strategy for winning credibility, acceptance, and integration;
excluding people of color from gay institutions; *selling* gay as white
to raise money, make a profit, and gain economic power; and daily

wearing the *pale protective coloring* that camouflages the unquestioned assumptions and unearned privileges of gay whiteness.[2]

This mirroring of the mainstream community to promote gay assimilation has meant ignoring allegedly non-gay issues such as "homelessness, unemployment, welfare, universal health care, union organizing, affirmative action, and abortion rights."[3] It has even ignored debates about immigration and asylum, as is evident in editorials in gay publications that suggest that focusing on immigrant rights would take away from gay rights. What such arguments ignore is that many in gay communities are members of immigrant groups and that significant numbers of people seek asylum specifically because they are gay. But of course, to be gay in America today is to be white. More specifically, it means to be white and well-to-do. This is obvious in the ways that gay organizations and businesses mark and market themselves to the larger society, both gay and straight. Gay publications tout the affluence of the gay community when fighting for advertising dollars.

Non-profit organizations and gay-identified businesses that serve a multiracial clientele are marked as being raced and, in turn, mark themselves as raced. Organizations such as Brother to Brother, Gay Asian Pacific Support Network, Hombres Latinos, among others mark the racial borders of patronage. Gay businesses, too, mark these borders. Bars that are populated by non-white clients or exist merely to support white male fantasies about gay men of color are marked with appropriately racialized names, such as the Voodoo Lounge in Seattle, Papicock in New York, and Red Dragon in Los Angeles. The Blatino Bronx Factory not only marks the club as raced but also quite blatantly specifies which races they are marking. Yet gay-identified organizations—both for-profit and non-profit—with mostly, and sometimes exclusively, white clientele are never marked in this way. Instead, they vehemently oppose such characterizations, arguing that they serve all gay people. It is never the Gay White Support/Social Organization, but rather, the Gay Support/Social Organization, the implication being that they speak for all gay people, a claim they make while ignoring certain voices. In this way, the concerns of gay white men become the de facto concerns for all gay people. Whiteness and maleness take center stage, and it becomes synonymous with gay where gay comes to mean white and white comes to mean gay.

One consequence of centering whiteness in gay life is that gay desire also comes to be marked by whiteness.[4] As Dwight McBride eloquently noted about the movie *Brokeback Mountain*:

> Ennis and Jack appeal to us in a context in which we have been prepared to receive a certain kind of gay man. He is white, masculine, straight-acting, good-looking, and therefore, sympathetic. All of this points to the centrality of whiteness and of white-on-white gay male relationships as sense-making norm that fuels the logic by which we ascribe value in the gay marketplace of desire. Gay white men know, and all of us who would have commerce in the marketplace know, that of all the variables that circulate, none are more central and salient than "the gift" of racial whiteness. Whites know they have it, others know they will never have it, and virtually everyone wants it.[5]

Within the gay marketplace of desire, whiteness comes to have currency while non-whiteness is perceived as a deficit. And gay men of color are constantly reminded of this alleged deficit. On the website Douchebags of Grindr, where users post Grindr profiles of offensive comments on "the world's largest social network for men," the most common are blatantly racist comments meant to signal disdain for men of color. The pervasiveness of such racist sentiments expressed by gay white men has led to a small explosion of sexual racism lit within mainstream publications where gay men of color share their experiences of racism by gay white men, particularly the ways that they are rejected as potential sexual partners or fetishized by them because of their race.

SEXUAL RACISM

Originally introduced by Charles H. Stember in his book *Sexual Racism: The Emotional Barrier to an Integrated Society* to explain the sexual nature of general racial hostility (such as resistance to desegregation and interracial relationships), the term *sexual racism,* within a gay context, has come to mean sexual exclusion and/or sexual fetishization based on race.[6] Although Stember's discussion was largely about heterosexual interracial desires, and much of what Stember argued has not (yet) made it into the new discussion of sexual racism among gay men, his work does include many of the building blocks for the way that the concept is presently used, including the racialized nature of what constitutes attractiveness and how racialized definitions of desirability influence relationships between gay white men and gay men of color and between gay men of color themselves.

A primary, and obvious, form of sexual racism among gay men, as noted earlier, is that of sexual rejection based on race, an occurrence that is widely reported by gay men of color.[7] The flip side of sexual rejection is sexual objectification based on race. In his essay "China Doll," Tony Ayres noted:

> It is an attraction to me because of my Asianness, my otherness. Again, this has nothing to do with who I think I am, my individual qualities as a person, or even as an object of desire. It is the fact that I conveniently fit into someone else's fantasy . . . And they expect me to be so flattered by the attention of a white man that I will automatically bend over and grab my ankles.[8]

The problem with objectification is that people come to be seen purely in terms of the stereotypical traits associated with the body. They become consumable products rather than individuals.[9]

The objectification of gay men of color further pushes them to the margins because their very desirability depends on their difference from the norm. As bell hooks has argued, "The commodification of otherness has been so successful because it is offered as a new delight, more intense, more satisfying than normal ways of doing and feeling."[10] Only when gay men of color can be defined as the "other," removed from the norm, can their objectification be worth anything in the marketplace of desire. In essence, the very difference that marks them as outsiders is the only currency they possess to trade for whiteness. But even then, as we will see later, race is currency only when it meets white expectations. That is, white men continue to determine the value of racial currency. Whether one is excluded or included as a potential sexual partner, sexual racism "reinforces ideas of racial hierarchy and stereotypes."[11]

Such racial desires, or lack of desires, are rarely understood as racial exclusion or racial objectification. Instead, they are explained as personal preferences.[12] Even gay white men who don't engage in egregious acts of exclusion and/or fetishization argue that such desires are simply personal preferences based on individual tastes. The true danger of sexual racism lies in its ability to hide, under the guise of being a personal preference, rather than be exposed as part and parcel of the larger system of racial oppression that depends on constructing one race as fundamentally inferior to another. In the face of such a clear pattern of favoring white men, even among gay men of color, the preference is anything but merely personal. That pattern betrays the larger structures of power that place a premium value on whiteness.

Sexual racism is more than simply excluding members of a racial group as potential sexual partners or objectifying them as sexual others even when they are desired. Whether one is sexually excited or left frustratingly flaccid by someone of another race is among the most trivial of concerns. What is important is that deeply embedded in those stereotypes about sexual attractiveness and sexual prowess that lead to one's seemingly personal sexual preferences is a very public distortion of the sexual worth of one group and the sexual bankruptcy of another that has roots in the larger system of racial maligning of minority groups deployed by the dominant group, specifically for the purpose of promoting white superiority, both structurally and culturally, and constructing the dominant group as having more worth. As Peter Jackson argued, "When desirability is linked with race, and when certain races are ascribed greater erotic interest than others, then to be a member of an "unsexy" ethnic group is to be equated with an inferior form of existence."[13]

Not only do gay men of color come to be seen as less desirable, they come to be seen has having less worth than gay white men, both inside and outside of erotic desires and sexual interactions. Expanding on the alleged undesirability of Asian men, Jackson added, "Asian homosexual men are simply 'not worth a fuck.'" That is, Asian men and other men of color become figuratively "not worth a fuck" because the white-centered ideology of desire makes them literally "not worth a fuck."

Being seen as "not worth a fuck" leads men of color to be perceived as not worthy of attention or resources within gay communities. Lacking desirability, the mere existence of gay men of color are negated and ignored. Allusions to invisibility are common in writings and media productions created by gay men of color. In *Tongues Untied*, Black film maker Marlon Riggs had this to say about San Francisco:

> I pretend not to notice the absence of Black images in this new gay life, in bookstores, poster shops, film festivals, even my own fantasies. Something in Oz was amiss, but I tried not to notice. I was intent on my search for my reflection, love, affirmation, in eyes of blue, gray, green. Searching, I discovered something I didn't expect, something decades of determined assimilation cannot blind me to. In this great, gay Mecca, I was an invisible man. I had no shadow, no substance, no place, no reflection.[14]

This invisibility is actively enforced. Take, for example, the *Advocate* magazine's cover of 2008 in which the magazine boldly claimed that "gay is the new Black" and characterized the fight for gay rights as "the last great civil rights struggle." In declaring gay as the new Black, the *Advocate* compartmentalizes gay from Black as if queer Black people were absent from the analysis of what it means to be gay and draws a boundary between what comes to be seen as two separate and distinct communities and movements.[15]

Yet these easy distinctions are not merely about compartmentalizing the social categories of Black and gay. As Siobhan Somerville argued:

> Such analogies implicitly posit whiteness and heterosexuality as the norm. To say that gay people are "like" Black people is to suggest that those same gay people are not Black. The underlying assumption is that white homosexuality is like heterosexual Blackness."[16]

implying heterosexuality + whiteness > poc + homo

Once erased, concerns and issues that may impact their lives can also be ignored. Issues of economic justice, racial discrimination, and police brutality, to name just a few, can be dismissed as not gay issues precisely because people of color are not gay. And if these issues are not gay issues, then they don't deserve resources or attention from members of the gay community. Because they are invisible, all kind of atrocious acts perpetrated against gay men of color and other queer people of color, such as the alarming rates of physical violence against Black trans women, can be ignored and dismissed. As if simply being negated and ignored isn't bad enough, sometimes the whiteness of gay spaces are actively policed to deliberately keep queers of color out.[17]

Because they are "not worth a fuck," they are easily marginalized and excluded from gay spaces as well. As Anthony Ocampo found in his ethnographic study of gay Latino men, gay spaces, as well as the aesthetics of those spaces, are perceived by gay Latino men to be an unwelcoming environment for non-white gay men. The men in his study note that presenting oneself, through clothes and manners, in a way that is counter to what are considered to be white norms carried an even greater risk of exclusion from certain venues, and even police harassment, in gay neighborhoods.[18] Gay venues are actively made and kept white through deliberate and conscious decisions by businesses and gay community leaders through a persistent promotion of whiteness as the norm.

Perhaps the most notorious example of this trend are the events surrounding Badlands, a popular bar in the Castro district in San Francisco. In the summer of 2004, Badlands became the site of weekly picketing after a group of racially diverse Bay Area residents filed a complaint with the San Francisco Human Rights Commission, the San Francisco Entertainment Commission, the California Department of Fair Employment and Housing, and the state Alcoholic Beverage Control Department claiming racial discrimination at the bar. Among the complaints were not only that the owner was practicing job discrimination at the bar by denying employment and promotional opportunities to non-whites, but also that non-white customers were being turned away at the door or expunged from the bar. Among the most obvious examples of this behavior was the

Example of discrimination in gay context

requirement that Black men provide two forms of ID at the door while white men were required to only show one.

An isolated incident might have been easily forgotten, but the events at Badlands struck a chord with the city's non-white gay and lesbian residents specifically because it fit a pattern of discrimination toward people of color. For them, it was just another incident in a long history of racial discrimination in the city's gayborhood. The policy of requiring multiple forms of ID from non-white patrons had a long history in the Castro, starting with the Mine Shaft, a Castro bar that required three forms of ID for men of color during the mid 1970s. During the early 1980s, an informal study conducted by the Association of Lesbian and Gay Asians found that multiple carding was a fairly widespread practice among gay bars in throughout San Francisco, not just in the Castro district. Should there be any doubt that such exclusionary tactics are directly related to sexual racism, one bar owner was quoted as stating, "It's a cruise bar, we would lose money because they don't want to cruise your type," in response to allegations that the multiple-ID requirements were racist.[19]

The practice of multiple carding was not unique to San Francisco. In Washington, DC, two bars, Lost & Found and Grand Central, were targeted by community activists for blatantly requiring two forms of ID from non-white patrons while allowing white patrons easy access. In 1984, the Boston Bar Study conducted by Men of All Colors Together Boston cited numerous examples of widespread discrimination at gay bars in Boston against Black men. Similar types of discrimination have also been cited in Los Angeles and New York. Even more troubling is that this type of behavior seems to be international, occurring anywhere gay white men come into contact with gay men of color. Rather than isolated events attributable to racist owners of single bars, the attempt to patrol the borders of whiteness in gay-owned business establishments seems to be a systematic practice to ensure that only certain types of people are allowed entry.

More recently, owners and staff of eleven Philadelphia gay bars and clubs were required to take a course on the city's antidiscrimination laws following an investigation by the Philadelphia Commission on Human Relations after numerous complaints of rampant acts of racism by several

Double card black men

businesses located in the city's gayborhood were made by patron
were denied entry for a variety of vague reasons. Of particular conce..
was a video of bar owner Darryl DePiano using anti-Black racial slurs
posted to YouTube in 2016. In the video, he is heard repeatedly using the
N-word and making derogatory comments about Black customers. A
community response, which resulted in the creation of a new rainbow flag
that added a black and brown stripe to the original design created by
Gilbert Baker, was met with caustic backlash by gay white men. Ironically,
many gay white men argued that the flag already represented all gay
people, despite the fact that bars, clubs, and other venues flying the flag
were actively engaging in discriminatory acts toward people of color.
Many gay white men argued that adding the colors itself was racist, given
that there was no white stripe.

In late May of 2019, another venue, Progress Bar in Chicago, was heavily criticized when one of their employees leaked an email sent to staff
members by the owners specifically banning rap music. Alleging that their
goal was to "promote a positive, happy, energetic, upbeat and most importantly . . . a FUN vibe," the email continued by stating, "We have imple-
mented a no rap rule effective immediately. This is not a suggestion!! If
you play RAP you will not be asked back. Anything vulgar, aggressive or
considered mumble rap (including certain Cardi B tracks and newer Nicki
Minaj) is off limits." A few days later, the bar posted a tepid non-apology
statement on their Facebook page arguing that there was no racial intent
and that people should not "read too much into this." The non-apology
was met with swift condemnation on social media with many noting that
the original email specifically mentioned Black-oriented radio stations as
examples of what not to play.

Not only does sexual racism limit access to gay spaces and render gay
men of color invisible within gay communities, thereby robbing them of
much needed attention and resources, it can also have detrimental effects
on gay men of color more directly and intimately. Experiences of sexual
racism among men of color are significantly associated with lower self-
esteem and lower life satisfaction among members of these groups.[20]
Sexual racism has also been implicated in the rising rates of HIV among
gay men of color.[21] One of the most deleterious consequence for gay men

of color may be the damage that sexual racism does to their relationships with other gay men of color. For many gay men of color, actively dehumanizing other men of color becomes the justification for their desire for white men.

Writer Keith Boykin observed that gay Black men use coded language about other gay Black men to reject each other as potential sexual partners. As Boykin observed, "In a culture that devalues Black males and elevates white males," Black men deal with issues of self-hatred that white men do not. "After all," he notes, "white men have no reason to hate themselves in a society that reinforces their privilege." Boykin argues that this racial self-hatred makes gay Black men see other gay Black men as unsuitable sexual partners. Obviously, such racial self-hatred is rarely understood as such. Instead, gay men of color who don't want to date other men of color simply rely on stereotypes to justify their sexual desires for white men over men of their own race and/or other men of color. Boykin argues that many Black men justify excluding other Black men as potential partners by relying on stereotypes of the uneducated, less intelligent Black man. Ironically, the same Black men who rely on these stereotypes to exclude members of their own race rarely enforce them on gay white men, as evidenced by Boykin's example of the gay Black man who has no problem with dating blue-collar white men but excludes Black men on the assumption that they are uneducated and less successful.[22]

This desire for white male companionship, alleged racial self-hatred, and competition for white men is not limited to Black men. Rather, it seems to be pandemic among gay men of color. Kent Chuang writes about how he tried desperately to avoid anything related to his Chinese heritage and his attempts to transform his "shamefully slim Oriental frame . . . into a more desirable western body."[23] Asian men also rely on racist stereotypes to justify their exclusive attraction to white men. One gay Asian man is cited as stating:

> For me, I prefer dating white men because I want something different from myself. I think that dating another Asian would be like dating my sister. I mean, we would have so much in common, what

would there be for us to learn about? Where would the excitement come from?[24]

Within this narrative, all Asians are presented as homogenous masses with each person being interchangeable with another. Ironically, white men who exclusively date white men rarely rely on such tactics. There is no need to argue, from a white male position, that dating other white men would be like dating their brothers. Also, the man's characterization of other Asian men as sisters points to the stereotypical ways that Asian men are seen in the larger gay community. Stereotyped as overly feminine, gay Asian men become unappealing to gay men who desire men who are masculine or allegedly straight acting.

The competition for a white "trophy boyfriend" among gay Latino men often hinders community formation. Rather than seeing each other as allies, gay Latino men may see each other as competitors for the attention of the few white men who prefer Latino men to other white men. One Latino man was quoted as saying:

> One of the things that I saw that really bothered me and I told them, I said, "What the problem here is everybody is after the white trophy. That's the problem here. And unless two people are comadres [godmothers], you don't want to have nothing to do with each other. But that's the problem. After the white trophy, nobody has time. And it's like, you tear each other down . . . viciousness, because you're after the white trophy. And to have a white lover is ooohhh! Don't you see?"[25]

After complaining to other Latino men about the pedestalization of white men among gay Latino men, this particular (gay Latino man) was labeled a "radical lesbian." The implication here is that any Latino man who chooses to be with another Latino man rather than a white man, which has come to dominate gay male sexual fantasies, must be a "lesbian," a woman who prefers other women. The limited definition of desirable masculinity within the gay community leads to white males being seen as men while men of color are placed lower on the hierarchy, much in the same way that the larger society creates a hierarchy of men and women.

CONSTRUCTING THE "GOOD GAY"

It would be a mistake to assume that whiteness is not actively maintained. Rather, the illusion of normalcy requires active maintenance of racial borders. White doesn't become normal because it is so, it becomes normal because we make it so. Whiteness is maintained not only through active exclusion of those who are non-white, but also through the active construction of whiteness as the norm to which the "other" is compared. In constructing whiteness, we also construct what it means to be a "good gay," selecting which gays have more social worth and are therefore worthy of social support.

Rather than isolated incidences of personal preferences, the construction of racialized desires is intimately related to the construction of the "good gay" and beliefs about which gays belong and which gays do not. As Roderick Ferguson observed, the alleged sexual deviancy of Black men and women have been the foundation upon which the alleged pathology of Black people were framed. Taking aim at canonical sociology, particularly the Chicago School, Ferguson highlights the ways that American sociology "imagined African American culture as the site of polymorphous gender and sexual perversions and associated those perversions with moral failings typically."[26] It is through this racial imagining of the Black other that Ferguson argues that the "white bourgeois family" came to be seen as the model of heteronormative life. It is only through Black pathology that white normality can be established. And it is through sexual deviancy that Black pathology was constructed.

Allegations of deviant sexuality and gender non-conformity were also deployed in order to pathologize other non-white people. David Eng traces the ways that beliefs about deviant Asian sexual practices and the alleged gender non-conformity among sojourning Asian men helped construct an Asian American male subjectivity that was simultaneously raced and sexed and helped frame Asian men as the simultaneously raced,

Racial settings + playing field

gendered, and sexualized other. It is not possible, as Eng demonstrates, to separate out the racializing of Asian men with the sexualizing of them.[27]

Likewise, Scott Lauria Morgensen's work demonstrates the ways that violence against Indigenous people was justified by marking Indigenous people as sexual and gender deviants. This violence, which took multiple forms, including expulsion, family disruption, and out-right genocide, were predicated on the assumption of a non-heteronormative other that not only justified the violence inflicted on Native populations but also simultaneously constructed white colonialism as patriarchal, (hetero)normal, and human.[28]

As Jasbir Puar argues, the ability to displace sexual perversity onto brown bodies has led to the rise of "homonationalism," a framing of gay rights through the lens of heteronormativity that advocates for, and prioritizes, normality and the "right" of gays and lesbians to enter into heteronormative institutions such as marriage and military service that helps to construct the "good gay."[29] Yet the push for marriage rights and full inclusion in the US military have come at a cost to those who do not, or cannot, meet the new heteronormative construction of the "good gay" precisely because they have been constructed as being its opposite.[30] This construction of the good gay necessarily involves constructing the bad gay to which the normality of the good gay can be compared. While these comparisons deflect attention from the dilemmas faced by people who are both racially and sexually marginalized, the larger problem is with the ways that these comparisons use race to construct a normative white gay subject, one deserving of sympathy not based on queerness but on whiteness.

In examining the ways that gay racial desires are constructed, I find that the deviant sexuality and gender non-normativity historically associated with gay men in general, such as sexual promiscuity and gender nonconformity, has been displaced onto men of color. Displacing sexual deviancy and gender nonconformity to men of color allows white men to claim normality. Yet the new gay normal comes at the expense of gay men of color. What is considered universally desirable and normal among gay men, and what comes to be seen as erotic fetishism, is deeply raced. Because the racialized desire for men of color are always marked as a deviation from the norm, even a preference for them helps mark the boundaries of normative sexual desires. When white men desire non-white men, it is often for the racial fetish of difference rather than normality.

Thus, sexual racism, particularly the erasing of men of color as potential sexual partners and objects of desire among gay men, is part and parcel of a larger project of racial erasing that conflates gayness with whiteness and earns equality and acceptance for white men at the expense of queers of color. Because of this, sexual racism can be directly implicated in the exclusion of gay people of color from gay spaces, the refusal of gay organizations to address any issues outside of those important to cis-white men, and the active demonizing of gay people of color. Once pathologized in this way, racism directed toward gay men of color comes to be seen as a "natural, normal, and inevitable parts of everyday life."[31] Because gay men of color are deviant, any injustice directed toward them can be blamed on them.

Because they are sexual pathologies, gay men of color, particularly gay Black men, are also more harshly punished for sexual indiscretions. Take for example the notorious case of Michael Johnson, known widely as "Tiger Mandingo."[32] On October 10, 2013, Johnson was arrested at Lindenwood University in St. Charles, Missouri, and charged with one count of "recklessly infecting another with HIV" and four counts of "attempting to recklessly infect another with HIV," both felonies in the state of Missouri. The story quickly went viral, with netizens harshly criticizing his actions. Unsurprisingly, the internet branded him a "monster," using both explicit and implicit racial undertones. Following his trial, Johnson received a thirty-year sentence for a crime that is rarely prosecuted when the perpetrator is white. Given the way Black sexuality is pathologized, it was an easy leap to see Johnson's actions as monstrous, and then an easier leap to punish him so severely. And whether you agree with the sentence or not, there is little doubt that it fit a larger pattern of harsh penalties inflicted on Black men over white men.[33]

In this book, I examine the ways that whiteness comes to be equated with normality and how the construction of whiteness is implicated in gay racial desires. I argue that gay racial desire, rather than being an accident, is indicative of the ways that whiteness becomes central to the larger imagining of gayness, marking the border between the good gay and the other at which the desire for white men becomes normative while the desire for non-white men becomes exotified. In order to do so, I take an intersectional and critical approach to the study of race and sexuality to uncover the various ways that whiteness comes to have more value in the sexual fields of gay desire. Specifically, I examine larger structural factors, such as the ways gay media construct gay white men vis-à-vis gay men of color, as well as the racialized nature of everyday sexual interactions between gay white men and gay men of color.

THE SOCIOLOGY OF DESIRE AND THE EROTIC HABITUS

As Adam Isaiah Green observed, sociological studies of sexuality have led to the development of a "large, rich, and diverse body of literature [on] sexual identities, practices, communities, politics and polemics."[34] Yet relatively little has been done to examine sexual desire, making desire the "elephant that sits upon the scholar's desk, seen by all but addressed by few." This is not, of course, a novel view. Barbara Risman and Pepper Schwartz remarked, more than three decades ago, that the constructionist views upon which the sociology of sexualities rests fail to directly address why or how erotic preferences originally develops.[35]

Much of the failure of sociologists to examine sexual desires may be the continuing belief that such desires are subconscious.[36] Rather than being influenced by larger social factors, sexual desire is thought to be a "basic, biologically mediated phenomenon."[37] Beliefs about the unconscious nature of sexual desires may lead to a reluctance among some scholars to impose a sociological lens to an area largely associated with psychoanalysis. To this I would also add the difficulty of operationalizing desire for the purpose of analysis and the difficulty of defining what constitutes desire. Nonetheless, because of this reluctance, sociology lacks a "framework for understanding the processes by which social structure shapes, impinges upon, and constitutes sexual ideation."[38]

The problem with a lack of a sociological framework for understanding erotic desires and ceding the exploration of desire as a field of study to psychoanalysis is that the language of desire often comes to focus on personal preferences rather than on social hierarchies. However, sexual partnering is deeply embedded in the larger social structures where sexual actors find themselves, and it occurs within a sexual marketplace where different qualities are considered more desirable. Individuals who possess desirable traits are therefore more successful while those lacking desirable traits are less so. But perhaps most importantly, what comes to be seen as desirable within a sexual marketplace is not random. Instead, it represents larger social structural values where members of some groups are assigned higher worth than members of other groups based on the amount of erotic capital they possess. And they possess more erotic capital because they are socially constructed to be perceived as having more worth.

Erotic desires are not neutral or personal. Rather, they are the result of the development of an "erotic habitus," where some traits, and some people, are believed to be desirable and other traits, and other people, as undesirable.[39] But what exactly is erotic habitus and how and why does it develop? In this book, I argue that a racialized erotic habitus develops among gay men through the whitening processes within gay media and gay social practices. These desires "reflect a symbolic hierarchy that is determined and maintained by the socially dominant in order to enforce their distance or distinction from other classes of society."[40] Constructing gay desires along race not only creates a hierarchy of desire but also helps mark gay whiteness as different from queer non-whiteness.

In terms of sexual desires, possession of those characteristics that are deemed more desirable by society provide individuals with certain levels of erotic capital. Among gay men, Emerich Daroya points out that "erotic capital consists of an intersection of body capital (muscularity), gender capital (masculinity), racial capital (whiteness), age capital (youthfulness) and class."[41] What is important to remember here is that the characteristics that make up erotic capital and provide some men with more sexual worth are not a given but a reflection of the erotic habitus. That is, there is nothing inherently natural about whiteness having more erotic worth.

Sexual desires, rather than being entirely internal and physiological and thus void of social influences, can be understood as being heavily influenced by social cues that mark some people, objects, and activities as being erotic and having erotic worth.[42] It is also important to avoid conflating sexual desire with sexual pleasure. While intimately related, desire should be understood as the wishes and wants that motivate our actions.[43] While pleasure may also be socially constructed, the meaning of pleasure is directed internally while the meaning of desire is directed externally.[44] Unlike the construction of pleasure that involves framing some physical experiences as pleasurable and others as not pleasurable, desire creates an external hierarchy whereby some objects or people come to be seen as either more desirable or less so, thereby coming to have more or less erotic worth.

In order to examine the hierarchy of desire, we must ask several key questions. How are racialized hierarchies of desire constructed and maintained within gay communities? What purpose do such hierarchies of desire serve and how are they implicated in the maintenance of white supremacy? How do these hierarchies of desire shape gay racial desires and how do they come to be performed by gay men? How do gay men of color both internalize and challenge these racial hierarchies of desire? To explore the complexity of experiences among gay men of color, I utilize multiple types of data from multiple sources, taking a methodologically wide stance to examine and explore the types of data that I believe are appropriate to the type of data being analyzed, while using the analysis of narratives as a central organizing theme for the book.

EXAMINING RACIALIZED SEXUAL DESIRES
AND ORGANIZATION OF THE BOOK

It would be safe to assume, without hesitation, that few other activities are so widely practiced among myriad groups of people, using a plethora of venues and mediums, than storytelling. Telling stories is one of the most universal forms of language use.[45] On any given day, we tell numerous stories. We tell stories about our work, about our hobbies, about things we've seen, and about our personal experiences. Yet stories are more than simply anecdotal accounts. They are structurally situated recollections that help narrators make sense of those experiences within a larger social context.[46] Individuals attempt to create a narrative that establishes coherent connections between various life events in an effort to understand these events as systematically related.[47]

Despite the importance of narratives in examining and constructing the larger structures of everyday life, narratives are often viewed with suspicion in sociology, particularly given the discipline's collective tendency to want to understand people's "relationship to persons, objects, and events as empirical statements about social phenomenon." However, narratives have always been present in sociological research, whether it be through case histories, personal interviews, or content analysis of written and/or visual texts.[48] This suspicion in sociology of narratives and narrative methods is perhaps rooted in what many commentators have dubbed the "physics envy" prevalent in the social sciences. According to Kevin Clarke and David Primo, many in the social sciences suffer from an academic inferiority complex, leading them to attempt to mirror their disciplinary methods along the hard sciences using the language employed by the latter.[49] This inferiority complex is perhaps best captured by Paul Krugman in recalling an Indian-born economist's personal theory of reincarnation. According to Krugman, this particular economist is said to have told his graduate economics class that "if you are a good economist, a virtuous economist, you are reborn a physicist. But if you are an evil, wicked economist, you are reborn as a sociologist."[50]

At first blush, it is easy to read this comment as having ranked the three disciplines hierarchically by scientific purity and worth. Yet as Krugman explained, how one interprets this statement is dependent on who one is. That is, an economist would interpret this statement differently from a sociologist. And as Krugman continued, "Good economists know that the speaker was talking about something else entirely: the sheer difficulty of the subject. Economics is *harder* than physics; luckily it is not quite as hard as sociology." That is, if an economist is virtuous, they may return to life to pursue an easier life of a physicist, but if an economist is evil and wicked, they will be forced to endure the more difficult life of a sociologist.

If we are to take Krugman's comments at face value, what exactly is it about economics that makes it harder than physics, and what is it about sociology that makes it harder than both? The answer to this question is precisely the reason that there are perils to an over-reliance on positivistic models of science when they are employed uncritically to the social sciences. As Marion Fourcade-Gourinchas noted, "What makes economics and sociology harder than physics is that it involves human beings, whose behavior is elusive to observe, difficult to understand, and impossible to predict."[51] Yet despite the difficulty of predicting, let alone understanding, human behaviors, the tyranny of methods that places hypothetico-deductivism at the pinnacle of knowing leads many to devalue theoretical models that do not find empirical support or to dismiss evidence that cannot be neatly framed along acceptable modes of creating knowledge. This model also leaves little room for analyzing empirical data that doesn't lead to a grand theoretical model. Yet there is much to gain, as Clarke and Primo point out, in simply examining data for the sake of learning something about the impact of social phenomenon on everyday life.

Taking seriously Clarke and Primo's suggestion that "social scientists would be better off doing what they do best: thinking deeply about what prompts human beings to behave the way they do," this book takes a decidedly humanistic stance toward what counts as data and how that data should be analyzed and interpreted.[52] Specifically, I frame the work using the tenets of critical race theory to guide data collection, coupled with critical discourse analysis for the analysis of data.[53] Also, I embrace Phillip Brian Harper's notion of "felt intuition" in thinking about my data.[54] As Harper notes, "Sex and sexuality are by definition evanescent experiences, made even more so in our sociocultural context by the peculiar ways that we negotiate them verbally."[55] Continuing his argument, he urges queer theorists to "take our objects of analysis on the terms that define them, if we [are] to make any headway whatever toward the increased understanding we supposedly seek." For marginalized members of society, Harper argues that "speculative reasoning often appears as the only tool we have by which to forward the type of critical analysis our situation demands, such reasoning itself is necessarily conditioned by the material factors in which it is undertaken, and those material factors without exception all have histories that themselves can serve to guide us in our critical work."[56]

Rather than being simply "guesswork and conjecture," speculative reasoning is "bound up with the material factors that constitutes" queer and racial subjectivity and can provide valuable insights and expand theorizing beyond what can be empirically observed while at the same time provides us the space to empirically observe what cannot be adequately theorized. Speculative reasoning allows us to move away from what many queer theorists have called the "fetishizing of the observable," allowing us to "embrace multiplicity, misalignments, and silences" that often mark the lives of marginalized people.[57] Doing so allows us to rethink various categories and categorizations and how these categories themselves are a result of larger societal constructions of what it means to be members of subaltern groups. My goal is not to reject the observable per se or to avoid categories altogether. Rather, it is to expand what we mean by *knowing* and to explore how researchers may fully embrace the research enterprise by bringing their whole selves into the process.

The various narratives that I present in this book were analyzed using the tenets of critical discourse analysis (CDA), particularly those that deal with written narratives but also applied to interview narratives as well as visual images. As a research perspective, CDA is interested in exposing the "power and control" embedded in text and talk by analyzing the hidden meaning embedded in discursive choices that are made by the writer or the speaker. Within this framework, "no usage of language can ever be considered neutral, impartial, or a-political."[58] Rather, language use is understood to be pivotal in the production, maintenance, and resistance of power relations. At the same time, the context in which a discursive product is produced also includes the power to produce, circulate, and deploy the product that is produced. The unequal access to the various modes of discursive productions then further enhances power differentials between groups. Because of this, I take seriously the perspective that narratives and visual images are "an instrument of power and control" used to construct a reality that benefits one group at the expense of another.[59]

A central tenet of CDA is that meaning is not inherent in the words used but are embedded in the choices made by the author in the way narratives are presented. Embedded within these choices are specters of power, domination, inequality, and bias. Stories are not told "as they are" but as they are interpreted, through the social context that writers and speakers inhabit. In addition, discursive products actively maintain a reality based on dominant group expectations of what that reality should be.

Rather than a clearly defined research methodology, CDA is a series of techniques that "involves the use of discourse analytic techniques, combined with a critical perspective, to interrogate social phenomena."[60] Doing so involves examining (1) how text is framed, that is, how text or talk is presented and what particular angle the author/speaker is taking, including the general mood of the text or talk; (2) what information is foregrounded, that is, what concepts are given textual prominence while others are in the background; (3) what presuppositions and/or insinuations are made; (4) which subjects are topicalized, that is, who the subject is and who the object; (5) what is omitted; and (6) how visual aids are used to support the narrators arguments.[61]

In chapter 1, I analyze thirty-five interviews conducted between December 2005 and August 2006 with gay men of color during the initial phase of the Ethnic Minority Men's Study, a larger quantitative study designed to examine the impact of discrimination, sexual partnership, and social networks on sexual risk behaviors among gay Black, Latino, and Asian Pacific Islander men living in Los Angeles, CA. Individuals were recruited from a variety of sources, including gay newspapers, notices placed in venues frequented by gay men, and organizations that target members of these groups. A theoretical sampling frame was used to ensure diversity among participants. Inclusion criteria included (1) being at least eighteen years old; (2) self-identified as Black, Latino, or Asian Pacific Islander; (3) being proficient in English; (4) reporting at least one male sex partner in the past six months; and (5) residing in Los Angeles County. The interview sample included twelve Black men, eleven Latino men, and twelve Asian Pacific Islander men. Sixteen men were between the ages of eighteen and twenty-nine years old, and nineteen were thirty and older. One of eleven Latino men and nine of the Asian Pacific Islander men were foreign-born. All Black men were born in the United States. Although the data were collected in 2005, the themes I uncovered have proven to be timeless in that sexual racism is a recurring topic in both the mainstream and gay media. With the advent of social media and dating apps such as Grindr that have come to facilitate convenient sexual interactions between gay men, the themes I have identified seem to have become more, rather than less, salient. Through these men's stories, I demonstrate that gay men of color understand the racialized nature of the gay sexual field of desire and that such racialized hierarchies have negative impacts that go beyond just sexual behaviors and partnerships. At the same time, I show that gay men of color are not simply victims of sexual racism but that they attempt to redefine what it means to be a gay man of color and actively confront sexual racism.

Chapter 2 offers an analysis of various gay media outlets in order to explore how these outlets construct racial desire through the centering of whiteness. Because what counts as gay media is nebulous, with many gay outlets targeting both gay and straight readers and most mainstream media including more gay content, I use a broad definition of gay media to include various publications, TV shows, and movies that have strong representation of gay characters or that address (homo)sexuality as a major topic. At the same time, to provide the chapter with needed structure, I focus primarily on *Out* magazine, the largest gay publication in the United States. I examine the covers of *Out* magazine published between 2000 and 2019 to argue that gay media outlets create an erotic habitus centered on desire for whiteness, while utilizing a variety of other media items to highlight the main arguments presented in the chapter. Using the theory of erotic habitus, I argue that gay media construct the desire for whiteness as normative while simultaneously constructing sexual desire for men of color as being a deviation from the norm. In this way, gay media helps construct a hierarchy of racial worth regarding not only what has social value, but also who has it.

Personal advertisements for sexual partners placed on the popular website Craigslist make up the data for chapter 3. During the month of January 2016, I searched all ads placed on Craigslist under the "casual encounters, men seeking men" category in the city of Los Angeles by men of color specifically seeking white men and white men specifically seeking men of color. Removing duplicate ads, there were 820 ads in total; 214 ads were posted by white men seeking Black men, 177 ads were placed by white men seeking Latino men, 116 ads were placed by white men seeking Asian men, 83 ads were placed by Black men seeking white men, 167 ads were placed by Latino men seeking white men, and 63 ads were placed by Asian men seeking white men.

There were many reasons I specifically chose Craigslist "causal encounters" ads over ads placed on other sites. Fear of researcher bias has long been a concern for scholars studying sexual behaviors and desires. Selecting online personal ads allows researchers to take an observational stance that removes the researcher completely and is unknown to the research pool. In this way, researchers are able to observe without interfering in any way.[62] I selected Craigslist rather than other online dating portals such as OKCupid and Grindr because Craigslist, at the time of data collection, required no registration or creation of a profile to post or view ads. This allowed users to remain completely anonymous and to limit their posts to descriptions of what they are specifically seeking in terms of sexual acts and the characteristics that they are seeking in a potential sexual partner. I limited my search to ads placed in the "casual encounters" section rather than the "dating" section because men post to this section specifically looking for sexual encounters.

Based on these ads, I found that interracial sexual encounters are often presented as a "new delight," something that should be more intense and more satisfying precisely because interracial sex is out of the ordinary. Craigslist ads placed by white men seeking sexual partners of another race for "casual encounters" often use racialized tropes in describing the requirements of the potential partner. At the same time, ads placed by men of color looking specifically for casual sexual encounters with white men use similar racial tropes in their own self descriptions.

Chapter 4 offers an analysis of the ways that racism gets denied by gay white men by examining articles and reader comments on popular gay websites, primarily focusing on *Queerty* and *LGBTQ Nation*, the two largest gay websites in the United States. I selected articles based on keyword searches that included terms such as *race*, *racism*, and *interracial*. After identifying articles on the two websites and engaging in an abbreviated version of grounded theory analysis, I engaged in a more focused method of data collection by exploring a smaller number of articles outside of these two websites that received widespread attention or were alluded to in the articles published in *Queerty* or *LGBTQ Nation*. In exploring the denial of racism, I focused more on the reader comments than on the articles themselves, as I was more interested in how racism gets routinely denied in everyday interactions. My rationale for focusing on reader comments rather than the articles themselves was that many of the articles were written by men of color and specifically discussed racism in the gay community. My goal was to explore how such accusations of racism are deflected and denied by gay white men rather than how they are presented by gay men of color. As the chapter demonstrates, gay men use a variety of tactics to deny the existence of racism in the gay community, including trivializing racism in the gay community, portraying the gay community as a racial haven compared to the larger society, deflating racism in the gay community with alleged homophobia in communities of color, accusing gay men of color of racism, and conflating racial preferences with sexuality itself.

In chapter 5, I examine various personal narratives written by gay men of color about interracial and intraracial desires and relationships published on various online magazines and blogs. Rather than focusing on specific publications, I used a modified grounded theory approach to data collection and data analysis. I began data collection using key terms such as "gay men of color intraracial desire," "gay men of color intraracial dating," "gay men of color interracial relationships," and "gay men of color intraracial relationships." I began with the highest ranked articles, coding them along the way and identifying various themes that emerged. Using the emergent codes, I engaged in a more focused data collection, paying particular attention to other narratives that were either linked or discussed in previous articles. I continued searching for new articles until I reached saturation, whereby no new themes emerged. This method led to a total of forty-two different articles for analysis. Gay men of color frame intraracial desires in three large ways. First, they may see intraracial desires as a personal journal toward racial awareness, a form of protection from racism by gay white men, and, most importantly, a political act that directly confronts and challenges gay white supremacy.

SEXUAL RESISTANCE

Despite the prevalence of sexual racism and the white-centered logic of gay desire, it would be a mistake to assume that queers of color are simply victims of sexual racism. Hierarchies of desire are never absolute.

Because the racial hierarchy of desire is socially constructed, it is actively challenged. Rather than passively accept racialized narratives of desire, gay men of color challenge the hierarchy of desire through counternarratives regarding both interracial and intraracial desires. Their response to sexual racism should be understood as forms of resistance practiced by queers of color in other arenas of life. Specifically, their sexual desires, whether in the ways they frame their erotic worth or in the ways they frame their inter- and intraracial desires, can be considered a form of disidentification.

According to Judith Butler, disidentification involves attempting to situate oneself (in terms of identity) both within and outside of the existing the identity discourses available to us.[63] This concept was perhaps best developed for queers of color by José Esteban Muñoz in his book *Disidentifications: Queers of Color and the Performance of Politics*. According to Muñoz:

> Disidentification is about recycling and rethinking encoded meaning. The process of disidentification scrambles and reconstructs the encoded messages of a cultural text in a fashion that both exposes the encoded message's universalizing and exclusionary machinations and recircuits its workings to account for, include, and empower minority identities and identifications. Thus, disidentifications is a step further than cracking open the code of the majority; it proceeds to use this code as raw material for representing a disempowered politics or positionality that has been rendered unthinkable by the dominant culture.[64]

For queers of color, disidentification involves taking the dominant narrative of what it means to be both raced and sexualized, repurposing those narratives, and transforming those narratives for their own purposes.

While Muñoz focused specifically on performances rather than the performativity of race and sexuality and how these performers transform existing narratives in their performances, his main argument—that queers of color have more options in how they resist racial and sexual oppression than simply accepting the dominant discourse about race and/or sexuality or rejecting the dominant discourse—can be used to examine how gay men of color take the dominant narratives about race and desire and racialized sexual desires within the gay community and build alternative narratives that reframe those dominant conceptions about race and sexuality.

Gay men of color do not simply accept the larger narratives about sexual worth and desirability, nor do they blindly conform to the sexual expectations of white men. Rather, they confront these narratives in numerous ways, even when it may appear that they are embracing them. Even when gay men enact racialized sexual stereotypes, they often do so in the employ of their own sexual pleasures. Often, gay men of color enact racialized sexual stereotypes while specifically excluding white men as sexual partners, decentering white desire. By decentering white desire even when they deploy racialized sexual stereotypes, gay men of color demonstrate that desire can be directed away from the white gaze and that such racialization of desire can performed outside of white men's fetish for racial difference. In doing so, they center non-whiteness as the center of desire rather than the margins.

Erotic capital:

Sexual value "type of currency"
↳ tall, white, attractive, fit, young, wealth

Notion of sexual field:

- Currency can hold diff weight
in different scenarios/areas/instances

CHAPTER 1

Very Few People Say "No Whites"

Sexual Racism in Gay Communities

BEACON HILL IS A QUIET NEIGHBORHOOD OF MODEST SINGLE-FAMILY homes on a stretch of land that sits a bit south, and a bit more east, of downtown Seattle. On a clear day, there is a sweeping view of Elliott Bay to the west and downtown skyscrapers to the north. When the weather is particularly good, which happens much more regularly than outsiders might imagine, a majestic view of Mount Rainier can be seen to the southeast. From there, it's a quick jaunt up Interstate 5 to Capitol Hill, Seattle's bustling gay neighborhood. But for Rolando Bautista, the distance between an imagined life on Capitol Hill and his actual life on Beacon Hill felt like an insurmountable chasm. For him, "It was really hard and it was very lonely" growing up on Beacon Hill. Compounding this were his perceived feminine mannerisms, which he suspects didn't help him make many friends or fit in with the other students at his school. Despite the fact that Beacon Hill was a predominantly Asian neighborhood with a significant Black population, he was never quite sure if the feeling of loneliness came from his being a person of color or "how much of that was due to knowing that [he] was different because [he] liked boys." Whatever the reason, he knew he didn't quite fit in.

After always feeling different from everyone else because of his attraction to men, he experienced his first night at a gay bar as surreal:

first gay bar experience = "freedom"

I still to this day remember the very first Friday night after I turned twenty-one when I went to Neighbours [a local gay bar]. That was the first gay bar that I ever went to, and I thought I had died and, you know, went to gay heaven with all the men dancing on the boxes and the music, and I remember feeling finally free and not being ashamed and not feeling alone.

common escape experience

In many ways, Bautista's initial experience on that first night was not unlike those shared by many other gay men for whom gay bars represent a refugee from a homophobic and heterosexualized world, a place where they can finally feel free, even if only for a night.

Gay bars have long been social anchors for gay men and women and the center of gay social life. But for Bautista, the sense of finally having found a haven was short lived. As he recalled:

I think it was a false sense of security and a false sense of, uh, a false sense of community . . . I thought I was going to be very easy to meet, you know, a guy and fall happily ever after and all the naiveness that you think. So I didn't know very much about how people were in the gay community, especially at the bars . . . I spent a lot of time just sitting in the corner, watching and observing, and then after a few times of just going to the bars, I started to feel like it was high school all over again.

After the first burst of euphoria faded, he was once again on the margins, watching from the sidelines and not really fitting in. This too is a common experience for some gay men, particularly men of color, as they find that within the gay bar, their "value," as defined within the erotic world of the bar, doesn't measure up to the standards that exist there. While many different characteristics may be assigned different levels of erotic worth in different types of gay bars, gay men of color come to realize that not only does their race afford them little erotic value and provide them little currency with which to negotiate social and sexual interactions, it actively hinders them from fully participating in the sexually charged life of a gay bar, leading many to sit in the corner and watch. For Bautista and many *[handwritten: Being rejected in a scenario of supposed Acceptance (still discrimination everywhere)]*

others, it's a second rejection, one that cuts particularly hard given the expectation of acceptance after what can feel like a lifetime of rejection.[1]

While mobile apps have afforded gay men a new way of sexually and socially connecting with other gay men, a disturbingly similar racial dynamic has been widely reported. Writing for *Vice* magazine, Manisha Krishnan observed, "They read more like signs you'd see affixed to the doorway of a 60s-era American diner than messages you'd encounter on a modern dating forum. 'No Blacks'; 'no asians'; 'WHITE ONLY!!' And that's a relatively benign selection."[2] *[handwritten: ← Example of discrimination again]*

The "they" to which Krishnan is referring are user profiles she found posted on Grindr, the most widely used and most widely recognized gay hook-up app. As Krishnan noted, these are the "relatively benign" comments. More blatantly racist comments, such as those collected by the website Douchebags of Grindr, where users have uploaded the profiles of thousands of "douchebags," betray an ugly underside to gay racial desire and the ways that such desires are conveyed. Comments such as "I block more Asians than the great wall of China," "Squinty eye, no reply," and "I don't speak Ebonics," as well as derogatory comments playing specifically on racial stereotypes, such as, "I don't like Asians, I like big cocks," or "Not into Black guys or other thugs," are routine. Rather than simply listing preferred characteristics, online sites and dating apps for seeking sexual partners have delved into venues for gay white men to openly flaunt and vocalize their racist beliefs. As Jeff Lau told Krishnan about gay dating apps, "It's like another world. . . . It's like an outlet for [gay white men] to act out on it and live out this white supremacist idealism." *[handwritten: gay sexual racism]*

The racism expressed by gay white men on Grindr should come as no surprise to any astute observer. Within the past few decades, a significant amount of literature on the experiences of gay men of color have demonstrated that contemporary gay life is marked by high levels of racism directed toward them by gay white men, with much of it manifesting itself as negative sexual attitudes toward, and sexual exclusion or fetishization of, non-white men.[3] Gay white men routinely and actively exclude non-white men as potential sexual partners or racially fetishize men of color when they do prefer them over other white men.[4] Despite many gay men's insistence that sexual exclusion and/or sexual fetishization is not

White gay men deny it

inherently racist, there is evidence that attitudes toward sexual exclusion are related to almost every identified factor associated with racist attitudes in general. Even gay white men who do not actively engage in acts of racially based sexual exclusion seem to be tolerant of racist behaviors from other gay white men who do.[5]

While the idea of sexual racism has been widely discussed in the popular press, and academic studies have also documented the racial hierarchy of desire in gay communities, most of these discussions have focused on whether sexual racism was indeed racism or just personal preference. Conspicuously missing have been attempts to systematically examine how such racialized hierarchies of desire and the practice of sexual racism are understood by gay men of color and the impact it has on them. Yet sexual racism and sexual desires cannot be understood outside of the larger erotic world of the gay marketplace of desire and how that erotic world is shaped by whiteness and the desire for whiteness. Rather than personal preferences, erotic desires are the consequences of the formation of erotic worlds in which whiteness comes to have more value and worth precisely because whiteness has more value and worth outside of erotic worlds. Rather than simply a matter of personal preference, racial preferences for sexual partners is evidence of a racialized hierarchy of sexual and social worth. And it is patterned and predictable because the erotic marketplace of desire among gay men places a premium on whiteness.

WHITENESS IN THE EROTIC MARKETPLACE OF DESIRE

According to Adam Isaiah Green, "Modern urban life is increasingly characterized by specialized erotic worlds designed for sexual partnership and sexual sociality."[6] These erotic worlds, marked by high levels of interpersonal interactions between various actors, where individuals come to seek sexual and social partners, can be considered a "sexual field." Both within and outside of gay communities, there are many diverse sexual fields where different constellations of traits come to be seen as more desirable than other traits. Age, body type, ways of dressing, and social class (at least the presentation of social class through clothing, consumption patterns, etc.), all become forms of sexual currency that become more or less valuable depending on the social setting. At a leather bar, the murals of "very masculine looking, muscular, hairy, 30- and 40-something *white men* clad in black leather chaps and boots" might imply that those are the men who are deemed most desirable by the bar's patrons, while posters of "20-something, shirtless, muscular, hairless men in athletic shorts, jockstraps, and similar attire" at the sports bar might signal the same for their patrons. "The representations of sexual desirability in these two bars communicate distinct structures of desire that favor distinct classes of sexual actors."[7] What is considered desirable in one location may not translate to another. The key takeaway is that in different sexual fields, different characteristics are considered desirable, and what is considered desirable or undesirable in one sexual field does not easily transfer to other sexual fields.

While the different types of sexual fields within the gay communities have been discussed and are now widely recognized, there has been less attention paid to the ways that such sexual fields and the erotic worlds they represent may be influenced by larger societal factors such as race.[8] This lack of attention to the sexual organization of erotic worlds along larger structural factors is particularly problematic given that much of an individual's sexual life occurs within an erotic world that is "consistently patterned within and organized by particular communities, social networks, organizations, and meaning systems."[9] That is, sexual desires are often influenced by larger social constructions of race, ethnicity, age, and class, and the social meanings given to race has always played a critical role in the construction of desire and desirability.[10] Imagining sexual fields as independent social arenas rather than a part of a larger organized social system leads one to believe that they are self-contained erotic marketplaces where those who possess valued traits are on equal footing, regardless of larger structural factors.

Yet sexual fields are not isolated arenas. They are embedded within a larger society whose values are reflected in what is considered desirable within a given sexual field.[11] As evidenced by Green's own accounts of his field work and by the statements made by participants in his study, race plays a pivotal role in defining attractiveness and desirability across various sexual fields within gay communities. Whether the specific field in question is a gay leather bar or a gay sports bar where different types of dress, degrees of muscularity, and amounts of body hair are deemed more desirable, race remains a consistent, and constant, marker of desirability across all different sexual fields within gay male communities.

A possible explanation for the durability of race across different sexual fields may be because unlike characteristics such as clothing, muscularity, and body hair, whiteness is a central organizing principle in gay communities.[12] In promoting equality through the normalization of (homo)sexuality at the expense of "non-gay" issues, gay organizations such as the Human Rights Campaign promote a monolithic image of the gay community as being rich, conservative, and white. Media images of gay men also use whiteness as a marker for gay normality. Because whiteness is an organizing principle of what it now means to be gay, and because gayness is now equated with whiteness, whiteness embeds itself in all aspects of gay life, even erotic ones. The centrality of whiteness as the organizing principle in gay life leads to the creation of a gay marketplace of desire where whiteness has a value, in and of itself, in sexual exchange. Because of this, whiteness transcends diverse micro-level sexual fields within gay communities and acts as a universal currency that supersedes all other characteristics deemed worthy within any given sexual field. Thus, it isn't enough for one to wear the appropriate clothes or possess the ideal muscle mass, if the clothes and the muscles aren't framed over a white body.

In some instances, even the traits deemed desirable within a sexual field seems to be negated by race. In my previous book, *Geisha of a Different Kind*, I quoted one gay Asian man who attempted to make himself more desirable at gay bars by changing his body through exercise:

> I had muscles where I didn't think you had muscles. I looked really good. I was down to 2 percent body fat, and every muscle in my entire body was obvious. . . . I used to go to West Hollywood where the non-rice bars were, and I could count on both hands how many times I got picked up or I could pick up, actually went to bed with somebody from a non-rice bar. It was horrendous. If I went by myself, I was standing in the only empty area of the entire god damn bar.

I used to have a ten-foot area around me, and people would avoid me. I couldn't believe it.[13]

So while muscularity may be the desired trait in a "muscle bar," the lived reality for gay men of color is that their attempts to develop or acquire the currency of desirability within those specific gay spaces, or sexual fields, is negated by their race. Put simply, across different sexual fields found within gay communities, race seems to trump all other characteristics.

Certainly, social and virtual sites where race itself is the blatant sexual currency exist. Within these spaces, men of different races interact primarily for the purpose of meeting other men of a specific race. In groups such as Long Yang Club and Black and White Men Together, race itself is the organizing principle of sexual interaction. While there are racial nuances to these groups that make them more than simply another sexual field, particularly Black and White Men Together that have a history of attempting to counter racial fetish as well as promote racial justice, members of these groups nonetheless initially join for the purpose of meeting men of a given race, not those who share similar tastes in clothes, have similar body types, or perform similar gender presentations.[14] Race has sexual currency precisely because it is the sexual product being consumed. But as I've argued elsewhere, even these spaces are often sites where whiteness has more value. When white men are seen as being few in number, these groups often fail to maintain themselves.[15] It is a sexual marketplace only in the sense that white men bring the currency of whiteness to "purchase" non-white sexual partners. Thus, white men continue to have the upper hand in sexual negotiations. Also, on many occasions, when gay men of color are sexually preferred by gay white men, they are often preferred not as individuals but because they fulfill racial stereotypes regarding sexual behaviors. Thus, gay men of color are only sexually desired if they fulfill the racialized sexual fantasies of white men. While they may be able to trade their race for sex within such racialized sexual marketplaces, their race has value only if it conforms to white expectations about race.

Given that race traverses different sexual fields, we must ask, How does race and the racial hierarchy of desire impact social and sexual relationships between gay men? While the sexual fields that Green identifies are largely physical spaces, is it possible to imagine race as a conceptual sexual field whereby beliefs about race and the values placed on race drive sexual desires across different social arenas? In order to address these questions, we must examine if race meets the criteria of a sexual field outlined by Green and examine if the rules of the field dictate sexual behaviors among participants.

A sexual field is easily identifiable based on a number of characteristics. First, "patterns in 'hooking up' systematically favor certain individuals or groups over others" and favored individuals or groups are easily identified in the interaction order by members of the field.[16] While individual actors bring differing levels of sexual capital with which they negotiate the field, the sexual capital available to them is not as much individually possessed as it is embedded within larger societal values that assign more social worth to certain characteristics. Within a sexual field, six key interactional processes occur: (1) actors' recognition that the sexual field is constituted by a set of relations anchored to competition and sexual selection; (2) the perception of a generalized other within the field, including knowledge concerning a given field's collective valuations of sexual attractiveness; (3) a formulation of one's own position within the sexual status order vis-à-vis intersubjective feedback and the development of a looking-glass self; (4) an assessment of others' positions within the sexual status order; (5) knowledge of the "game" – including how to conduct a successful self-performance, the construction of an optimizing front and proper filed-specific demeanor; and finally, ideally, (6) the ability to "save face."[17]

Put simply, sexual desire within any sexual field is based on a hierarchy of desirable traits, with some individuals possessing more of those traits than others. Some individuals come to be seen as more desirable than other individuals depending on the traits that they possess that are valued by the specific sexual field in which they operate. There also needs to be recognition among individuals regarding their own social position based on those collective traits rather than individual ones. In order to determine whether race is, in fact, a conceptual sexual field and explore how race itself is implicated in gay desire, we need to examine if race acts as an organizing factor in gay sexual desires. One way to address this particular question is to examine the sexual fields perspective using a sexual racism lens.

In his book *Boystown*, Jason Orne argued that sexual racism is "a system of racial oppression, shaping an individual's partner choices to privilege whites and harm people of color" that manifests itself structurally, culturally, and interactionally.[18] First, structural sexual racism limits the availability of partners within the social environment. While this can involve physical segregation of gay men of color and gay white men into different social locations, structural sexual racism also includes marginally integrated "mixed bars," where gay men of color and gay white men occupy different areas of the establishment. Cultural sexual racism involves the creation and maintenance of patterns of social and sexual interactions based on racialized sexual stereotypes that lead to objectification of men of color as well as the culturally constructed definition of who is "hot." Finally, interactional sexual racism involves the active discrimination against members of minority groups. While some are overt, such as statements like "no fats, no femmes, no Asians" on online dating apps, interactional sexual racism also includes more subtle actions, such as bars changing music or enforcing dress codes to limit the number of men of color or gay white men and warning other white men to avoid certain clubs based on the race of the clientele. These three dimensions of sexual racism operate to not only construct white men as being more desirable but also to construct men of color as being less desirable and therefore socially undesirable as well. If we think about race as a conceptual sexual field through the lens of sexual racism, then we should find that gay men of color are structurally, culturally, and interactionally excluded based on the perceived desirability of race.

Despite the structural nature of sexual racism, it often hides under the guise of personal preference, masking racist actions as a reflection of personal taste rather than racial exclusion. Yes, sexual preference for a certain race does manifest itself as a personal taste in a certain "type" of man on the individual level. Yet to borrow a quote from Susan Sontag, "The rules of taste reinforce structures of power."[19] It isn't simply that white men are considered more desirable in gay communities but that there is a pattern of preference for white men, even among gay men of color, that hides the larger structures of power that place a premium value on whiteness that drives the preferences we believe are personal. Not only do gay men of color prefer white men as sexual partners, they are also much more likely than even gay white men to exclude members of their own race as potential sexual partners. Men of color who state a sexual preference for another race are overwhelmingly likely to prefer white men, with 97 percent of Asian men, 90 percent of Latino men, and 88 percent of Black men who prefer men of another race stating a preference specifically for white men. Rather than individual preferences, these patterns of racialized preferences seem to be the result of larger structures of power and racialized beliefs. Given the patterns of preferences that favor white men over men of color, we can conclude that race itself is an organizing principle of desire among gay men.[20] And if race itself is a conceptual sexual field, how do gay men of color perceive, negotiate, and experience social sexual interactions within that particular field?

THE UNDOUBTABLE DESIRABILITY OF WHITENESS

If race is a conceptual sexual field, there should be widespread recognition regarding which individuals are more desirable based on racial, rather than individual, characteristics. Gay men of color recognized that being white afforded white men with more opportunities for sexual contact than gay men of color. When asked about looking for sex online, one gay Asian man said:

> Caucasian tend to work very well for many people, and there's very few people that say "no whites." You know, some do say "no whites," but it's very rare compared to other ethnicities. . . . You almost never fail to be a Caucasian. . . . But for ethnic people, there tends to be more bias. Like you see a lot of places, "no Asians" or "no Blacks" or "only attracted to whites and Latinos" and stuff. And it's everywhere.

According to many men of color, white men were seen as being universally desirable among gay men. Rather than being limited to specific physical spaces such as leather bars or twink bars or to specific websites and dating apps, the desire for whiteness was said to be "everywhere." Thus, being white was perceived to "work very well" in securing sex. This isn't surprising given the widespread belief that whiteness works well everywhere, even those sexual sites that allegedly cater to different "types" of gay men.[21]

It wasn't simply that being white gave white men an advantage when it came to seeking sexual partners but that being non-white specifically hindered gay men of color from finding sexual intimacy. Gay men of color understood that not being white made them less desirable to potential sexual partners, even other men of color. This was particularly problematic the more stereotypically racialized physical features one possessed. As one gay Latino man shared:

> It's like the more European that you have, the better off you proba-
> bly are. And then the more like indigenous you look . . . it's not the
> same. It's different, so I think there's a definite preference. . . . I'm
> convinced that I probably inherited more of one, like my mother's
> side of the family, which has Zapotecan Indian grandmother, great
> grandmother at one point, so . . . that definitely expresses itself in
> the way that I look. . . . It's kind of a source of insecurity.

While some white men may argue that their preference for other white men has more to do with shared social experiences, the sexual exclusion of gay men of color by gay white men is not about place of origin or dif-ferences in cultural values. Instead, it is specifically about how one looks and the more one looks European, the more one can be successful in finding a sexual partner, regardless of cultural or social backgrounds. Collectively, gay men of color understood that whiteness was the currency that held the most value when seeking sexual partners, not shared cultural practices, life experiences, or any other characteristics.

There was also a recognized racial hierarchy that non-white men understood. Gay men of color were aware of the racial hierarchy within gay communities and knew where to place themselves within that hier-archy. As the man quoted above went on to state:

Well, I figured, I realized that my situation wasn't as bad. It sounds terrible, but I, you know, you always have to think about Black gays, and I think their situation is probably a hundred times worse than mine. . . . You reassure yourself by looking at other people and sort of recognizing the racial hierarchy and kind of establishing where you fit in that.

This isn't to suggest that the nuances of the racial hierarchy were widely shared by all gay men of color. Instead, many men, based on their own personal experiences with dating, put their own race at the bottom. In discussing the racial hierarchy, a gay Asian man said:

I guess there's a social hierarchy . . . sexually . . . in our community and where certain ethnic groups or racial groups are still seen as the model ideal, you know, form of beauty and Asians definitely not the top. It's more toward the bottom, you know, if not the bottom. . . . So that . . . I feel marginalized already there in the sexual market, you know, the sexual community.

Other men were more diplomatic in not placing non-white men into specific rankings where one group of gay men of color was above another. However, they were all nonetheless well aware of the primacy of whiteness in sexual attraction. A gay Black man had this to say:

Like if you were to go to like Micky's or Rage in West Hollywood, you don't see too many Black people. If you do, they'll . . . hug up on white guys. And nothing wrong with that, you know. You like what you like. But . . . if you're Black you wouldn't go to West Hollywood looking for a Black guy, you know. You'd go to one of the little Black clubs or bars they have, the few they have and hope you find something decent.

As is obvious by his statement, there was widespread recognition that mainstream gay spaces were organized largely to cater to white desires, and whiteness was the currency of desire within these spaces. As he noted, gay men of color within mainstream gay spaces were also there seeking white sexual partners. For those whose desires ran counter to the dominant narrative of racial desirability, opportunities for sexual contact were even more limited.

For many gay men of color, race became an issue only after becoming more involved in gay communities, testifying to the power of a racialized sexual field in dictating desirability and how gay men come to see themselves as sexual beings within a gay sexual field. One gay Asian man who grew up in Phoenix, where he was one of only five Asians in his school, had this to say about his first experiences with a gay community:

> And at the time, the fashion was "the fashion," meaning not just clothing but the whole, the public taste in the gay world, and the kind of what was en vogue then, was this very white, preppy, Ralph Lauren image. Literally, I mean with you know, the Izod shirts and the Topsiders, and so I felt out of place. . . . But I mean, I remember feeling like I needed to conform to that. I remember feeling like, you know, I remember being very aware that my general look and everything was not what was en vogue.

Although his recollection about his entrée into the gay community was focused largely on fashion, he went out of his way to note that the fashion included not only what one wore, but the whiteness associated with what one wore. Later, he went on to explain further, using Abercrombie and Fitch as an example of how fashion that is valued in the gay community is marked by whiteness. Thus, the "gay look" that comes to be equated with being fashionable and, therefore, desirable is not only available to white men but comes to be *equated* with white men. Because of this, attempts to acquire nonracial traits or characteristics that have value within a specific sexual field become futile for men of color. Without possessing the very whiteness that clothing brands such as Abercrombie and Fitch come to represent, men of color simply do not get the same benefit of those clothes. An argument can be made that these clothes come to have value in a sexual field precisely because they are marked as white.

For some gay men of color, learning that their race was not valued was a gradual development that formed within the context of seeking a sexual partner within a gay community. As one gay Asian man said:

> I don't think I was probably conscious of it for a long time. I think it was probably, I just attributed it to people online, flaky. But then it became obvious, you know? Asian was the key word that made a lot of people, probably at least half the people online, just stop talking altogether. I think it's really, I don't know, it's really saddening that in a metropolitan city in our current times that that still happens, but I think it happens just as much as ever. I think there's just so much racism, maybe not as overt but I think it just shows that racism changes, manifests in different ways.

This growing awareness that their race made them somehow less valuable to other gay men and that their race placed them in a disadvantaged sexual position, placed gay men of color in a situation that led them to learn how to navigate the sexual terrain directly in response to the racial hierarchy of desire that they encountered.

LEARNING TO PLAY THE GAME

One result of the participants coming to understand what is desirable within any sexual field is that they come to learn how to navigate within the field in order to gain access to those who possess more desirable attributes. One could say that participants within the field learned how to play the "game."

Given that attempts by men of color to acquire nonracial characteristics such as body type or clothing were negated by race, many gay men of color come to realize that playing the game involved possessing physical characteristics that are stereotypically associated with members of their racial group in order to trade white perceptions about race for whiteness. As one Black man said:

example of trying not conform to stereotypes

You know, the Black man myth, you know. You know, it'd better be big, you know, you've to big lips and big, big feet. You've got to be, you know, have a really big dick. Oh, he's got a big one, you know, a lot of different things like that.

Men of color realized that possessing certain physical traits made them more desirable to some gay white men who fetishize men of color. For gay men of color, these physical characteristics were often marked by racial stereotypes about penis size, body hair, and stature, widely shared within and outside of gay communities. They understood which stereotypical racialized characteristics were considered desirable by white men, and they framed their erotic worth along those characteristics. At the same time, simply possessing physical traits associated with members of their group was not enough.

For many of these men, playing the game involved meeting the sexual expectations, in terms of sexual behaviors, of gay white men as well. According to one gay Asian man:

> That's usually what people expect of me, is I'm going to bottom. You know. I will top somebody, if they want me to, I'm not opposed to that at all. But generally speaking, you know, people are usually wanting me to bottom. . . . It's like, and probably other minorities are this way, too. I mean, it's just, you know, it's not rocket science, it's like minorities are used to you know, having the crumbs, you know, or being offered the crumbs. You know, they don't speak up, they don't protest, you know, if they don't like something. They feel like particularly where, you know, it's a white person involved, that they need to acquiesce to that person. And I felt that way, and I would say that most minorities feel that way, if not nearly all.

The racial dynamics in gay communities not only determined which physical characteristics were deemed more desirable when possessed by men of color but also what type of behaviors were desirable from men of color. There behavioral expectations influenced how gay men of color interacted with gay white men. Because gay white men were considered more desirable, therefore possessing more worth, they were viewed as having a stronger bargaining position when it came to sexual activities.

Often, this meant presenting themselves as fitting stereotypical behavioral expectations and highlighting their stereotypical physical characteristics. When gay men of color could not fulfill white expectations, they found themselves in a disadvantaged position for sexual partners compared to the men of color who could. As one Latino man noted:

> You know, it's just the whole image of that [machismo], it's just hard because people who like Latins and stuff like that, that's what they see, that's what they want. And when you can't deliver that, it's, you know, it's, they don't like their bubbles being burst.

When asked to elaborate, he added:

> Most white people tend to have like this fixed image of what a Latin person should be or do or act. Yeah, like it's, you know, like the whole penis thing is kind of funny. You know, people think that all Latins have like this huge penis and stuff like that, you know, and it's like no, we're people. It's pretty much average like everybody else unless you meet someone who's just exceptionally large, you know. And they get really disappointed when, you know, they don't see that on you. So god forbid if a Latin person had his, like, foreskin cut off. Then that would like really freak them out.

As the above man states, the inability, or the unwillingness, to fulfill white male sexual fantasies about men of color made it difficult for him to find sexual partners. For some gay men of color, the need to play the game led to significant personal reflection, questioning whether sex was worth the playing into white male fantasies.

Gay men of color also understood that in order to secure a white sexual partner, they needed to fit existing racial stereotypes about them. After describing gay communities as being unwelcoming to gay Black men, one

Black man had this to say about the type of Black man that might be better accepted by gay white men:

> Now if you happen to be a big black masculine guy with maybe a big black dick then yeah, maybe they may be more accepting, maybe might like you or whatever. 'Cause gay men across the board seem to have issues with feminine guys and, you know, stuff, stuff like that.

Clearly, gay men of color understood that only some men of color, those who fit the stereotypes imposed on them by white men, were considered to be desirable—and even then, only to a small subgroup of gay white men who were specifically attempting to fulfill fetishized sexual desires.

But for gay men of color, playing the game also comes at a cost. Once the sexual fantasy was fulfilled, many gay men of color noted that their utility became less for gay white men. As one Black man shared:

> One of the learning experiences that kind of brought me to a place of, you know, not running after a relationship . . . there's also been other situations where, you know, maybe I've had sex with some-one and after I've had sex with them, there's an avoidance or just a, there's a look, it's, you know, almost as if a fantasy might be ful-filled for them but as an individual, you know, that's what they wanted, that's all they wanted, and they're done, you know.

As the above quote demonstrates, gay men of color were placed in a dif-ficult situation in navigating the racialized sexual field. On the one hand, the desire for whiteness marked them as less desirable than white men. At the same time, finding sexual partners, specifically white sexual part-ners, involved fitting the very same stereotypes that led to them being excluded by other gay white men who did not hold the same types of racial fetishes. Unfortunately, even when gay men of color managed to fulfill gay white racial fantasies, they found themselves discarded when the fetish was fulfilled.

A sexual field is not a neutral playing field where individual preferences determine who is valued and who is not. Because some characteristics are valued over other characteristics, individuals are accorded varying levels of worth based on the larger collective beliefs about which characteristics are desirable and which are not. This hierarchy of desire leads to negative consequences for those who are seen as being less desirable.

One of the most negative consequences for gay men of color was a feeling of marginalization in gay communities. As one gay Asian man shared:

> Frustrating, you know, if I'm online and people just, you know, see that I'm Asian and they just bypass me or in the sex club they just walk by me without looking or without acknowledgment, you know. So I feel marginalized, I feel isolated, I feel, you know, yeah, not wanted.

Other gay men of color repeatedly expressed the sense of feeling unwanted and marginalized, and it wasn't just the sense that they were not being acknowledged by gay white men but rather that the entire atmosphere of gay-identified spaces was seen as being unwelcoming to men of color. When asked to expand on why he felt unwelcome at gay bars, one gay Black man stated:

> If you're a Black, if you're a Black gay man and you're out, you're out of the closet, you, you don't feel accepted by the white gay community because for the most part, white men are into white men. I live in West Hollywood, and I don't feel as if, do I, do I feel like that's, that's my community? No, that's my neighborhood, I live there. But that's not my community.

For some gay men of color, the feeling of exclusion was based on both race and perceived social class. When asked to describe a specific situation when he felt out of place, one Latino man said:

Maybe because I'm not wearing, you know, the right type of clothes or I don't look exactly like the mold that, you know, is dancing at the party. They're tall, you know, blond and blue-eyed or tall.

For this particular man, his feeling of alienation had to do with both not being blond and blue-eyed as well as not wearing the "right type of clothes." Given the atmosphere of the gayborhood and the businesses found within the gayborhood, many of the men stated that they often avoid being in the area at all. The tendency to avoid gay spaces was found across all racial groups and relatively widespread, leading to further alienation for gay men of color.

Given the centrality of race to the way that they are treated within gay communities, gay men of color spent a significant amount of time thinking about sexual racism. As one Latino man said:

Well, I'm preoccupied with racism, I think. And very jealous and very bitter about a lot of stuff in my life. I felt I missed my youth. I felt I never really had the sort of sexual appeal that is often associated with youth so a lot, a lot of problems that I've experienced have sort of stemmed from that I think. It's anger, bitterness, resentment, all that sort of thing. . . . I just became kind of obsessed with it, you know, to what extent does my race have something to do with my failure to date people that I want to date? Yeah, it's been a recurring issue.

Experiences of sexual racism led men to feel resentment toward other gay men and to the gay community in general, further leading to alienation and isolation from predominantly gay spaces and social circles.

Ironically, sexual racism made it difficult for gay men of color to develop connections to other gay men of color. As one gay Black man stated:

And it's like, if you do see another Black person, normally, I guess, there's some unwritten code that if you're Black, you know, you just speak to another Black person just 'cause you're Black, you know?

But it just seems like in West Hollywood, that unwritten code doesn't stand. You might see a Black person in a club, and you might speak to them. For whatever reason, they might not speak back.

When asked to describe his experiences with other Asians, a gay Asian man said:

> I don't associate with Asians too much. Like, I only have about three Asian friends. Like, I talk to them in good terms and stuff. So, and plus, with the Asians, I don't usually, if I happen to be in the community, I don't usually just come out, because my preference is not Asian, so then it's no big deal for me.

Not finding other Asian men attractive led to his having minimal contact with other gay Asian men. Gay men of color often discussed seeing other men of color as competition for limited number of white men who preferred men of color as sexual partners. Because they were competing for white men, it was difficult for them to build strong friendships with members of their own race. Ironically, many of the men discussed how they were different from other gay men of color, with some arguing that they have a difficult time finding sexual partners because they did not fit the stereotype for their race.

The negative experiences of gay men of color with sexual racism placed gay men of color in a difficult position in terms of dating. While many stated a sexual preference for white men, they also questioned the motivations behind the white men who showed interest in them. As one gay Asian man stated:

> Or . . . people who want Asian only, you know. Are they asking for someone who, just because they love Asian cultures, or because— or they like the Asian body, you know, the type of feel to it, or is there more than that? Are they looking for someone who's submissive? Are they looking for someone who they can push around? Or are they looking for someone that they can . . . showcase? . . . So I

want to have a better idea of where they're coming from before . . .
I want to meet, before I meet up with them.

This shared sentiment that white men who were exclusively attracted to
men of color were less desirable than other white men was widely shared
among gay men of color and traces back to the way these men are also seen
by other gay white men. Because the white men who specifically sought
out men of color as sexual partners were seen by other white men as somehow lacking, they were, for the most part, the least desirable white men.

Ironically, gay men of color came to hold similar views of other racial
groups. One gay Black man had this to say:

> I hate to say this, but I think certain races, . . . as far as sex-wise,
> are known to be more open to trying new things or to play certain
> roles. And I want to say like, ok, Asians, maybe they're viewed as
> being like submissive. And so like if you're a top or whatever you
> know, you want somebody down. You want to find you an Asian
> 'cause you know they'll submit to you, and if you'd like somebody
> that wants to do everything, go find you a white boy. You know,
> white people, they do it all, you know. . . . And you know, Black
> people, you know, well, I guess they're just freaks. You know, they've
> got big dicks and they do whatever they do and you know, that type
> of stuff, you know, crazy stuff.

Because of these beliefs, gay men of color were also less likely to express
a preference for other men of color, including members of their own race,
further limiting their options. When asked to describe the type of men
he finds attractive, a Latino respondent stated:

> Well, I guess I prefer someone around my age or older. And then
> Caucasians and Latins. I don't go for Asians or for African Ameri-
> cans. I'm just not attracted to 'em. . . . Latin people, I've noticed, I
> don't know if I should speak on it, but tend to get together maybe
> as a second resort . . . So I've only dated like white guys and no
> African American people.

When asked about their own sexual attractions, very few of the men indicated that they preferred members of their own race as sexual partners, while many stated a preference specifically for white men. This was surprising given that many of the men also indicated that they did not necessarily have a "type" in terms of age and/or body types, but nonetheless indicated a racial preference for white men.

RESISTANCE AND CHANGE

Despite the constant and considerable focus on white men, many gay men of color recognized the racism embedded in sexual desire, whether they were excluded or fetishized. As one gay Asian man noted:

> I do feel like I get fetishized a lot. Online or just where older white males want to date me. And at the same time, I also experience not being liked by other people because I'm Asian and because the whole stereotype of not being desired because you're Asian.

Several of the men indicated that sexual racism was, indeed, a racist act and therefore should be confronted as a racist act. As one gay Black man said:

> I call this the decade of the angry white male anyway. . . . I mean, things like you even read online. "Not into Black, not into Black or Asian. No offense." That's fucking offensive. To categorically deny people. We all have our preferences. But to say friends or, to me that is the most, just, you know, disdainable thing, and I find that I've never tolerated that here.

Other gay men of color also noted that sexual racism was an issue of racial power, not individual preference.

For many gay men of color, resistance and change also involved attempting to create a non-white gay aesthetic that would make them feel more authentic as men of color. One Latino man shared a story about a friend who eventually found a "gay Latino" aesthetic after attempting to conform to what he believed it meant to be gay:

> For example, there was a guy . . . who once told me . . . when he first came out, you know, he completely plucked out his eyebrows, . . . dyed his hair blond, bleached blond, and started just wearing extremely tight clothes even though that wasn't him. . . . Why? Because he thought being Latino and gay, that's what he had to look like. . . . It was until he got older that he saw that, "You know what, that's not me. . . . I'm a guy who likes wearing my baggies and my tank top and just sticking my hair back, you know?" I mean, I think as a Latino, yeah, we experience trying to find our place without having to conform to the stereotypes of what a gay male needs to look like.

Interestingly, the man quoted above also shared that he no longer hangs out in West Hollywood area—the gayborhood—despite acknowledging that the area was the first place he went to explore and discover his sexuality. When another Latino man was asked to expand on his statement that he no longer dates white men or hangs out in West Hollywood, he replied:

> I had gone to Micky's, Rage, Mother Load, but those are not my kind of places. I don't like that music, techno. I think it's just too queeny for me. I don't like it. I'm more, I guess, . . . a roughneck, like a Mexican. I'm more into the Latino style more. I've tried a little bit of Britney Spears and all that kind of, but it's just not me. It's just not me.

Both men framed their movement away from what they perceived was the gay community by first discussing the ways that the gay community was not necessarily welcoming of gay men of color.

Also, even when their own sexual desires were directed toward white men, some men saw changes among younger men of color. More importantly, they saw these changes as being positive for them as a whole. One gay Asian man stated:

I see a lot of young Asian guys that are completely different than I was when I was that age. You know, . . . they have a lot more kind of outward pride, it seems. And they also have a lot more unity between them. There's like this whole Asian brotherhood thing, and also Asians who date Asians, which was not the case when I was that age. You know, it was really all about mostly white guys that date Asian guys, and Asian guys dated white guys. Now there's a lot of Asian guys that date Asian guys. So that in itself tells me that . . . the self-image thing is improving. You know, the self-esteem thing, because . . . we're finding each other more attractive than we ever have.

Thus, while his own sexual preference was for white men, he saw the growing number of Asian couples as having a positive impact on the way that gay Asians were perceived. So while personal preferences were slow to change, attitudes toward those preferences were becoming more critical.

CONCLUSION

Within different sexual fields, certain traits and characteristics come to have more value than others when seeking a sexual partner. Gay venues often reflect such preferences through a multitude of different types of bars, such as leather bars and sports bars, which cater to different "tastes." But sexual fields cannot be understood outside the social context in which they develop. Not only do sexual fields represent larger societal beliefs about social worth, but they also actively reinforce them. In terms of race, the very way that the sexual marketplace for gay men is organized by race offers gay men of color fewer opportunities for finding sexual partners in the same way that larger beliefs about race limit opportunities for people of color in general. Because whiteness is a central organizing principal in contemporary gay life that is actively used to promote gay normalcy and assimilation, whiteness comes to have value across seemingly different erotic worlds.

Structurally, gay spaces come to be seen as largely white spaces, and they become actively unwelcoming of gay men of color, leading many of them to avoid such spaces. Culturally, whiteness comes to be equated with desirability. The desirability of white men was not limited to other white men. Instead, gay men of color indicated that white men were also preferred by men of color. More than simply a preference for white men, there was also active exclusion of men of color by white men and by other men of color. When white men did prefer men of color as sexual partners over other white men, gay men of color understood that their desirability was based on largely stereotypical traits associated with their race. Thus, gay desire is characterized by high levels of sexual racism that marks gay men of color as being less sexually desirable than gay white men or only desirable specifically because they are a racial fetish.

The racial hierarchy of desire had several negative consequences for gay men of color. First, gay men of color often reported having to "play the game," in order to find sexual partners. That is, they often engaged in sexual activity for the pleasure of white sexual partners, making their own sexual needs secondary. More damaging was the impact that sexual racism had on the self-esteem of gay men of color. Gay men of color often felt marginalized and frustrated in gay communities as a result of their sexual exclusion. Thus, sexual racism had both a sexual and social consequence for gay men of color.

Despite these problems, many gay men of color reported ways that they actively confront sexual racism. A primary method was to challenge sexual desires based on racial fetishes. But a more significant change was in the ways that gay men of color began to see other men of color as potential sexual partners. Several of the men, even those who preferred white men, viewed the rising and visible number of gay men of color dating each other as a challenge to the belief that only white men were sexually desirable.

Examining sexual fields theory through the lens of sexual racism demonstrates that larger social structural factors such as race directly influence personal interactions at the micro level. These structural factors often cancel out the other sexual norms and values that may be found within any given sexual field. Much of what is considered to be unique preferences within sexual fields, such as styles of dress and body sizes, are also raced. Thus, what is considered desirable within sexual fields can also be said to have a racial basis in that certain types of clothes and body shapes are not race-neutral. That is to say, cultural artifacts used by gay men to signal desirability are also white.

Examining the sexual fields perspective through the lens of sexual racism also allows us to better understand how larger social structures influence and impact the ways that seemingly personal desires are rooted in a larger system of racial hierarchies and racial beliefs. Here, I turn to Sharon Patricia Holland's argument that sexual desire cannot be understood without thinking about race, nor can racism be fully examined without grasping the role that sexual desires play in maintaining racial hierarchies.[22] Racialized desires, whether to exclude or fetishize, are marked by race. Because of this, we cannot separate desire from race as if desires are race neutral. Whether one excludes or includes, race is implicated in that decision. By bringing these two perspectives together, we can demonstrate that intimate encounters are often dictated by larger racial structures and that larger racial structures are maintained through intimate encounters.

- Preference is to be white bc it doesnt ever hurt anyone / a disadvantage

- Theres still racism in the gay community
  - more accepted if youre gay + white than gay + poc

CHAPTER 2

Do You Have a Hot White Guy?

Gay Media and the Production of Racialized Desires

IT BEGAN, AS THESE THINGS SO OFTEN DO NOW, WITH A SEEMINGLY random thought thrown out into cyberspace. On March 28, 2016, Sony Music songwriter Jesse Saint John tweeted a criticism of the gay media with the message "'Gay media' needs to reevaluate their content when the major corporations' ad campaigns they're covering are more progressive than them." These advertisements, part of the larger push for gay consumer dollars, have been heralded by some gay rights groups for allegedly being inclusive of the gay experience while simultaneously being criticized by others for presenting an image of the gay community as largely white, male, and upper-class. While Jesse Saint John may not have specifically meant to point out gay media's lack of racial inclusivity within his broader and more generalized comment regarding gay media's tendency to push a middle-class, homonormative image of the gay community, rapper Mykki Blanco took Saint John to point and noted gay media's specific privileging of white men by tweeting a collage of gay magazine covers with the tagline, "How can you see this shit and feel 'apart of the community' or even Progressive???" In a series of subsequent tweets, Blanco continued, "I wonder everyday if 'Gay Media' in 2016 are at all embarrassed when you go to their websites/content and it's only shirtless white guys?" and "I think I will probably be dead before White

Gay Media ever becomes inclusive, I think none of us living now will ever see it LMAO."

Blanco's criticism gained even more traction after blogger-activist Viktor Kerney, using the hashtag #GayMediaSoWhite, responded to Blanco's tweet with their own observations on gay media. Soon, #GayMediaSoWhite began trending. As others joined the conversation, they launched a firestorm of criticism against gay media, noting that when people of color are portrayed at all, it is to talk about sexually transmitted diseases, tragedy, or homophobia in communities of color. Others expanded the criticism to include "mainstream" gay organizations such as GLAAD and HRC, with one commentator tweeting, "They'll campaign if a baker won't make gay wedding cakes but don't care about issues affecting LGBT POC, like homelessness" and another tweeting, "Valid issues queer people of color face gets overshadowed by GLAAD and HRC fundraising galas and marriage equality." The hashtag was later used to criticize the phone app Gmojiz, a gay emoji app, for including only white emojis, with the one exception of an emoji representing drag icon RuPaul. On whatever media platform, be it television, movies, or social media, the overwhelming consensus among gay tweeters of color and their allies was that gay media, in all its forms, is overwhelmingly white.

But something else is going on. It isn't just that people of color don't make it onto the cover of gay magazines or are rarely, if ever, featured as main characters in gay-themed movies or television shows, but that gay people in general are less likely than cisgender straight white men to be featured on the cover of a gay magazine or play the role of a main gay character. A survey of gay magazine covers by John Walker for *Fusion* found that the most likely person to be feature on the cover of a gay magazine was a straight cisgender white man who graced 45 percent of the magazine covers while making up 0 percent of the gay community.[1] Likewise, gay characters in major motion pictures and television shows are more likely to be played by straight, cisgender white men.[2] Straight cisgender white men are also noticeably over represented in gay pornography targeting men. It isn't just that gay magazine covers, gay-themed movies and television shows, and gay male pornography uniformly feature white men, but that they only feature a certain kind of white men, preferably straight. And if not straight, allegedly straight-acting.

A good example is the 2015 film *Stonewall* directed by Roland Emmerich. The famed director, whose films have grossed over $3 billion worldwide, is widely considered to be the most successful openly gay director in history and has been widely praised by gay media for having championed gay causes. The admittedly fictional account of the gay liberation movement that was set in and around the 1969 Stonewall riots marketed itself as capturing the moment in history "where pride began." Yet the release of the first theatrical trailer led to widespread condemnation and ridicule by gay people of color for essentially whitewashing the historic event. As Richard Lawson wrote in *Vanity Fair*, the film depicted the historic moment for the gay rights movement through a "white, bizarrely heteronormative lens" that all but erased people of color or simply treated them as comic sidekicks to the fictional white protagonist specifically engineered to appeal to straight audiences.[3]

Emmerich's response to the criticisms, which included telling *Buzzfeed News* that he "didn't make this movie only for gay people, [he] made it also for straight people," was telling of the ways that gayness has come to be defined. He further went on to say, "I kind of found out, in the testing process, that actually, for straight people, [Danny, the imaginary protagonist] is a very easy in. Danny's very straight-acting. He gets mistreated because of that. [Straight audiences] can feel for him."[4] Emmerich later told the *Guardian* that "Stonewall was a white event, let's be honest" and attributed his inclusion of people of color in supporting roles as "political correctness."[5] In Emmerich's version of gay history and gay imagery, the inclusion of people of color is not for accuracy but for appeasement.

The whiteness of gay media or the presentation of the gay community as largely white, middle-class, cisgender, and male is driven by a carefully crafted image of contemporary gay life specifically designed to win acceptance for gay white men through a possessive investment of whiteness that normalizes gay white men by othering people of color.[6] As Allan Bérubé noted about the push for gay acceptance:

Some gay organizations and media began to aggressively promote the so-called positive image of a generic gay community that is an upscale, mostly male, and mostly white consumer market with mainstream, even traditional, values.[7]

Thus, the importance of #GayMediaSoWhite wasn't that it exposed the lack of diversity in gay media, but that it exposed something much more problematic: the homonormalizing of gay America, specifically for the benefit of straight audiences, that itself has now become ubiquitous. Rather than gay liberation, the goal of gay media seems to be appeasing straight audiences in order to make gay people more acceptable to them. But this acceptance comes only to white cisgender men and often comes at the expense of everyone else.

Whiteness in gay media not only constructs gay white men as normative but also normalizes gay desires on whiteness. Through the centering of whiteness, gay white men are provided more erotic worth than men of color. Whiteness comes to be seen not only as normal, but as desirable. At the same time, constructing whites as normative also depends on constructing non-white groups as deviant.[8] As Viktor Kerney observed, in the few occasions when gay men of color are presented in gay media at all, they are constantly pathologized. When gay men of color are equated with sexual depravity, it further reinforces the normality of gay white men and provides straight audiences with the image of the "bad gay" to which the "good gay" can be compared.

In this chapter, I examine how gay media outlets present men of color differently from how they present white men. Although I explore a number of different publications and websites, I anchor my analysis on *Out* magazine, given its role as the most widely read gay magazine in the US and its reputation as an arbiter of the gay lifestyle. I examined all one hundred issues of the magazine published between 2010 and 2019. I embellish the findings from this analysis with observations of the gay website Adam4Adam, the now defunct gay porn magazine *Inches*, and *Attitude* magazine. Unlike with *Out*, I do not offer, nor claim, a systematic analysis of the other sources. Instead, I use them to support the analysis from *Out* magazine. In examining gay media outlets, I find that not only do these media outlets construct the desire for whiteness as normative, but also simultaneously construct sexual desire for men of color as being a deviation from the norm. While white men are presented as being uniformly and universally desirable, men of color are presented as either lacking sexual worth or having sexual worth only to fulfill a sexual fetish. Specifically, I argue that gay media, in multiple forms, creates a racialized erotic habitus in which white men come to have more sexual value.

THE EROTIC HABITUS AND THE MATTER OF IMAGES

As noted earlier, sociological studies of sexuality have done little to examine sexual desire, making desire the "elephant that sits upon the scholar's desk," leading to a lack of a sociological "framework for understanding the processes by which social structure shapes, impinges upon, and constitutes sexual ideation."[9] One consequence has been that desire comes to be seen as being entirely internal and personal. Yet there is ample evidence to indicate that sexual desire follows a racialized pattern and seems to be heavily influenced by a socially structured sexual marketplace where members of one race come to be seen as being more desirable than members of another race.[10]

To address this rather large elephant, Adam Isaiah Green introduces us to the theory of "erotic habitus." According to the author:

> Erotic habitus is a socially constituted complex of dispositions, appreciations, and inclinations arising from objective historical conditions that mediate the formation and selection of sexual scripts. The concept rests on the principle that sexual desire is oriented to the social world through historically specific erotic habitus that differentially invest particular objects with erotic meaning, while rendering other objects neuter.[11]

Erotic desires are not random, neutral, or personal. Rather, these desires arise from larger structural factors that construct some traits, and some people, as desirable and other traits as undesirable. Much in the way that Pierre Bourdieu theorized habitus to be embodied in the individual,

Green theorizes erotic habitus to be similarly embodied, driving our sub-conscious desires, making these desires seem natural and normal. Our sexual desires, particularly our preferences for "our type," come to be understood as being the result of personal preferences rather than larger social structural influences.[12] Yet Green's main point is that these desires are not personal but are the result of larger structural cues that creates erotic meaning. Individuals internalize these cues, thereby seeing some objects as erotic and other objects as neuter. This process then "orients the undifferentiated biological libido toward particular social forms."[13]

But what exactly is erotic habitus and how does it develop? As can be expected, Green relies heavily on Bourdieu's concept of habitus to develop his theory. According to Bourdieu, habitus is a "system of acquired dispositions functioning on the practical level as categories of perception and assessment or as classificatory principles as well as being the organizing principles of action." That is, habitus shapes the way we understand the world, interpret the events around us, and drives our values and beliefs. Specifically, habitus is "society written into the body, into the biological individual," making our values and beliefs, as well as our actions and our way of life, appear natural and self-evident.[14] Individuals primarily engage with the world in a way that their habitus predisposes them to do, thereby reproducing their already existing worldview. These practices then lead to the creation of doxa, situations in which "the natural and social world appears as self-evident." Yet the self-evidence of the natural and social world "goes without saying because it comes without saying."[15] That is to say, what is seen as self-evident is due to the "complicitous silence" of community members that help to maintain the habitus of any given community.[16]

At the same time, habitus is not only a "structuring structure" but a "structured structure" as well.[17] That is, Bourdieu's use of *habitus* bridges the long held "structure or agency" debate within sociology by arguing that habitus not only guides individual and collective actions but that these actions also shapes it. Thus, habitus is not fixed but is shaped by individual and collective actions.

But habitus is not simply a way of life of a particular social group. It also extends to our tastes—in food, art, and clothing, to name but a few— which also come not as a result of our natural and personal preferences, but as a result of our immersion into different types of communities that result in different levels of exposure to different cultural products. Thus, different tastes in the types of food that we prefer, the types of activities that we enjoy, and the type of music that we find pleasing that appear to be a reflection of different personal tastes are instead a reflection of different levels of exposure and cultural training.

These objects of desire "reflect a symbolic hierarchy that is determined and maintained by the socially dominant in order to enforce their distance or distinction from other classes of society."[18] In fact, the "social order is progressively inscribed in people's minds" through the production and distribution of cultural artifacts and control of educational institutions that continue to create and maintain social hierarchies.[19] The act of creating and maintaining these social hierarchies are an act of symbolic violence, one that is "exercised upon a social agent with his or her complicity."[20]

Culture reproduces inequalities between individuals and groups by reinforcing the belief that some objects have more worth than others. While individuals may attribute their tastes to individual factors, and different groups of individuals may have different tastes, there arises a general agreement as to which objects are better than others. In this way, habitus is simultaneously "the product of structure, producer of practice, and the reproducer of structure."[21] Thus, our alleged personal preferences for certain types of sexual partners is a reflection not merely of personal tastes but of larger structural beliefs about which characteristics are more desirable than others.

In terms of sexual desires, possession of those characteristics that are deemed more desirable by society provide individuals with certain levels of erotic capital. Emerich Daroya points out that among gay men, "erotic capital consists of an intersection of body capital (muscularity), gender capital (masculinity), racial capital (whiteness), age capital (youthfulness) and class."[22] What's important to remember here is that the characteristics that make up erotic capital and provide some men with more sexual worth are not a given but a reflection of the erotic habitus. That is, there is nothing inherently natural about whiteness having more erotic worth.

As Bourdieu notes, there is a process by which the values and beliefs of the dominant class come to be universally held through a system of

Erotic capital

cultural products that mark some objects are worthy and other objects as less worthy. Through cultural products, members of the dominant group make their habitus universally desirable. This ability to use cultural products to shape the values and beliefs of subordinate groups may be the most insidious type of social domination as it "represents the deepest and most insidious penetration of the social order at the level of the unconscious."[23]

Gay media represents a powerful collection of cultural products that construct erotic habitus among gay men. As Richard Dyer has argued in his influential essay "The Matter of Whiteness," racial imagery is central to the way that societies dictate who has value and who does not.[24] Thus, the problem with gay media isn't that it excludes people of color per se, but that it actively constructs cisgender "straight-acting," if not simply straight white men as having value. The relative absence of gay people of color in the gay media doesn't simply lead to the assumption that white people are "just people" who aren't raced, it leads to the assumption that those who are not "just people" are problematic. How gay media represents race is more than about simple lack of representation of people of color or the privileging of white men. Rather, the centering of whiteness leads to a "condition of white racial domination where white values, ideas, aesthetics, preferences, and privileges are made to appear as normalized, taken-for-granted basis in which to navigate the social world."[25]

~~READING REPRESENTATIONS~~ Image of Magazine

Focusing our attention to the cover of the French magazine *Paris Match*, Roland Barthes implores us to consider what may be "read" from an image. At first blush, the cover image is deceptively simple: a picture of a young Black boy, in a French uniform, saluting what can only be imagined as the, not pictured but implied, French flag. As Barthes notes, the image is meant to signify that France is a great empire wherein all the nation's subjects, regardless of color, faithfully serve under the flag. To accomplish this, Barthes argues that the various signifiers—that is, the elements of the image itself, the signified, the concepts found in the image such as *soldier* and *flag*—unite to form a sign with a rather simple message: a soldier saluting a flag. The message is then linked to a second set of signifieds, specifically the broader themes about French colonialism and the ideological beliefs about it to create a myth. In this case, the myth of the French empire that signifies that "France is a great Empire, that all her sons, without any color discrimination, faithfully serve under her flag, and that there is no better answer to the detractors of an alleged colonialism than the zeal shown by this Negro in serving his so-called oppressors."[26] Clearly, there are contested meanings that can be attributed to French colonialism, and the *Paris Match* cover is signaling a very specific meaning of it. The media landscape offers plenty of opportunities for individuals and groups to challenge dominant narratives, especially about race. In addition, how an image is read is also influenced by an individual's social location. That is, individuals differently located within the social structure may, and often do, read the same images and narratives differently.[27]

Whether one believes in the alleged benevolence of French colonialism or acknowledges the brutality of it, the meaning inferred by the image is nonetheless universally interpreted specifically because the various signifiers already contain in them a shared cultural knowledge that allows for the interpretation. We can disagree with the message itself, but the point is that the meaning is interpreted similarly.

This shared interpretation is possible because the media provides the basic frames for how the world should be interpreted using various tactics focused on the use of representations. And representations work because they provide social meaning and allow us to "regulate and organize our conduct and practices, [and] help to set the rules, norms and conventions by which social life is ordered and governed."[28]

Focusing back on gay publications, I would like to turn your attention to the August 2010 issue of the *Advocate*, the oldest and largest LGBTQ publication in the United States. This particular issue featured a cover image of musician Jake Shears of the Scissor Sisters with the tag line, "A Day in Gay America." The thematic issue included photos of people throughout the country taken on the same day, thereby presenting, as the cover teases, "a day in gay America." Given that the cover image is meant not only to introduce the story but to also frame how and what readers should think about the topic of the issue itself, it's telling that "a day in gay America" is represented by a young, physically fit, cisgender white man that Andy Towle of *Towleroad* characterized as "beefcake."[29] This image works precisely because we've come to equate gayness with whiteness and maleness. And specifically with a type of whiteness and maleness that embodies gender norms and marks gay men as being "just like" straight men, with the exception that they just happen to be gay. As Audre Lorde observed about the "mythical norm" of who is an American, the mythical norm of who is gay is clear.[30]

Likewise, in an interview in the July 2006 issue of *People* magazine, the flagship digest of suburban straight America, Lance Bass, one of the members of the phenomenally popular 1990s boy band 'N Sync, proudly declared, "I'm gay." More a confirmation of lingering rumors about his sexuality than a declaration of a shocking fact, Bass took the opportunity to share his personal journey of coming out, including trials with family and friends and his own internal realization that he couldn't "truly have a relationship with a woman," despite, in case there were any doubts about his manliness, "definitely" having been with them.

After sharing what can only be described as a quintessential, if not formulaic, coming out story, Bass ended the interview by stating, "I want people to take from this that being gay is a norm. That the stereotypes are out the window. . . . I've met so many people like me that it's really encouraged me. I kind of call them the SAGs, the straight-acting gays. We're just normal, typical guys. I love to watch football and drink beer."[31] In denouncing the stereotypes of gay men and declaring himself a "straight-acting gay," Bass relied on the trope of the "normal" gay man who is just like everyone else, except of course, gay. While perhaps still novel to non-gay readers in 2006, the trope of the masculine straight-acting, and most importantly, normal gay man had come to dominate the cultural narrative of what it means to be gay even prior to Bass's interview. And gay men have long begun to identify as "just like" straight people, with sexuality being the key, if not the only, difference. Rather than a routine shift in the way that society has come to view gay men, this image was carefully and intentionally crafted by gay leaders and gay organizations specifically for the purpose of winning wider social acceptance. This heteronormalizing of gay life has placed masculinity at the forefront and has led to masculinity coming to represent a central cultural value that marks gay men as "normal." As David Halperin points out, "The slightest allusion to gay male gender deviance sparks immediate resistance because it poses a threat to that scenario: it defies the current dogma that there is no difference between gay people and straight people and therefore no intrinsic obstacle to gay assimilation."[32]

So entrenched is the image of the straight-acting gay white man in the popular imagination that an openly gay celebrity who doesn't aspire to meet the new manly norm becomes notable for not meeting those norms. As writer Peter Moskowitz wrote on *Splinter*, "Adam Rippon is not only gay, but our first nationally recognized and respected faggot."[33] So widespread is the image of cisgender white men as the de facto representation of gay men that an openly gay celebrity deviating from that norm is actually newsworthy.

Yet the creation and dissemination of such representations is not neutral. Rather, representations are deeply inscribed in power relations.[34] More often than not, those who control the means of creating and distributing representations that often work to define what is normal, and in the process define who belongs and who doesn't, create a parade of images and narratives that construct the dominant group as being normative. The images of white men work to define white men as normal, as belonging, and defines the desire for white men as universal and natural. The universal desire for white men is not inconsequential. It marks white men as having more worth and more value and endows them with erotic capital that grants them advantages far beyond simply being considered attractive. Thus, desire for white men becomes normal.

Collectively, these images help to create a white racial frame through which whiteness comes to be seen as having more value and worth through the collective sharing of beliefs and preferences.[35] Even images that at first glance appear race neutral represent collective racial assumptions held by whites. Given that "images contain no inherent meanings . . . the meanings attributed to them are created solely by society's shared investment in them," these images represent a collective shared investment in whiteness by certain segments of the gay community.[36] How gay media represents race is more than about simple lack of representation of people of color or the privileging of white men. Rather, the centering of whiteness leads to a "condition of white racial domination where white values, ideas, aesthetics, preferences, and privileges are made to appear as normalized, taken-for-granted basis in which to navigate the social world."[37]

GAY IMAGES AND THE CONSTRUCTION OF WHITENESS AND RACIALIZED DESIRE

During the summer of 2012, graphic designer Aram Vartian was contracted by popular Washington, DC, nightclub JR's to design a flyer for a special Summer Olympics–themed event. But when Vartian delivered his design, which featured a shirtless Black model, David Perruzza, the manager of the club, wrote back, "I don't know how to be pc about it but do you have a hot white guy? That's more our clientele." When contacted by *MIC*, which broke the story on January 28, 2017, after Vartian publicly shared screenshots of the original message on social media, Perruzza defended his actions by stating, "I won't apologize for it, because I don't think there's anything wrong with that for what was going on at the time. Everything was Abercrombie models and pretty boys."[38] Perruzza also pointed to the club's monthly "Arabian Nights" promotional event, where "Muslim music" is played, as evidence of how JR's was a warm and welcoming place for people of color. In Perruzza's accounting, it is clear that the designation "pretty boys" only applies to white men and being warm and welcoming to people of color is to use them as exotified marketing gimmicks.

While it's easy to condemn Perruzza's action as outlandish and annoyingly racist, it's difficult to blame him for believing that a "hot white guy" would resonate more with his clientele than an equally attractive Black man. While online comments seem to suggest that the clientele at JR's, back then as now, is overwhelmingly white and people of color attest to feeling unwelcomed at the club, the flyer was not necessarily meant to represent the type of person who attends the club, given that so very few people actually look like models that are used on flyers, billboards, and the like, but rather the type of men the club's clientele desires. Sexualized images used by gay bars on advertisements, flyers, and in the clubs themselves overwhelmingly feature "hot white guys" to cement the erotic habitus of the clubs. Thus, Perruzza's actions aren't at all surprising given the centrality of whiteness in the logic of gay desire. And while not all white men fit the image of the "hot white guy" envisioned by Perruzza, these images still allow non-muscular, non-masculine, and non-successful white men to claim white privilege insofar as "whiteness confers a generalized social privilege [for] anyone who can successfully claim whiteness."[39] These images work in two ways, by establishing the erotic habitus of gay social spaces as largely white spaces while simultaneously providing erotic worth to white men who inhabit those spaces.

As John Walker discovered in his short survey of gay magazine covers, the overwhelming number of gay magazine covers feature cisgender white men.[40] The men are not simply cisgender but, more often than not, they are also straight. Between the years 2010 and 2019, cisgender white men appeared on the covers of sixty-six of one hundred issues—fully two-thirds of the covers during this ten-year period. Of these, white men appeared alone in slightly more than half the covers. Non-white men were featured alone on only eleven of the covers, with women, particularly white female music stars, making up the remaining solo covers. In the *Out* magazine universe, cisgender white men are the norm.

Yet for the sake of my argument, it isn't just that cisgender white men are the most likely to be featured on the cover of *Out* magazine, but that they are presented in such a way as to make whiteness normative and sexual desires geared toward white men the default by sexualizing white men but either neutralizing or sexually pathologizing men of color. During the entire period, only thirteen non-white men appeared on the cover of *Out* magazine. Of these, non-white men appeared alone in only ten issues. Among the covers that featured non-white men alone, one was President Obama, and one was RuPaul. The remaining eight followed a predictable pattern. The July 2011 issue featured Michael Irvin for the annual sports issue, and the March 2014 issue featured Devonté Hynes for the annual music issue. Internet celebrity Rickey Thompson was featured on the cover of the November 2018 issue, a special issue devoted to "The New Queer Black Male." The other July cover in 2011, also sports related, featured white rugby player Ben Cohen. Notably, while Cohen was described on his cover as "rugby's big man" who is featured "up close and personal" as a member of the gay community, Irvin was portrayed as an ally, outside of the gay community, discussing the "gay brother he loved and lost." In this way, Cohen was presented as someone who may be potentially available as a romantic or sexual partner, but Irvin was not.

These themes of sports and music carried over into the covers that feature other Black men. The August 2014 issue featured Michael Sam holding a football, while the March 2016 issue had a cover of Jussie Smollett, whom the magazine crowned as being "Empire's undisputed darling." Yet despite being labeled the "undisputed darling," Jussie Smollett was largely desexualized, appearing fully clothed and only from the shoulder up.

Only two Latino men graced the cover of *Out* magazine alone during the 2010–19 period. Ricky Martin was featured on the cover of the February 2018 issue, which corresponds to his role of Antonio D'Amico, Gianni Versace's long-time lover who was Italian, which attested to Martin's ability to pass as white on the FX channel's true crime anthology, *The Assassination of Gianni Versace*. Javier Muñoz was featured in one of five covers for the "Out 100 issue," in 2016. Previous to the February 2018 issue, Ricky Martin was also on the December 2010 issue as a part of an ensemble for the "one hundred most compelling people of 2010" issue.

No Asian man appeared alone on the cover of *Out* magazine during the entire period, with the exception of Darren Criss, who by his own boasting "[looks] like a Caucasian guy," in the March 2011 issue.[41] The only other Asian man to grace the cover of *Out* magazine during this period was designer Alexander Wang, who appeared as a part of an ensemble with photographer Ryan McGinley and film maker Dustin Lance Black as part of their "tastemakers" issue, which provides the magazine's readers with a "user's guide to style." As the above examples demonstrate, men of color virtually never make it onto the cover of *Out* magazine outside of specially themed issues or to mark specific themes that are either explicitly racialized or closely associated with people of color.

Unlike men of color, white men are routinely sexualized on the covers of *Out* magazine and are used to mark the boundaries sexual desirability. The most striking demonstration of this are the images used for the annual "hotlist" issues. While some years feature women on the cover, the accompanying images for the covers present the subjects with different amounts of erotic worth. The 2010 hotlist issue featured Christina Aguilera, and the

2011 hot list issue featured Adele; all the other hotlist issues featured white men on the cover. More telling is the different ways the two white women were presented and described compared to the white men. While Christian Aguilera "reclaims her fame," and 2011 is the "summer of Adele," Channing Tatum, who appeared on the 2012 hotlist cover, was described as "the total package," and Matt Bomer, who appeared on the 2014 and the 2017 covers, was described as the "Hollywood love bomb," specifically alluding to his sexual appeal to gay audiences.

Returning to the British magazine *Attitude*, originally used by Blanco in their tweets criticizing "gay media," we see a similar pattern of normalizing desire for white men while either neutralizing or fetishizing desires for men of color. Much like *Out*, the covers of *Attitude* feature overwhelmingly cisgender, mostly straight white men; Blanco and numerous other activists focus in on *Attitude* for a reason. Yet the interesting point of comparison isn't that cisgender white men grossly outnumber anyone else on the covers of the magazine but that they are presented differently from everyone else in a way that marks them as sexually desirable. Take, for example, the September 2017 issue featuring country musician Steve Grand. In all respects, the cover is fairly typical of what one would expect from the magazine—a cisgender white man photographed in a sexually suggestive pose. This cover formula is employed by the magazine repeatedly—except of course, when the cover image is that of a woman, a man of color, or a white man who is less gender conforming.

Even when men of color are photographed for the cover less than fully clothed, they are robbed of their erotic appeal. The different erotic worth presented by the cover featuring pro wrestler Anthony Bowen, who is Black, compared to the erotic worth of the cover image of rugby player James Haskell, who is white, is a case in point. While both men appear shirtless, Bowen is presented smiling and standing tall, as he would in a public place, perhaps after winning a wrestling match. Haskell, by contrast, is photographed leaning back in an erotic pose, staring seductively into the camera. The copy accompanying the image is also telling. While Bowen is apparently "learning to love his scars and [embrace] his bisexuality," James Haskell "might just give you one" if you need a snog, a British slang term for deep kissing and "making out."

The stark difference in racial representation is most evident in the different formula employed for the cover images used in the UK version of the magazine and the Thai version. Although published as a Thai edition, with a print edition largely available only in Thailand, the magazine largely publishes in English, despite the fact that English is rarely spoken or read outside major tourist centers popular with Western visitors. While not publicly advertised as such, it is possible that the magazine, much like the now defunct *Oriental Guy* magazine, targets white readers, selling Asian men as a commodity. But if Asian men are sexual commodities for consumption by white men, what type of commodity are they?

The contrasting way white men are routinely portrayed on the cover of the UK version of the magazine and the way Asian men or portrayed on the Thai version of the magazine are telling in terms of the different gendered attributes considered desirable in men of different races. Unlike men of color featured on the covers of the UK version of the magazine, the Asian men featured on the cover of the Thai version are heavily sexualized, perhaps even more so than the white men on the covers of the UK version. Yet the ways they are sexualized and presented are starkly different. The UK cover featuring rugby player Thom Evans proclaims that he "is not in the Olympics but he is in his pants [and] is the total package." Here the allusion to the "total package" when referring to his pants is explicitly sexual and specifically sexualized through his penis. Likewise, the way that men are presented on the cover images of the Thai version are also explicitly sexual. Yet they are sexualized differently. Here, we turn to James Berger's distinction between being nude and being naked.[42]

At first blush, the distinction is not clear. That is, both being nude and being naked is to be in a state of undress. However, "to be naked is to be oneself. To be nude is to be seen naked by others and yet not recognized for oneself. A naked body has to be seen as an object in order to become a nude . . . Nakedness reveals itself. Nudity is placed on display."[43] That is, nakedness implies power and freedom, to be undressed for one's own sake. Nudity, on the other hand, is to be undressed for the enjoyment of others.

While men on both the UK and the Thai editions of the magazine are usually less than fully dressed, the white men featured on the covers of the

UK edition, such as Evans, are naked, while the Thai men are nude. Evans stands firm, staring scorchingly into the camera, almost daring the reader. The Thai models look longingly into the camera, teasing the reader with a striptease. Their undressing is for the reader, not for themselves.

Similar methods of sexualizing white men while neutralizing men of color can be found on gay websites as well. In *Adam4Adam Blog*'s regular "hot or not" column, for example, images of white men and men of color used as the art are presented differently, regardless of the topic. The white man whose image was used for "Hot or not: Army men" was shirtless, abdominal muscles flexed, wearing a tiny white speedo showing off his bulge; the Black man whose image accompanied the "Hot or not: Military men"—virtually the identical subject—was fully dressed, smiling into the camera as if taking a picture for Facebook. The implication here is that in answering whether the man pictured is "hot" or "not," the reader's answer should be "yes" to the white man, but can be left open to interpretation for the Black man.

This pattern of normalizing desire for white men while pathologizing or neutralizing desire for men of color is evident in another set of blogs, one titled "Hot or not: Monster cock," and another titled "Hot or not: Big cock." The image used for the "monster cock" column is that of a well-endowed white man standing alone, while that used for the "big cock" column is a photo of a Black man's penis, cropped without the rest of his body, with a white man looking on in near disbelief. The erotic sentiment aroused by the picture of the white man is that of normalized desire for well-endowed men, while that aroused by the white man looking incredulously at the Black man's penis is that of oddity. It is also telling that the image of the Black man's penis is entirely dislocated from the man himself and exists only in response to a white man's gaze.

The normalization of desire for gay white men is also found outside of media outlets that specifically target gay audiences when articles feature gay content. In a 2017 article on the popular online news and lifestyle site *BuzzFeed*, journalist Jon-Michael Poff introduced readers to "22 NSFW gay sex scenes that always get the blood flowing."[44] The overwhelming majority of the twenty-two scenes featured white men, so much so that reader Duke Pepper asked in the comments section, "Did you purposely set out to make this entire list only about white men or was that accidental?," and reader Steven Timothy wrote, "Something's not quite white here. I mean right. It's not quite right. I mean it's all white." To be fair, the list of twenty-two NSFW sex scenes did include a scene from the Netflix series *Sense8* featuring two Latino male characters and a scene from the television show *How to Get Away with Murder* between a white male character and his half-Asian partner. Yet it's also worth noting that all three of these non-white characters have what can be considered physical features stereotypically associated with white men.

Poff was certainly not lacking in examples of gay sex scenes that feature non-white men that he could have drawn upon. As reader Khalil Goodman wrote, "There are hot Black POC men scenes that I am surprised did not make it on here, such as the first scene between Noah and Wade on 'Noah's Arc,' the first time Kal and Tariq have sex on 'The L.A. Complex.'" The lack of sex scenes featuring men of color is all the more surprising given that the movie *Moonlight*, featuring gay Black male characters, was the recipient of an Academy Award for best motion picture less than six months prior to the publication of the *BuzzFeed* article. The movie, the first gay-themed film to win an Academy Award for best picture, should have taken center stage on any list of films of interest to queer audiences.

While an argument could be made that the twenty-two scenes featured in the article were the result of a reader survey conducted a week prior to publication and that the responses to Poff's earlier article requesting reader input did include many of the scenes that readers suggested, equally important to consider are the examples that the author used while soliciting reader input to begin with. In the short article asking readers "Which TV or movie gay sex scene always turns you the fuck on?," Poff offered six examples of such scenes, all but one of which featured white men.[45] While several readers offered the scene in *Sense8* as an example of a sex scene that "always turn you the fuck on," it was not included as an example in the original request. While the scene featuring Jack Falahee and Conrad Ricamora, who play the gay couple Connor Walsh and Oliver Hampton on the television show *How to Get Away with Murder*, was included in the original survey request, it's telling that the only sex scene included in the original article included a heteronormalized gay couple whose white half is clearly the "man" in the relationship while the Asian man plays the more submissive partner.

White men are also presented as being normative of sexual behavior itself. On September 10, 2018, an online article appeared on *Out* titled "9 types of tops you encounter in the sack," written by Zachary Zane.[46] Using a feature image of a young, lean and muscular white man, the author tells readers that "while all tops want one thing, they sure have a different way of going about it," and that "tops come in all sorts of breeds." Through the article, the author introduces us to the nine types of tops, including the "faux-porn star" who "screws like he's on set, putting on a show" and the "impatient top" who is "so horny and ready to go that he forgets that foreplay is a thing." While photos of nine different men are used to highlight an example of each type of top, they are all uniformly white. Apparently, tops come in "all breeds," but all the "breeds" come in one color.

MEN OF COLOR AS RACIAL FETISH OR RACIAL EXCEPTION

When men of color are presented as potentially sexually desirable, they are virtually always marked with their race. In a pair of articles from *BuzzFeed* titled "21 gorgeous Asian men guaranteed to make you thirsty" and "A definitive ranking of Latino men who caused your sexual awakening," the men are presented as sexy men of color rather than just sexy men, much akin to being told that a man is attractive for an Asian guy, a Black guy, or a Latino guy.[47] Given the liberal leanings of *BuzzFeed*, it is likely that the magazine included these articles specifically to fight the stereotype that men of color are not sexually desirable. Articles such as Kevin J. Nguyen's 2017 piece "Why Aren't Asian Men Sexy?" specifically attempts to challenge the assertion that Asian men are not sexy.[48] Despite these good intentions, *BuzzFeed* routinely publishes articles on and about "sexy" men that feature only white men while not marking the men as white. The website's tendency to include a few men of color in these universal "sexy" lists only works to further normalize whiteness as being equated with normative desires given that lists that feature mostly white men, and lists that feature only white men are not racially marked.

Given that desire for white men is normalized, desire for men of color is often marked as the exception to the rule. In an *Adam4Adam Blog* article titled "Hot or Not: Shemar Moore," written by the website's marketing/social media director "Dave," the author writes, "His face and look are so different from any other Black guys out there because of his interesting mix. Moore's father is African American and his mother, who was born in Roxbury, Massachusetts, is of Irish and French-Canadian descent."[49]

While dozens of readers chimed in making 146 comments and most were simply short affirmations such as, "very hot!!!!," and the over-whelming majority of commenters agreed that Shemar Moore is, indeed, "hot," many comments were marked with caveats about Black men, such as, "I'm not normally attracted to Black men, but Shamar Moore [*sic*] is so good looking, he transcends race or ethnicity." Comments marking men of color as exceptions were by no means confined to those made about Black men. A "Hot or not" column featuring half-Asian model/actor Daniel Henney garnered such comments as, "I am not normally attracted to Asian men but yes I find Daniel Henney. Nice smile & nice muscles. Yep I would sleep with him."[50] Compare these to the "Hot or not" column about red heads that was published in 2012.[51] Despite garnering 282 comments, not one reader described redheads as "Not usually my type but . . ." While many readers commented that they had a special affinity for redheads, none saw this as an exception to their normative sexual desires.

The tendency to racially fetishize sexual desires for non-white men is most evident in gay pornography. Perhaps nowhere was this tendency more obvious than on the covers of the once popular *Inches* magazine. Although now defunct in the age of online pornography, *Inches* and the various subtitles within that genre demonstrate the ways that gay white sexuality is normalized at the expense of gay men of color. Published by the Mavety Group alongside a number of other gay porn magazines, *Inches* was among the most widely circulated gay porn magazine until Mavety folded in 2009. Unlike Mavety's flagship magazine, *Mandate*, *Inches* attempted to cultivate a diverse audience with the publication of *Inches*, *Black Inches*, and *Latin Inches*. It's telling, of course, that *Inches* was simply called *Inches* while the other two were specifically marked with race. Yet even beyond this racialized distinction, the presentation of the models used in the magazine was embedded with the racial logic of desire.

In both *Black Inches* and *Latin Inches*, Black and Latino men were uniformly presented as sexual fetishes through outfits that stereotypically signified gang membership or criminal activities and were posed in such a way that would suggest sexual aggression and brutishness. Complete with do-rags and gang tattoos, they represented an unabridged, raw, perhaps even criminally taboo sexuality. Yet the white men featured in *Inches* were rarely objectified in this way. Instead, they were most often presented as the boy next door, the universalized image of what a gay man is supposed to be like envisioned by director Roland Emmerich when he invented the fictional character of Danny for the film *Stonewall*—an image that, according to Emmerich, would resonate with all audience members, regardless of race or sexuality.

CONCLUSION

If desire is a product of the larger social structure, then the question to be asked is, How do desires get constructed and where do the ideologies of desire gets disseminated? As this chapter demonstrates, one particular site where whiteness is relentlessly promoted as the standard of desirability is in mainstream gay publications and the ways that these publications represent gay white men.

As Richard Dyer reminds us, "Racial imagery is central to the organization of the modern world."[52] Examining media products is critical in thinking about how we come to perceive race and desire given that media representations reflect a "system of values, ideas and practices" that help "establish an order which will enable individuals to orientate themselves in their material and social world."[53] Rather than a neutral presentation of the social world, media representations reflect power differences between those who have power and those who do not. As film maker Jean Luc Godard is reported to have stated, "There are no just images, there are just images."

It should be obvious from the above discussion that white people, in media products imagined and produced by white people, rarely if ever mark whiteness as a race. Instead, white people are presented as just people, and "there is no more powerful position than that of being 'just' human. The claim to power is the claim for the commonality of humanity."[54] White people are everywhere in media representations, but whiteness is nowhere. Within gay media, white men are invisible in the sense that they are normalized. Thus, they become the default in the absence of racial markers or cues. Specifically, desire for white men comes to be seen as the default of desire, whereas desire for men of color is an exotic taste that needs to be explained or framed as different from what one would normally desire. When gay men of color are desirable, they are desirable because they offer a distraction from the norm, an unusual delight that would otherwise not be indulged.[55]

Yet often, discussions about desire tend to focus largely on the psychodynamics of desire rather than its larger social structures. The tendency to use an entirely psychoanalytic framework for understanding sexual desire, particularly as it relates to racialized sexual desires, leads to such desires being understood as personal preferences by those who hold a racial preference for sexual partners. However, "the way in which sexual partnering is organized is not random, genetically determined, or uniform."[56] Rather, sexual desire follows a predictable racial pattern despite individual explanations for their own racialized desires.

As Peter Jackson has noted, racialized gay desires are not a form of cultural diversity, but "a tightly structured hierarchy in which white men are indisputably at the top of the sexual desirability stakes."[57] The problem with a hierarchy of sexual desirability isn't simply one of who gets sex and who doesn't or even a matter of who has sex with whom. It isn't simply that white men don't want to have sex with men of color, it is that the belief that gay men of color are not "worth a fuck" is deeply imbedded in larger systems of racist beliefs and behaviors that *make* gay men of color not "worth a fuck." Thus, racialized desires aren't simply a matter of personal preference but a reflection of the larger social structure in which race operates as an organizational principal to mark some as being better and more desirable than others.[58] A queer hierarchy of desire exists because a racial hierarchy exists. In this way, racial desire is a reflection of larger social structures that constructs one race as being superior to another along multiple different dimensions, including erotic ones.

Perhaps the tendency to use men of color to promote whiteness is most problematic because there are ways that gay media outlets can stop centering whiteness as the de facto marker of desirability or normalcy. The recent revamping of the popular gay dating site Adam4Adam, for example, relaunched in late 2018, features a variety of images of men of different races and sizes. Although they are all primarily younger, these images as a collection point to how sexual desires can be de-centered from whiteness.

As a collection of images, the revamped website portrays a variety of men in various parings, demonstrating that there is no natural or logical parings based on race. Rather than promoting desires for white men as normative, it presents those desires as just one of many possible desires that gay men can have. More importantly, it does not frame for the reader who, based on race, should take a more active role or a more passive role in sexual interactions, leaving the decision open for interpretation. Although the revamp did not last long, it did demonstrate new possibilities of desire.

This chapter was an attempt to examine racialized gay desire and the hierarchy it creates, through the framework of an erotic habitus. Gay media constructs an erotic habitus that constructs white men as being universally desirable and men of color as being desirable only in so far as they are an exotic distraction from the norm. This is accomplished by not only bombarding gay readers with images of white men but also actively presenting white men as the default category of sexualized desire and the default measure of a normative gay sexuality.

CHAPTER 3

All Horned Up and Looking for Some Fun

Performing Racialized Desires on Craigslist

A LEISURELY STROLL THROUGH THE GAY PORN SECTION OF A VIDEO rental store makes clear the active erotic othering of men of color in the gay sexual imagination. Titles such as *Black Ballers*, *Black Jaw Breakers*, *Black Sex Pack*, and *Black Hot Rods* racially mark gay desire.[1] While the video stores of yesteryear may be unfamiliar to younger readers, the most harried glance through any of the multitude of gay porn websites would convey a similar truth. On the website *Gayempire*, the handful of videos featuring predominantly non-white casts to make the list of the top best-selling gay porn videos of all time include such titles as *Tight Asian Man Holes*, *Black Balled*, *Inter-racial Interrogation*, *All Black Gay Footage*, and *Black Brigade*. Yet none of the films featuring predominantly white casts, which make up the vast majority of the bestselling porn movies, are raced. Instead, they have titles such as *ManWatcher*, *Frisky Summer*, and *How the West Was Hung*, normalizing desire for white men by making them universal. The point isn't only that the videos that feature men of color specifically mark them as sexual others, but that videos comprising of all white casts never do. There are no videos titled *White Cowboys*, *White Gomorrah*, *White and Horny*, *White Workout*, *White Raven Gang Bang*, *White Ballers*,

White Muscle Machine, White Gang Bang, White Men in White, White Balled, White Jaw Breakers, White Jacks, White Sex Pack, White Brooklyn Beef, White Jocks and White Cocks, White Hot Rods, White Patrol, White Heat, or *White Street Fever,* all of which have Black counterparts.[2] In gay pornographic desire, white is the unmarked category of universal sexual desire. Pornographic videos featuring white men don't need to be marked with race when the assumption is that any gay viewer will find the videos tantalizing. Yet pornographic videos that feature men of color need to be racially marked because race itself is what is being sold, rather than just the sex.

But this leisurely browse through a gay porn section of the local video store also exposes the gendered nature of racialized gay desire. As Dwight McBride observed:

> On many of the most readily imaginable stereotypes about Black masculinity, these films do not disappoint viewers who bring to them a desire for a variety of Black manhood closely associated with the brutish, the socially and economically disempowered (though never physically or sexually), the violent, and a fantastic insatiable animal sexuality that will fuck you tirelessly and still be ready for more. . . . The genre that has the most to teach us, for our purposes, is interracial gay porn. . . . In the interracial genre, Black men are portrayed in consensual sex scenes with white men, and more often in rape or gang bang scenes in which the white man plays the passive role.[3]

What McBride's observation tells us is that interracial desire among gay men is not only raced, but also gendered. More importantly, it is gendered in a specific way. It isn't simply that Black men are "more" masculine than white men, but that they are "dangerously" masculine.

In doing research for his book *How to Bottom Like a Porn Star,* writer Mike Alvear discovered that interracial gay porn is targeted largely to white consumers and reflects what porn producers believe white audiences want. In his essay reflecting on those experiences, he quoted a white porn producer as stating, "Most of the white guys who watch interracial porn want the fantasy of submitting to a tough street thug."[4] What are being shown in these films are white fantasies about Black sexuality. Whether it is Black-on-Black sex or Black-on-white sex, the images presented by racialized gay porn is that of the brutish and sexually unrepentant Black man that fulfills white fetishized desires. Black-on-Black films allow white viewers, or middle-class Black viewers, as McBride notes, to imagine an unbridled, raw, almost animalistic sexuality, while Black-on-white films allow them to engage in an imagined sexual domination without actually being dominated in real life. As Jarrett Neal pointed out, watching interracial gay porn featuring "homo-thug" Black men and submissive white men allows gay white men to "indulge their private sexual fantasies while allowing racist and stereotypical beliefs regarding Black men to persist."[5] Black men become valuable within the marketplace of sexual exchange only if they can fulfill white sexual fantasies as sexual objects rather than as sexual subjects.

Often, the fetishization of the Black men focuses on the stereotypical beliefs about Black men's penises as evident in nude photographs of Black men, taken by white men, and meant for white (straight, gay, male, and female) consumption. Describing the famous (or infamous) *Man in Polyester Suit*, by Robert Mapplethorpe, Susan Gubar eloquently pointed out that the image of a Black penis may be seen as "even more dangerous than far more violent, contorted shots like, for instance, [Mapplethorpe's] self-portrait with a handle inserted into his anus."[6] While Gubar's analysis demonstrates that *Man in Polyester Suit* is much more complex than what appears on the surface and raises a number of important contradictory questions, the image of a Black man's penis "provides the white imagination with an escape route from the boredom of the family romance, the pieties and proprieties of customary roles."[7] Reducing Black men to a penis also hypersexualizes them.

The hypersexualization and fetishization of Black men have a long history in the US. Born of white fears and justification for the enslavement of Black men and women, Black masculinity has long been constructed as inherently aggressive, hypersexual, and threatening.[8] And gay porn, produced and consumed by white men, display these sexual fears and fantasies.

Latino men are fetishized in gay pornography similarly to Black men. Western media accounts, and primarily Western pornography, have historically depicted Latino men as hypersexual and hypermasculine, "whose raw sexuality functions as an unquestionable sign of their inner primal machismo."[9] Ray Navaro, in a discussion with Richard Fung, noted that representations of Latino men as either campesino (peasant farmer) or criminal was a recurring and consistent theme in gay porn marketed to gay white men. As Navarro observed, these images of Latino men focus less on body type than on signifiers of social class. As he argued, images of Latino men seem to be a "class fantasy collapsed with a race fantasy, and in a way it parallels the actual power relations between the Latino star and the producers and distributors, most of whom are white."[10]

The collapsing of class fantasy and race fantasy is also on display in non-pornographic media products geared to gay viewers such as the HBO series *Looking*. A pivotal storyline of the series was the on-again, off-again relationship between Patrick Murray, a twenty-nine-year old video game designer who moved to the Bay Area to attend college at the University of California, Berkeley, and Richie Donado Ventura, a barber who grew up in San Leandro, a working class suburb that borders Oakland's south end. Patrick and Richie's relationship is fraught with cultural misunderstandings that pivot on both their racial and class differences. What's interesting about the show is that Richie is not the only recurring character of Latino descent. One of the three protagonists, Agustin Lanuez, played by Frankie Alvarez, is a Cuban American from Coral Gables. Unlike Richie, however, Agustin is classed similarly to Patrick, having also attended Berkeley and heralding from a wealthy Miami family, and his racial background, unlike his class background, is rarely highlighted. It isn't simply that Richie's class background is highlighted in the series; rather, it is that his class background is specifically linked to his race, whereas Frankie's race is erased. Richie's presentation, which embodies the homeboy aesthetic as discussed by Richard Mora, emphasizes both his race and class background, marking the relationship between Patrick and Richie as being out of the ordinary, whereas the class aesthetic embodied by Frankie mitigates the racial difference between him and Patrick.[11]

Much like the hypersexualized image of Black men that has its roots in American slavery and continues to be deeply ingrained in white supremacist notions, the use of Latino men as a criminal element must also be understood within a sociohistorical context.[12] Similar to the way historic representations of Black male aggression continue to be deployed against them to justify current incarnations of racism, the historic representations of Latino criminality continue to be used against Latino men.

This use of Black and Latino men as sexual fetishes specifically for certain types of aggressive sexual fantasies further "reinforces the fear-based prejudices that white supremacy thrives on."[13] A popular genre in gay porn is an adult version of cops and robbers, where all the prison guards are played by white men and the criminals are overwhelmingly Black and often, Latino. Here, class fantasies collide not only with race fantasies, but also with racial imagery of crime. In the larger American imagination, Black and Latino men are often stereotyped as more likely to engage in criminal activity, and Black and Latino neighborhoods are more likely to be perceived as having higher levels of crime, regardless of the actual level of crime within those neighborhoods.[14] A prime example is the website Gay Patrol that markets itself as "Your source for the Real Dirty Gay Cops" where "power hungry and horny cops take control of our Black population and fuck them."[15] Even in the few films in which the roles are reversed, with Black actors playing the prison guards and white actors playing the inmates, the narrative arc still relies on the brutishness of Black sexual partners, such as Black prison guards sexually abusing white inmates.

These racialized gendered stereotypes of Black and Latino men translate into the actual sexual marketplace where sex is traded for money. In his study of male sex workers, Trevon Logan found that Black men who conform to stereotypes of hypermasculinity and sexual dominance are significantly better rewarded financially when engaging in sex work, and those who failed to meet these stereotypes experienced a financial penalty. A similar, but less significant finding was reported for Latino men as well.[16]

While portrayals of Latino men as criminal elements are common, they are also often portrayed as Latin lovers, a stereotype with a long history in film and television that started with Rudolph Valentino, an Italian immigrant who rose to fame by playing "the dashing and magnetic male Other."[17] Yet what sets the Latin lover apart from the other stereotypes of Latino men has been the characterization of Latin lovers as having lighter skin than Latino gangsters and laborers and coming from an aristocratic background rather than an impoverished one.[18]

If Black men, and to a lesser degree Latino men, represent one extreme of the gender binary marking racialized desires, then Asian men represent the other. Unlike gay porn that features Black or Latino men as brutish sexual thugs who fulfill white men's submission fantasies, gay Asian men are presented as the feminine partner, ready for masculine domination.[19] Unlike Black and Latino men who receive a premium in sex work for being a top, Asian men are the only racial group to not receive a premium for being a top or receive a financial penalty for being a bottom.[20] While Black and Latino men are specifically sought after by potential white partners for being aggressive sexual tops, Asian men are not. Similarly, while Black and Latino men are found to be less desirable by white men if they are sexual bottoms, Asian men are specifically sought after to take that role.

Within gay porn, Asian men are uniformly depicted as submissive bottoms eager to please their white male partners. Whereas Black men are hypersexualized, Asian men are "collectively seen as undersexed."[21] But I want to extend this argument a bit further and note that Asian men are seen as undersexed only when it comes to being active sexual partners, but they are overtly sexual when eager to fulfill the sexual needs and desires for white male partners.

This isn't to imply that Asian men are exclusively portrayed as sexual bottoms. In his analysis of porn star Brandon Lee, arguably the first Asian porn "star," Nguyen Tan Hoang points out that the performer is a sexual top.[22] Yet what makes Brandon Lee notable and worthy of academic inquiry as a performer is the very fact that he deviates from the norm. The attention he receives as an Asian top is due entirely to the peculiarity of an Asian top, thus reinforcing the Asian role as bottoms. His popularity comes not from the normalization of masculine Asian men in gay porn but his very peculiarity. He is the exception that proves the rule.

The gendered sexualization of men of color is hardly unique to gay porn. Gendered tropes of sexuality are rampant in mainstream media as well. The oversexualization of Black racialized bodies and desexualized Asian racialized bodies is evident in a skit titled "Flashlight," which aired on the late-night comedy show *MAD TV* in 2006. In the skit, two white men are stranded in a park when their car breaks down. The skit's central comic theme revolves around the two men shaking a motion-powered flashlight in order to get it to turn on. Lines such as "That looks hard" and "I'll keep yanking it" make a not-so-subtle allusion to male masturbation. The central punch line of the skit comes toward the end, when two police officers, one Black and one Asian, arrive to investigate the scene. Immediately, the Black police officer whips out an oversized black MAG flashlight. When the giant flashlight fails to work as well, the Asian police officer states, "Just use mine," and takes out a miniscule penlight, garnering the biggest laugh of the skit.

The skit succeeds in eliciting laughter because the audience understands the sexual and racial undertones of the joke. Not only do they understand that the flashlights represent penises, they also understand that the big black flashlight and the little penlight represent the doxa of racialized penises. When it comes to penis size, the epitome of male bodily embodiment, Black men are big and Asian men are small. When it comes to masculine embodiment, Asian men come up short. Yet at the same time, Black men miss the mark by being outside of what would be considered a normal penis size. Like Goldilocks finding some soup to be too hot and some too cold and some beds too hard and some too soft, Black male bodies and Asian male bodies are portrayed in the skit to normalize white male bodies as being "just right." It isn't simply that Black men's penises and Asian men's penises deviate greatly in size from one another, but that there is a norm from which deviation is possible. Even while gendered racial stereotypes are widespread outside the gay imagination, it can be argued that gay men are more likely to buy into these stereotypes than others.[23]

Much as the over-sexualization of Black and Latino men can be traced to historic racial experiences, the undersexualization of Asian men also has long historical roots. As Nayan Shah noted:

In the nineteenth and early twentieth centuries Chinese and Japanese American men and women were depicted as depraved, immoral, and racially inassimilable to US society. US immigration restrictions, labor migration, and recruitment patterns contributed to predominantly male Chinese, South Asian, and Filipino migration. This "bachelor society," with its lopsided gender ratios, has been cast as a tragedy of sexual and social alienation. Historians have critically interpreted the lurid and sensationalist imagery of Asian American bachelor vice to understand broader patterns of sexualized and gendered race-making that buttressed racial antipathy and segregation. The racial caricatures that circulate in the nineteenth and twentieth century media of effeminate men, treacherous women, and subservient women reinforced the perception of the "Oriental" race as gender atypical and sexually nonnormative, bereft of sexual agency.[24]

These historic stereotypes of Asian men, while directly opposite to the sexual stereotypes of Black and Latino men, nonetheless served the same purpose of positioning white sexuality as normal. Perceptions of gay white men not only lack the racialized gendered stereotypes associated with men of color, they are seen by both gay white men and gay men of color as being normative by which gay men of color are measured.[25]

Although the way men of color, particularly Black men and Asian men, are portrayed in gay media are on opposite ends of an imagined gender continuum, the point to be made is that both groups are othered through a whitening process that normalizes white men and constructs the sexual behaviors of white men as normal. While the emasculation of Asian men is obvious, images such as those produced by Mapplethorpe emasculates Black men by hyper-masculinizing them "by fixing [Black men] at the physical level of the penis, [these images] contribute to those dangerous mythologies of Black male predation on white women that were often used to warn against miscegenation."[26] Similarly, submissive portrayals of Asian men help to reinforce white male superiority. Either way, these images work to make sexual desires for men of color seem outside the norm.

Not only do sexual markets designate quality among the pool of eligible partners by dictating who is desirable and who is not, they also dictate expectations about how sexual interactions will occur.[27] Because "racial groups are imbued with gendered information, such that Asian men are perceived to be feminine and Black men are perceived to be masculine," expected sexual behaviors may also be gendered.[28] The racial hierarchy of desire not only establishes white men as being more sexually desirable than men of color, it also outlines the rules of engagement during sexual and social encounters between white men and men of color. Not surprisingly, sexual behaviors among gay men of color are sometimes dependent on the race of their sexual partners.[29] One arena where we can observe sexual behaviors performed are online personal ads placed by gay men seeking sexual partners.

A website used by gay men seeking sexual partners may seem like an odd place to explore how racialized desires get articulated. However, gay men have long used the internet to search for sexual partners, with estimates running as high as 94 percent of gay men having used the internet to do so.[30] Whatever the actual percentage may be, it would be safe to assume that cyberspace has now become the busiest and most sexually charged meeting place available to men, a "technological tearoom" of sorts, to borrow a phrase.[31] Websites often allow users to explicitly place and search for ads based on specific personal criteria such as age, race, and sexual roles that allow individuals to cater their ads to targeted readers. Because of this, online spaces can be considered more authentic articulations of sexual desires, as they provide users with the ability to "engage more directly with their desires, develop and express their fantasies, and approach potential partners with these desires and fantasies in mind."[32] In online spaces, there is no more cruising, no more guessing, and no more negotiating what one desires or expects. At the same time, there are also no more discoveries of delights. One does not become sexually excited by a potential sexual partner but becomes sexually aroused by an imagined other and goes online seeking someone to fulfill their already existing desires. Because of this, examining personal ads allows us to explore the characteristics, both physical and behavioral, that users deem sexually desirable.[33]

Not only do these ads allow users to specifically target the demographic groups that they desire, they also allow users to market themselves by highlighting the traits that they believe will be desirable to others. "Dating advertisements are a revealing site for examining the social construction of identities, identities that are deemed desirable and marketable in a specific cultural context."[34] Personal ads can act as "a location of autobiography," where "advertisers [can] often construct their ideal selves in their personal narratives."[35] Through personal ads, advertisers create their most desirable self, in the process they highlight the personal traits that they believe make them desirable to the sexual partners they seek. Advertisers construct not only an idealized sexual partner, but also a belief in what that sexual partner would want from them. Personal ads allow for the "creation of a racially, gendered and sexualized self and others" and become sites where negotiations of race and sexuality are publicly salient and "become public occasions for invoking and distributing a host of myths and fantasies about race and sex."[36] Rather than challenge stereotypical notions of race and sexuality, personal ads often reflect existing racialized notions about how someone of a certain race is "supposed" to behave sexually.

The problem here is that stereotypes about sexual behaviors are always embedded with racial stereotypes, and vice versa. Stereotypes linking race and sexuality are legion. Within gay personal ads, these stereotypes get amplified rather than diluted. Evidence suggests that these stereotypes are also widely shared among gay men of all races and there is widespread agreement about the sexual proclivities of different men based on race.[37]

While studies of racial preferences in online personal ads are few, gay men are significantly more likely than straight men to explicitly state a racial preference for sexual partners.[38] Race is not only a criteria for online sexual partner selection among gay men but also a way to exclude potential sexual partners as well as to specifically facilitate interracial connections.[39] Although these studies offer important insights, they fail to capture the ways that racial preferences get articulated.

In this chapter, I examine online personal ads placed by gay white men seeking non-white men as sexual partners and ads placed by non-white men seeking white men on the "casual encounters" section of Craigslist to examine how racial desires are performed. I pay special attention to the ways that men market themselves and how they describe their preferred sexual partners specifically based on racialized characteristics. "Casual encounters" offers us a unique opportunity to isolate sexual desires given that, unlike traditional personal ads, these ads are explicitly meant to find partners exclusively for sex. In discussing these ads, I present them as they were originally published, with spelling, capitalization, abbreviation, and punctuation left intact. I do so in order to offer the most authentic representations of the way that these men market themselves and describe the objects of their sexual desires. Because these ads were placed in the "Men Seeking Men" section, I also assume masculine gender identity.

WHITE SEEKING BLACK/BLACK SEEKING WHITE

Erica Owens and Bronwyn Beistle observed that "whites and Black sexual contact, more than any other, is a cultural trigger of which otherwise latent racism become overt." Citing Joel Kovel's groundbreaking work on white racism, the authors argue that bodily contact between Black people and white people is confounded by an irrational fear of Blackness.[40] White people fear, the authors contend, that contact with Black people will "result in a sudden, and perhaps permanent, invasion of their own being."[41] As Lynne Segal noted, "Black is the colour of the 'dirty' secret of sex, relentlessly represented in the image of Black 'boy' as stud, and Black woman as whore."[42] These sexual stereotypes are also placed onto Black men, both gay and straight. Gay Black men face multiple derogatory sexual stereotypes and are perceived to be sexually promiscuous, aggressive, and insatiable as well as sexually "dirty."[43]

In the larger white imagination, Black sexuality is taboo precisely because it is believed to be outside the norms of sexual decency. Given this, it isn't surprising that white posters often frame sexual exchanges with Black men as "dirty" and clandestine. As one white poster wrote:

Traveling cocksucker seeking BLACK cock from cities off the 405: 39yo bi on the dl, nasty cocksucker who swallows n bttom's bare back will be traveling south on the 405 from San Fernando to Seal Beach and i'm hoping to suck n swallow some thick, white ropey cum out of some thick Black dicks before i get home to my wife tonight. If you are interested send your cock pic. Thanks.

A point I want to make here is that the above poster is not interested in photos of the potential sexual partner's face or body. Instead, the primary interest seems to be on the penis. For many white men, a "Black cock" seems to be an entity unto itself that is separate from the Black body all together.

As Frantz Fanon explained, the Black man, as a complete human being, no longer exists in the white sexual imagination. Instead, "one is no longer aware of the negro, but only of a penis. The Negro is eclipsed. He is turned into a penis. He is a penis."[44] As one white poster wrote:

Seeking BBC for NOW: All horned up and looking for some fun. Hit me up if interested and in or near Burbank, I can host. white, masculine, moderately hairy, very discreet, DDF and negative, vers bottom. Email me your age, stats, and pic lets do this now. I crave big Black cock, want to worship it and then submit to you while you plow my tight hole.

For the man who posted the above ad, a "big Black cock" (BBC) is something to be worshiped, a theme that runs through many of the ads placed by white men seeking Black men. Yet as Cornel West has noted, the expected large penis of a Black man is a metaphor for hyper-sexuality that is both pleasurable as well as dangerous.[45]

Given the tendency to equate Black men with his penis, the majority of ads placed by white men specifically looking for Black men explicitly state a desire for men with large penises. For example, one white poster wrote:

Bi white guy looking to suck Big Black Dick Mature Men only (50's +++): Suit & Tie – bi sexual masculine white guy in West

> L.A. – good looking and very clean – ISO Mature and Older than
> 50's Black Males that enjoy being orally serviced and maybe more.
> Str8 – Married – Thugs – Bi-sexual black men welcum? All body
> types as long that you are hung. I can travel or host in all LA areas.

As the poster notes, "All body types as long that you are hung." For him, characteristics that many may perceive to be usual in terms of what one should find physically attractive about another human being such as height, weight, and eye color no longer matter. Instead, any Black man will do as long as he is "hung," reducing Black men of all shapes and sizes to a penis, and a large penis at that. For white men, what is desirable in Black men is the allegedly large penis that is attached to him.

Often, the desire for Black men and their alleged "BBC" is part and parcel of the desire for sexual aggression. For example, one white poster wrote:

> **Dad wants BBC:** white Dad wants a younger bbc to take control
> and use me til he is satisfied. You: younger hung (9+ thick) in shape
> or lean, confident and comfortable with dominating an older guy.
> I can host or? Pvt. Discreet, accommodating, refreshments. Open
> to scenarios. Send stats, when avail and needs in reply.

Because Black sexuality is associated with unbridled aggression, Black men are expected to be the sexual aggressors. As one white man posted:

> **looking for a Big Black Daddy Cock to use me:** im tall, fit, bubble
> butt, hairy, drug and disease free, 7cut. I like to suck, get throat
> fucked, dominated, and fucked hard and deep. give me a big cock
> and make me your sissy, im open to being xdressed, fill my boi
> pussy with your hard hung cock, please be drug and disease free
> too and please respond with pics and stats or I will not respond.
> I like older men, Please be 9in+ or very thick, big dicks make me
> feel like a sissy, I like to watch straight porn while being used. im
> open too 2 Black men for double penetration.

Black men are often sought for what can be considered more "dangerous" or "uninhibited" sexual encounters, particularly related to sexual fantasies of overt domination. One white poster wrote:

wm seeking my Black Master: white male is searching for his Black master to serve,. Worship, be used and satisfy. I am five-eleven, goodlooking, 180lbs, brown & hazel, no std's, submissive and obedient, definite with nice ass. I have excellent oral skills as a cock servant should and very much enjoy worshiping my masters cock.. I wish to serve my masters needs and I am open to what they are. I am good submissive servant that enjoys being one and I am hoping to find a Black master to utilize my skills.

In the above ad, the poster uses a master/slave narrative, a form of sexual fetish that has come to be known as "race play." While there may be pleasure in race play, a major problem with it is that it is deeply rooted in beliefs about white supremacy, whether the slave is played by a Black person or a white person.

In comparison to the way white posters construct ideal Black sexual partners, they construct themselves as being less sexually aggressive. One white poster wrote:

Bukkake guy for Black Dicks: innocent white guy loves warm facials from a small group of masc Black men. beat your big dick and see your and your bud's loads cover my face. Slap those dicks on my cum covered face. I don't bottom, just looking for facials. be normal.

When seeking Black partners, white men present themselves as being more innocent and less sexually unbridled. Thus, the assumption is that it is the Black man who will introduce white men to sexual depravity. As another white poster wrote:

Black Men: I'm looking to hang with at least one Black man sometime today. Even better if you have friends to bring. I haven't done this before, and would love to have the experience. I'm a good look-ing, in shape white dude. The guy(s) must be in shape. I can host at my place. I'm DDF and discreet: you should be too. Drop me a line and let's set this up ASAP.

In the words of the above poster, this is a new experience for him, as he has never "done this before." Nonetheless, he would "love to have the experience," which he believes Black men can provide.

For their part, Black men who post online seeking white partners for sex often portray themselves the way white posters may fantasize about them. As one poster wrote:

Hot BBC top looking: Handsome total top man looking for "only" white fem sissy bottoms who love BBC. You need to be smooth body all over, nice then fem body, nice shape bubble butt, and a total bottom. 6'4", 190lbs, caramel smooth skin, nice tone rip ath-letic body, chill and relax attitude, with a very very thick uncut 10" cock. Looking for someone who enjoys long play time sessions and very open minded. Can't host but very be willing to get a room in my area or if you can host even better. If you like what you heard and see, please reply a.s.a.p. so we can make arrangements. No picture, no reply. Will send more pictures with your reply and pictures.

Many Black men utilized racialized sexual tropes in their own ads when seeking white sexual partners, marking themselves as being more sexually aggressive than their potential white partners.

Even Black men who did not play into the racial imagery of white men such as the poster below nonetheless had to address the white sexual imagery in their ads if they were seeking a white partner:

Looking for White Top into Black Bottom: I'm a Black bottom sub, athletic, clean-shaven face, very trimmed, drug-free, HIV Neg and STD free (Jan 20th this year), and seeking an older (mid 50s on up+, can be flexible) white Top with no facial hair and is HIV neg and STD-Free. I received a number of replies from those who are just experimenting or those who are subs themselves, but am looking for someone who truly is into interracial play. Let's exchange photos and go from there. Into oral, 69, massage, frot, getting fucked.

As obvious from the ad above, Black men prefer a wide range of sexual roles. Unlike white posters who have a clear preference for aggressive Black tops and construct their imaginary Black sexual partners as more sexually aggressive and domineering, gay Black men do not uniformly fit into white racial fantasies. However, it should be observed that this particular Black poster specifically notes that he has received a number of messages from assumedly white men, who are also sexually submissive, seeking a Black partner. Thus Black men who did not fit the white sexual imagination were nonetheless repeatedly placed in the position of having to address white sexual desires in their ads.

WHITE SEEKING ASIAN/ASIAN SEEKING WHITE

Compared to the ads placed by white men seeking Black men, the ads placed by white men seeking Asian men were decidedly different in sexual expectations. One poster wrote:

Looking for asian son/daughter: I'm a fatherly type white man who is attracted to nice, young (but legal) asian. Maybe you are a sweet asian boy who is curious about being with a guy, I'm basically straight but have an attraction to smooth and emo/fem asians. I can host at my home and we can enjoy some 420 and just relax together. I'm open to helping you explore your self identity, as well as any sexual fantasies that you many have. I'm very open minded—so feel free to be honest with me about what you need or want in terms of being with a dad type. If you have any interest in dressing, I have lots of things you could wear. My main objective is to meet a nice person and make you feel safe and comfortable. Please send a photo and I will return a photo of myself.

The above ad demonstrates a number of themes found among ads placed by white men seeking Asian partners. First, there is an expectation that the Asian partner would be more feminine than white men. More importantly, the theme of Asian sexual inexperience was also prevalent in a number of ads.

Whereas Black men are expected to be sexually dominant, Asian men are required to be sexually submissive to white partners. The vast majority of ads placed by white men seeking an Asian sex partner are from self described tops looking for bottoms. This isn't surprising given the long history of feminizing Asian men in contemporary American media, both gay and straight. Having roots in Western colonial domination of Asian countries, Asian men have long been stereotyped as being more feminine and more submissive than white men as part and parcel of colonial justification and Western homoerotic fantasies about the "mysterious" east.[46]

White men often sought Asian men with more feminine physical features as well. As one white poster wrote:

> **asian guys are hot:** I love the slim smooth asian guys I see at the gym and around town. they look great with their clothes on and even better with their clothes off. I'm a masculine bi white top 5'9" 170 uncut cock shaved crotch hiv-neg play safe looking for a sexy hiv-neg asian bottom (18–48) for daytime sex. host or travel. get back with pix and info. thx.

For the poster who placed the ad above, his desire for Asian men revolved around perceived conceptions of them being more feminine and sexually submissive than white men. In the way that Black men fulfilled white sexual fantasies revolving around the need to be sexually dominated, Asian men were expected to fulfill white sexual fantasies of needing to dominate.

Contrary to the ways white men seek Black men with large penises, few ads posted by white men seeking Asian men specify penis size. When penis size is mentioned at all, the ads placed by white men seeking Asian men specifically seek men with smaller penises. One poster wrote:

I love your small dick: what's the big deal with big dicks? I like guys with small, boyish-looking dicks. I'm a masculine bi white top 5-9" 170 uncut hiv-neg play safe looking for a smooth small-hung hiv-neg white /asian/latino bottom (20–4) for daytime sex. host or travel. get back with pix and info.

Another white poster wrote:

HOT ASIAN WANTED: Short hot Asian BB bottom wanted for NSA fun. small dick preferred, the smaller the better). I'm HIV-.

Desire for a smaller, smooth Asian man was a recurring theme found among the ads placed by white men seeking Asian men for sex.

While few of the ads placed by white men seeking Asian men specified that they were seeking sexual partners with a big penis, many of the white posters specified that they themselves possessed a big penis. One white poster wrote:

Looking for young Twink that can host, Thick 7 inch's waiting: Nice tall chill very clean thin strong white 38 155, 7" cut, thick 6.5 girth male hosting tonight for thin twink petite or tiny guys men CD TS Asian ++++ Mostly top but verse here.. Please be thin petite or small framed smaller the better younger the better 420 pnp

Like the other ads placed by white men, the above ad demonstrates a number of themes found among ads placed by white men seeking Asian men. First, the Asian man is expected to be smaller, thinner, and younger than the white men. While the poster presents his "7" cut, thick 6.5 girth," the only physical demand he makes of his potential partner is a "thin petite or small frame." Unlike the "big Black cock," that becomes the center of pleasure in encounters between Black and white men, encounters between Asian and white men placed the white penis at the center.

Unlike Black men who demonstrate a wide pattern of sexual behavior despite white fantasies about them, the ads placed by Asian men indicate that most Asian men seeking white partners attempt to fit sexual stereotypes in order to attract them. One Asian poster wrote:

Come take my panties off daddy then fuck me: I just got a new pair of panties and I would like to find an older married white or hairy top daddy to come pull them off as I suck your married cock then pull them off as I bend over so you can Fuck me like you do your wife. I live alone and discretion is a must. Your clear face pic and stats get mine. I am just a regular guy, not a cd or T girl. I am into kissing, sucking, massaging and if you like to rim a clean smooth tight asian asspussy ++.

Another Asian poster wrote:

seeking a hung pATy Top (U host): Seeking hung pATy Guy. Straight acting to blow clouds while you are getting sucked. Me: hwp good looking asian with lean body type and bubble ass. You: HWP and with no problem to get hard when you party. Big and hard party cock a plus. Email full stats and your pics if you want me to reply. prefer to travel No into back and forth. White young daddy type with big dick++++++

The ads above highlight the most common themes found among ads placed by Asian men seeking white men. First, white men are expected to be older, more masculine, and possess larger penises than Asian men. Second, white men must be willing to take charge of the sexual situation while the Asian man submits to him and provides him with sexual gratification.

Much like white men who make a Black man's penis the center of sexual desire, Asian men place the white man's penis at the center. As one poster wrote:

Cute asian w/ nice ass looking for a quick fuck: Cute clean asian total bottom looking for a hot clean cock to fuck me hard and deep before it gets any later. 5'9 with a great ass and muscular body with some love around the waste. Prefer clean white top with a huge dick.

Yet another Asian poster wrote:

anonymous young Asian Ass for you to fuck: Are you looking for a tight Asian ass to fuck? Are you interested in an anonymous scene? I'll send you my address, door will be unlocked. You enter and I'll be blind folded and ass up. You drop your pants, put a condom on, and then pound my pre lubed Ass. Fuck me and then leave after you've cummed. I'm a young Asian guy 21 years old. Send your body and cock pic. Good looking and in shape guys ONLY. No fat, obese or ugly guys. Only muscle jock white guys can fuck this tight Asian ass.

The poster states that he is seeking an "anonymous" sexual partner and that he would be "blind folded and ass up," apparently unable to see his sexual partner. Nonetheless, he states that he prefers "only muscle jock white guys." And like many of the other ads placed by Asian men, the poster highlights his ass as the main physical characteristic that white partners should be attracted to. In his mind, it is his ability to meet white sexual fantasies of dominating an Asian man that makes him desirable to "muscle jock white guys."

When Asian men believe that they do not meet the physical expectations white men may have for Asian men, they rely on other non-physical yet equally racialized characteristics. One gay Asian man seeking a white partner posted this ad:

Asian cub looking for regular top friend: I'm a 24 y/o asian cub, not fat, 5'8" hairy. Certainly not some fantasy model but I make up for it with my submissive and always hoping to please personality. I'm 100% clean, kinda new at this too, but willing to take directions and lessons on how I can please you better. I'm looking for someone local who can host, and after our first meet just call or text each other whenever we get horny. I have a really tight super low mileage ass and a mouth wet and ready anytime. Into most fetishes and roleplaying, love to wear girly things if you have some.

Because the above poster does not meet the expected physical characteristics of being slim and smooth, he markets the non-physical traits that he believes white men would find attractive, namely being submissive, eager to please, and sexually inexperienced. In this way, the above poster is able to market himself as being potentially desirable to white men who may be seeking Asian men not only for their stereotypical physical features but also their stereotypical personality traits.

Among Asian men, the sexual fantasy they sell to potential white partners is not the ability to be sexually dominated by a man with a big penis but to use their own penis to sexually dominate another man. Within this fantasy, white men are always older and bigger and possess larger penises, while Asian men provide tight asses.

WHITE SEEKING LATINO/LATINO SEEKING WHITE

In the gay imagery of desire, Latino men are either conflated with Black men or with white men. As discussed earlier, Latino men are often stereotyped as being dark-skinned gangsters or criminals, but they are also portrayed as lighter-skinned Latin lovers. Given this unique racial placement of Latino men as being similar to either Black men or white men, it isn't surprising that Latino men are usually not as sexually excluded by gay white men or other men of color as Black and Asian men are.[47] This racial placement of Latino men in the sexual imagination of white men may be why Craigslist ads placed by white men seeking Latino men don't show a consistent pattern in terms of sexual role preferences. Unlike ads placed by white men seeking Black men that showed a clear pattern of preference for sexual tops and ads placed by white men seeking Asian men that showed a clear pattern of preference for sexual bottoms, ads placed by white men seeking Latino men were as likely to indicate a preference for a sexual top as they were to indicate a preference for sexual bottoms. Similarly, ads placed by Latino men seeking white men also showed no pattern of preferences for sexual roles. Additionally, a significant number of ads placed by Latino men seeking white men described themselves as "versatile," that is, able to take both the top or bottom position during sex.

Unlike Black men or Asian men, Latino men were more often than not included as another preferred racial group rather than an exclusively preferred racial group with the majority of ads placed by white men seeking Latino men including them as either/or rather than an exclusive preference. Most men seeking Latino men, for example, were seeking either white or Latino, either Black or Latino, or either Asian or Latino. It was in these groupings that specific requirements for sexual role preferences appeared. Consider this ad placed by a white man seeking either an Asian man or a Latino man:

> **Could REALLY use a blow job!!** Horny in Hollywood. Vgl white guy 5'8: 155 need my vein drained now! Come by you can suck my cock, (I'll suck yours if you like). and then I'll shoot my hot load down your hungry throat or all over your face. You decide. Host only. NSA. Straights and Bi welcome. Clean and DDF. Near Hollywood and highland. Looking for NOW. Latin & Asians always a big PLUS!!

The following quotes are taken from ads placed by a white man seeking either a Black man or a Latino man:

> **7 inches hosting california city:** home along 7inches looking for bigger bbc or Latin. Horny white guy 7 inches 29 horny show cock pic 1st pic and size. please be At least 7 inches no old dudes.

Another white poster wrote:

> **Need some good dick:** Weather's good fuck me. I'm so horny and bored tonight. Email me if you're a hot, MASC top who's down to get kinky I'm 5'8", 125, white. Skynny, nice butt. Black and Latino ++ I have some bomb 420+. E-Mail ME WITH PICS IM DOWN AS LONG AS THIS IS UP

White men seeking either Black or Latino men tended to specifically look for aggressive sexual partners to take the top role, while those seeking Asian or Latino men tended to seek submissive sexual partners. In the larger white imagination, when Latino men were equated with Black men, they tended to be aggressive, dangerous sexual partners but were submissive docile partners when equated with Asians.

Craigslist ads placed by Black men or Asian men seeking white sexual partners rarely indicated a preference for their own race as well. Yet unlike Black and Asian men, Latino men seeking white men were more likely to indicate a preference for white men in addition to other Latino men rather than an exclusive preference for white men. For example:

TIGHT HOLE: CURIOUS TO GET FUCKED FOR THE FIRST TIME. I'VE SUCKED DICK AND JO, BUT NEVER HAD A DICK UP MY ASS. MASCULINE DL FOR THE SAME ONLY. LATIN HERE. MOSTLY INTO WHITE OR LATIN GUYS. CANT HOST. LOOKING FOR TOPS.

A Latino man seeking a bottom placed this ad:

wanna fuck?: hey horny today and looking for a hot toned, athletic or muscular, white or latino bottom. Can host for a few hours. Hit me up with pics and stats. B negative and disease free, and please be discreet. Any time after 6pm I cant host. I'm twenty eight years old latino about a buck eighty and have a six inch thick uncut cock. looking for safe play.

As evidenced by the ads above, sexual expectations for, or from, Latino men were not as rigid as for Black men or Asian men in that Latino men sought either a white or Latino sexual partner to be the bottom or the top. While there were many Black men seeking sexual tops and even a few Asian men seeking sexual bottoms, Black men were more likely to seek sexual bottoms and Asian men were much more likely to seek sex tops. Yet these patterns were not evident in ads placed by Latino men.

White men who seek either another white man or a Latino man placed ads that were different from those placed by white men seeking either a Latino man or an Asian man, and white men seeking either a Black man or a Latino man. For those seeking either another white man or a Latino man, the ads were largely neutral, and there was no discernable pattern. Like white men who only seek other white men, the ads included those placed by white men who were tops and white men who were bottoms in roughly the same proportion. One white poster wrote:

> **DL bi guy want dick:** What's up? Bi DL married here looking for something similar. Not super picky but would like my age or younger white of Latin who want to kick back j/o and maybe give head. Lets meet up and see what happens. I'm a regular everyday Joe type of guy looking for the same. Hit me up with stats and a pic if you ask for a pic.

What's telling about the above advertisement is that the white poster repeats that he is "looking for the same."

A notable exception to the lack of a pattern among white posters seeking only Latino men or either white men or Latino men were the white men who peppered their ads with Spanish slang words. These men were much more likely to seek Latino men who were sexually aggressive and domineering:

> **WHITE BOTTOM to bitch out for HOMIES/CHOLOS/ MEXICANS:** Very clean and discreet white bro here, shaved head, go-t, on the downlow – real masculine and chill, love to bitch out for some good dick. If you're blazin' with your friends and just need someone to hook up some good head, higt me up. I'll throat you all good and swallow that load. Or if you need to pound one out, I can bend over and give it up. Only into other downlow bros, horned up str8 homies who just need to blow.

Another white man posted this ad:

Voracious White rimpig craves DL Latino verga and culo: Are you athletic, beefy, MACHO and NASTY in bed? Do you crave having a white puto's TOUNGE service your ALL MALE MACHO culo and erect verga over and over til you blow your load into his mouth? Would you REALLY ENJOY taking a lonnng slow piss into your white puto's mouth while he's sucking your uncut Erect verga? Do you love watching your personal puto pig sniffs and licks and worships your huge erection and then dives down into your culo for some deeeep cleaning of your Macho hole with his puto nose and tongue? to kick back, spread your legs wide and open and let a VORACIOUS white COCKSUCKER AND EXPERT ASS EATER sniff, kiss, lick, worship, suck and eat your SUPERIOR CULO AND MANHOOD! YOU can't get ENUF COCKWORSHIP and REALLY ENJOY GIVING DIRTY VERBAL ABUSE! YOU are ALSO INTO FEEDING YOUR PISS and GETTING RIMMED FOR HOURS! I'm 5'7", 160, nice looking, mature, 54, muscular, masculine, cocksucker who LOVES SUCKING UNCUT VERGA and MACHI CULO!

White men who tended to use a much more blatantly racialized language tended to view Latino men as sexually aggressive and dominant and more likely to engage in what some may consider deviant sexual acts. However, white men who used Spanish terms such as "hombre" or "papi," were the exception rather than the rule.

CONCLUSION

In Craigslist ads, interracial sex is often presented as a "new delight" something that should be more intense and more satisfying, precisely because interracial sex is out of the ordinary. When men look for inter-racial sexual partners online, they are not looking for the normal ways of doing things but rather project their racialized sexual fantasies on poten-tial sexual partners.[48]

Taken together, the images of men of color in gay pornography and other gay media products discussed in chapter two can be understood as a type of "controlling image." As Patricia Hill Collins observed, controlling images are specifically "designed to make racism, sexism, poverty, and other forms of social injustice appear to be natural, normal, and inevitable part of everyday life."[49] Media images of gay white normality or desires for white men are specifically deployed to make racial preferences and racialized hierarchies of desire appear natural and normal while simultaneously making sexual desires for men of color as a fetish. Within the world of Craigslist mediated hook ups, interracial sex is often presented as a "new delight, more intense, more satisfying than normal ways of doing and feeling."[50] When men look for interracial sexual partners online, they are not looking for the "normal" ways of doing things but rather project their racialized sexual fantasies on potential sexual partners. Ironically, racialized sexual encounters are an arena where race is both immaterial and infinitely salient.[51] Rather than blur racial boundaries, interracial desires help to create and maintain perceived racial differences through sexual behaviors that are racially marked and marketed.

At first blush, it would be easy to claim, as some commentators have, that the higher rates of interracial relationships among gay men compared to straight men is evidence that race matters less to gay men than it does to straight men. To make this argument, however, we would need to decouple racism from eroticism, as if the physical act of having sex with someone of another race can somehow inoculate sexual actors from the influences of a racist society. Yet as Sharon Patricia Holland points out, race and racism are central to the ways desire is constructed.[52] These Craigslist ads demonstrates that gay men use racialized sexual tropes to define and frame their sexual desires. In the most intimate of spaces, within the confines of the most intimate acts, race comes to take on more salience rather than less.

In the control and employ of white producers and white consumers, these images mark men of color as the sexual other that reinforces the sexual normality of whiteness. At the same time, as this chapter demonstrates, men of color utilize these racial tropes in the pursuit of their own pleasure. One possible interpretation would be that these men have internalized the racial and racist tropes about men of color. As we will see in chapter 5, accusations of internalized racism among men of color who pursue white men as sexual partners is widespread. While it might be argued that the use of these tropes in constructing desire is uniformly problematic because they specifically construct desire for white men as normal and universal while constructing men of color as a sexual fetish, the use of such tropes in the pursuit of pleasure may be a bit more complicated. Take, for example, this comment from a gay Asian man whom I quoted in *Geisha of a Different Kind*, about finding white men for sex :

> I had to figure out what sort of stereotypes these guys wanted and to match those stereotypes. I'm not exactly the submissive type, but I could shut my mouth. I'm not exactly a passive guy, but I could roll over on my back. You know, I mean, I can compliment, I can manipulate with the best of them. If they request and I could get a fun night of it, I did it. . . . I remember talking about that with some of my friends and they got upset because they were foreign-born and they didn't think they could match all the stereotypes that I could as easily.[53]

It's difficult to argue that the man quoted above has internalized the racist tropes associated with Asian men. But he uses his knowledge of those tropes for the purpose of seeking sexual pleasure, giving him an advantage over Asian men with less knowledge of such tropes.

It's possible that gay men of color do not embody these sexual expectations per se. That is, their own sexual preferences do not conform to white expectations.[54] To reconcile the contradiction between the construction and deployment of such racist tropes and the actual use of such tropes, we may need to make a better distinction between desire and pleasure if we are to fully examine the ways that racialized sexual images impact sexual lives and behaviors.

While uncoupling desire and pleasure is beyond the scope of this book, a trio of scholars—Jennifer Nash, Mireille Miller-Young, and Ariane Cruz—have provided us with a new framework for understanding racialized images and the use of such images by people of color, particularly as they relate to racialized sexual pleasures. Rather than perceive racialized sexual images as only sites of violence and oppression, these works have asked if it is possible that such images can be both sites of violence and pleasure.[55]

While acknowledging that racialized and sexualized images of men of color created by white men can, and do, have negative consequences, it is also possible that men of color can deploy those same images in the pursuit of sexual pleasure. When desire is raced, using race in pursuit of sexual pleasure is one possible way that gay men of color can disidentify with these tropes.[56] Mireille Miller-Young, for one, suggests that Black men can take up stereotypically racialized images and create "new spaces for desire and pleasure through counter-fetishization."[57]

It is possible that rather than simply internalizing these images, gay men of color embody racialized stereotypes for the specific pursuit of "race pleasure," a pleasure found in "hyperbolic racialization and uncomfortable enjoyment in embodied racialization."[58] Like the gay Asian man quoted above, gay men of color may "negotiate the minefield of representation" in order to find racialized sexual pleasure in them.[59] Through a more modest form of race play, in which they take on stereotypically raced sexual roles, gay men of color may be finding pleasure in "the charged, complex, and contradictory relationships between racism and rapture."[60] In fact, for some men of color, deliberately using racialized violent stereotypes may work in finding sexual partners if the end goal is sexual pleasure.[61] In chapter 5, I return to these themes to examine the ways gay men of color frame what it means to have both interracial and intraracial desires.

CHAPTER 4

Dan Savage Wept for Obama

Gay White Men and the Denial of Gay Racism

IN LATE 2013, *QUEERTY* PUBLISHED AN ARTICLE BY KEVIN CLARKE titled "PHOTOS: A history of hairy guys."[1] As an expanded review of his book *Beards, An Unshaved History*, Clarke shared his personal reflections about how he came to write a book about men's facial hair, along with some interesting tidbits he had learned along the way. Among articles published on *Queerty*, little was remarkable about this one, and there was nothing deliberately racialized about it. Its significance lies, in fact, in its unexceptional display of the norm: as is true of virtually all articles published on *Queerty* that are not specifically about race or racism, all the images accompanying the article were of white men.

The lack of any images of men of color accompanying the article didn't go unnoticed. "Once again the lack of beautiful minority men is striking," wrote a reader calling themself Bear Aspirin. Observations that articles on *Queerty* generally lack representations of men of color are repeated, in one form or another, on many of the articles that appear on the website. Despite the widespread observation that gay media almost exclusively caters to white men, the next comment, posted in response to Bear Aspirin, is also typical. In their response, a reader calling themself Faggot rhetorically asks:

Minorities vis-à-vis which country (countries) exactly? Which hirsute minority (minorities) would you have liked to have seen represented? Aren't the hirsute a minority in their own right?

The three question response by Faggot demonstrates several things that are representative of the way gay white men respond to accusations of racism in gay communities. First, it directly challenges the accusation of racism by attempting to shift definitions of *minority* in favor of whites or to minimize the racialized status of men of color. Also, it attempts to belittle Bear Aspirin's comment by suggesting that *minority* is a contested category. Here, Faggot makes an entirely numeric argument about what constitutes a minority group, based on a physical characteristic rather than a social one. Using this definition, virtually anyone can be a member of a minority group if we narrow the definition of what constitutes a minority to virtually any characteristic that one might possess. Faggot's comment only makes sense if the category *minority* does not have a historic reference to those who are denied rights and privileges granted to members of the dominant group. This method of defining what constitutes a minority group erases power and domination embedded in an unequal status system, based not on numbers but on political and social power. Together, the three rhetorical questions minimize the concern raised by gay men of color by trivializing them and taking them out of context.

Rather than being an isolated incident, Faggot's comment is representative of the ways racism is routinely trivialized or minimized by readers of gay publications. When *Queerty* posted a short story on the Urban League of Atlanta presenting a Champions of Justice and Equality Award to Dan Cathy, the vocal anti-gay CEO of the Christian fast-food company Chick-fil-A, in late 2013, readers were understandably irate.[2] Many of the comments were thoughtful, such as this one written by a poster calling themself calista:

There's a statue of Dan Cathy in the downtown Atlanta business district since Chick-fil-A was founded in Georgia. I suspect that he or his marketing team bought this 'honor' to deflect from all the bad publicity they've been getting.

Many other posters were less refrained in their racist vitriol. One poster calling themself Hephaestion commented, "Dottie Johnson [head of the Urban League] has a lot o' 'splainin' to do!," a phrase often erroneously ascribed to Desi Arnaz's character on *I Love Lucy* but hearkening back to stereotypical and racist characterizations of alleged Black speech patterns from 1980s television sitcoms. Others were even more blatantly racist, as exemplified by a poster calling themself Ben Dover: "Fried chicken? I guess this award might make sense if the Urban League also gave an award to a brewer of 40 oz Malt liquor. Oh, and a heroin dealer while they're at it." Later, another poster calling themself DarthKitsune wrote, "So it boils down to urban people praising a guy who makes fried chicken? You go ahead and give this guy an award, have Uncle Remus present it while you're at it."

When other posters took issue with the racist tone of comments such as those made by posters like Ben Dover and KarthKitsune, their concerns were met with further trivialization. A poster who objected to Ben Dover's racist comment was told:

Your anger is misplaced and you're throwing around the 'r' randomly and meaninglessly. Save it for the Urban League for its wallowing in self-hatred and racism and reinforcing negative Black stereotypes.

Ben Dover's response to their comments being racist are noteworthy. In their defense of their original comment, Ben Dover does not offer any explanation as to why their comment was not racist but instead dismisses criticisms as being meaningless. Ironically, as they accuse others of throwing the "r" around randomly, they offer a stereotypical and racist portrayal of the Urban League, a national civil rights group, as being racist. The assumption is that they are racist toward white people. Their use of racist stereotypes to describe the Urban League is entirely lost on them as they accuse the organization of reinforcing negative Black stereotypes, stereotypes that they apparently hold.

Gay people of color are trivialized as well. When *Queerty* ran a column titled "Seven LGBT African-Americans Who Changed the Face of the Gay Community" during Black History Month in 2012, many of the comments were thoughtful, with some listing others who did not make the list.[3] Yet a poster calling themselves Isaac C wrote:

> All of these people are pretty much irrelevant in the grand scheme of things outside of racial/color representation, which I guess is important enough for some people. I certainly don't consider most of them a part of the GLBT rights movement.

And when *Queerty* published a short story featuring five Black LBGTQ blogs in 2016, a commenter calling themselves Stachedı responded, "Unless you're Black, I don't see why you would even read those blogs."[4] Here, Stachedı makes a clear distinction between Black and non-Black people. These blogs, despite being written by queer people, were unworthy of being read by non-Black people, regardless of their sexuality.

These attempts to trivialize racism by readers of gay websites should come as no surprise. Within the gay press and from prominent gay white writers, there has been a long history of denying that racism in gay communities is a problem that needs to be addressed.

In one tongue-in-cheek article titled, "I'm grateful to be gay: Otherwise I might have been a horrible person," published on the website *Slate* in late November of 2014, Mark Joseph shared a number of humorous ways that he is grateful to be gay, including not having to worry about birth control or peppering his speech with "dude" or "man."[5] After listing the things he does not have to worry about because he is gay, Joseph offered a reason to be grateful specifically for *being* gay, rather than just not straight:

> What if, given the privilege of heterosexuality, I turned against all the vulnerable and disadvantaged people, who, as a gay man, I inherently empathize with? As part of my job, I regularly read the writings of people in whom something has broken or withered— people who have lost the ability to see the humanity in others. I

put myself in the mindset of people who dehumanize and vilify and hate. I become intimately acquainted with the twisted beliefs of those who, encountering a person they don't quite understand, lash out with cruel loathing and immoral rage. . . . Because I am gay, it is basically impossible for me to become one of these people. . . . Gay people are born with empathy for the underdog, whether we like it or not. We've all played the role of the outcast, the weirdo; we've all faced prejudice and discrimination and sorrow and self-loathing. Those of us who emerge from the darkness gain newfound will and determination. But we can't shake that fundamental desire of justice, that yearning for fairness for those despised by society.

According to Joseph, the redeeming quality of *being* gay, rather than just not straight, is that it provides immunity to the normal societal woes of racism, sexism, and classism.

To be fair, the column was met with ridicule from readers who vehemently objected to his claim that being gay naturally led to being more empathetic to other marginalized people. Some commenters defending the author even suggested that perhaps the column was satire. Yet many comments posted in response to the article supported the notion that this is not an isolated view among significant proportion of gay white men.

The idea that gay men are naturally less inclined to be racist than others is repeated in subtle ways in numerous other writings by gay white men. In an article titled "Are We More Racist Than Straight Men?" published on *Queerty* in 2015, author Mike Alvear wrote:

I seriously doubt gays are more racist than straights. I just think witnessing or experiencing racism is more profound when it comes from us. After all, we're a group that is systematically discriminated against at all levels of society. When we see or experiences members of our tribe doing what's done to us it has a powerful impact. Because it's more memorable we tend to project out and think there's a lot more of it than there really is.[6]

Alvear follows this statement with an example of his "good friend" who is "gay, Latino, and has an Arab-sounding name" who experiences consistent acts of racism yet "constantly uses the 'N' word and spouts off some of the most hideously stereotyped racist garbage you've ever heard." There are several problems with Alvear's statement. In defining *we*, Alvear clearly limits the definition of gay men to gay white men. While the racism of his good friend is blatant, the examples he provides of racism by gay white men can be read as trivial, which allows him to make the claim that the reason we might believe that gay white men are more racist is because it is just more memorable when they engage in it, not because it might be true. Also, his use of his good friend, who happens to be Latino with an Arab-sounding name, helps to deflect from white racism and suggests that racism is something that any racial group is capable of practicing against another racial group.

Often, attempts to portray gay white men as being racially progressive utilize comparisons of gay acceptance of race to the alleged homophobia in communities of color. In a blog post published after the passage of Proposition 8 in California on the website of the *Stranger*, an alternative newspaper in Seattle, written by Dan Savage, arguably the most famous gay columnist in America, the author had this to say:

> I'm thrilled that we've just elected our first African-American president. I wept last night. I wept reading the papers this morning. But I can't help but feeling hurt that the love and support aren't mutual. I do know this, thought: I'm done pretending that the handful of racist gay white men out there—and they are out there, and I think they're scum—are a bigger problem for African Americans, gay and straight, than the huge numbers of homophobic African Americans are for gay Americans, whatever their color.[7]

Savage's comments present gay white men as widely accepting of Black people, providing the Black community with "love and support." The fact that gay men overwhelmingly vote for Democratic candidates is never mentioned. Instead, gay men voting for Barak Obama is presented as a show of "love and support" for Black Americans. However, some have suggested that gay white men were less likely to vote for Barak Obama than they were to vote for generic white Democratic candidates. Viewed this way, it can be argued that Obama's race actually prevented some gay white men from voting for him over a generic Democratic candidate, far from the "love and support" that Savage claims that gay whites lavished on Obama.

Savage also minimizes the problem of racism in gay communities by alleging that there are only a "handful" of racist gay white men, despite the fact that gay men of color report having experienced more racism from gay white men than from straight people in general. In doing so, he simply dismisses the overwhelming evidence that gay men of color experience more racism from gay white men than from the larger society. Arguing that racism in gay communities is only the actions of a "handful" of racist gay white men removes the role that gay white men play in creating institutional patterns that promote racial hierarchies.

The notion that voting for Barak Obama was a show of solidarity and support for Black communities was repeated again in a 2008 *Advocate* article by Michael Joseph Gross titled "Gay Is the New Black?" According to Gross, "The combination of Obama's win and gay people's losses inflicted massive whiplash. We were elated, then furious."[8] The message, as with Savage's, was that voting for Barak Obama, the Democratic presidential candidate, was a show of support for Black America. While Gross's article was much more objective than Savage's blog post, Gross still managed to imply that gay white people were not only not racist because they had cast a vote for a Black man, but that the fact that they cast a vote for a Black man demonstrated how not racist they were.

The denial of racism is certainly not unique to gay white men. Rather, it should be understood as a part of a larger pattern of widespread racial denial. Within the past few decades, the normative climate for what can be said in public about one's personal racial views has dramatically shifted, and it is now unthinkable that individuals expressing blatant racist views would be tolerated by civil society.[9] Parallel to this change in what is considered appropriate to vocalize about race in the public sphere has been a radical change in the way that society views people it thinks of as being racist. In a nation that once praised the Ku Klux Klan as protectors of white women's virtue and a last-line defense against "Black brutalism," political leaders are required not only to distance themselves from current and past members but to actively and publicly disavow them. To this end, a significant amount of mental and emotional energy is expended denying that their actions were racist, denying having racist beliefs and/or attitudes, and avoiding accusations of being a racist.[10] Not only that, those pointing out racist acts and beliefs attempt to avoid directly accusing others of being racist, even as they bring attention to acts of racism.[11] The taboo against being a racist is so damaging that both the accusers and the accused enter into a carefully choreographed beating around the bush in order to help save face.

The denial of racism is not simply about distancing oneself from racist acts. It also represents a form of impression management whereby individuals attempt to present a positive self-presentation in a society that has come to see blatant racist beliefs and action as inappropriate and the holding of racist beliefs and engaging in racist acts as morally and ethically suspect. To be accused of racism is to be accused both of engaging in a despicable act and of being a despicable person. Ironically, the belief that one can only practice racism if one is a bad person and/or that racism is a conscious hate for members of another race may hinder the ability of many white people to see systemic and structural racism, because they practice and maintain structures of racism themselves.

It should go without saying that denial of racism is hardly evidence of an absence of it. Yet here I am having to say it. Rather than being absent, contemporary racism simply manifests differently from the overt, blatant forms of racism common in the past. Contemporary racism is more subtle, often couching racist sentiments along less openly egregious lines and operating invisibly on the structural level of society.[12] Nonetheless, when examined carefully, acts of modern racism betray the racist assumptions and sentiments that continue to shape life in the United States. This social taboo against expressing racist sentiments more openly and blatantly have led to the development of discursive practices meant to protect speakers against accusations of racism while only thinly disguising the racist narrative itself. Under these conditions, the denial of racism becomes an arsenal in the active maintenance of racist beliefs and practices. As Teun van Dijk has noted, "One of the crucial properties of contemporary racism is its denial" with the discourse of denial playing a pivotal role in the maintenance and reproduction of racism.[13] The denial of racism is central to the promotion of the colorblind narrative that has all but replaced overt, government sponsored, and socially sanctioned acts of racism in promoting racist policies and beliefs. Unlike the blatantly racist talk of the Jim Crow era, the narrative of colorblind racism is "slippery, apparently contradictory, and often subtle" but nonetheless accomplishes the same goals.[14]

Examples of such denials are legion. Perhaps best exemplified by such qualified disclaimers as "I'm not racist but . . . " or its numerous cousins, such as "I have nothing against Black people but . . . ," such denials of racism allow speakers to simultaneously make racist generalizations about members of minority groups while disavowing their statements as being racist. Narrative attempts to frame one's racist comments as coming from someone who doesn't hold racist views is hardly the only method of discursively denying racism. Practices aimed at denying racism come in a variety of forms and allow speakers to disavow racism while simultaneously making racist generalizations.[15] In one form, speakers engage in act-denial, in which they strenuously deny that their statement or actions are in any way racist. In another, there is control-denial, in which speakers argue that what they said was an accident. Intention-denial allows speakers to imply that the listener misinterpreted their statements. Goal-denial allows speakers to deny responsibility for their statements by arguing that they did not intend to be offensive or to make a racist statement. Teun van Dijk also notes acts of mitigations, which can take the form of downtoning, minimizing, or using euphemisms when discussing issues of race.[16] Taken together, these acts of denial allow speakers to openly voice racist beliefs while maintaining face as a nonracist person.

There are also more complex methods of denial. Speakers may ground their views as being a reflection of the external world rather than any personal sentiment that they might possess. Rather than blatantly expressing a negative sentiment about an outside group, speakers may present an "uncomfortable fact" as evidence that members of the outgroup routinely fail to adhere to acceptable social norms. Individuals may adamantly claim that they have nothing against various groups but have issues with how they behave. In this way, the groups being criticized are blamed for the negative sentiments that may be directed toward them. The problem is that social norms themselves are a reflection of the ability to define certain behaviors, values, and morals as being normative and other behaviors, values, and morals as being deviant and, therefore, worthy of disdain.[17]

Another way racism is denied is by simply defining it in a way that excludes certain acts directed toward people of color as being racist or suggesting that racism is simply a universal act that impacts both whites and people of color equally. As I described in the introduction to this book, an event hosted by a mainstream gay organization run by mostly gay white men that hosted a "Race Forum" where the organizational leaders announced that the forum would be an opportunity to discuss race but not racism, since "anyone can be a racist," a definition that few people of color would share. When defining racism, whites tended to do so in a much more limited way, often limiting racism to overt acts of discrimination directed by one individual against another, while Black people are more likely to define racism using broader criteria that is able to capture the much more subtle ways that racism operates on the structural level.[18]

The limited definition of racism favored by whites specifically requires a belief in the superiority of one race over another and active acts of racial discrimination directed toward members of a racial minority group. When adhered to rigidly, this limited definition makes it impossible to adequately determine if an act or a person is racist; the inner workings of a person's belief are, after all, inaccessible. One simply cannot be accused of being a racist or engaging in racism if the definition of racism excludes any act that can be dismissed with the excuse that no prejudgment or active discrimination, based on the belief that some races are inferior, took place.

An accusation of reverse racism is another tactic that is often used to dismiss accusations of racism. Accusations of racism are also often dismissed as "playing the race card," and those making such claims are often accused of being racist for seeing racism where it allegedly does not exist.[19] Yet, as many scholars have pointed out, "racism requires both prejudice towards a group of people based on the social construction of race *and* the power to oppress those groups of people."[20] This power to oppress an outgroup lies both with individuals and with the larger social structure in which one group is dominant over another.

The denial of racism can also be achieved collaboratively with other individual actors or with other members of one's group.[21] At the same time that individuals defend themselves from accusations of racism, they also defend other members of their group, or their group in general, extending the denial of racism to include assessments about social groups. These types of denials occur within larger social contexts through public discourse created and disseminated by governments, the media, educational institutions, corporations, and other organizations to demonstrate how the entire group is racially enlightened.[22] The collaborative denial of racism may be even more problematic being that it denies both personal negative feelings and attitudes toward members of minority groups and hides larger structural issues under the guise of not being a racist society.[23]

Examining reader comments on articles about racism published on *Queerty* and *LGBTQ Nation*, the two largest websites targeting gay audiences, offers us a good insight into how racism is denied in gay communities. My interest here is not to make generalized claims about whether gay communities are more racist than non-gay communities or if gay men of color experience more racism within gay communities than outside of them. I am also not interested in how often gay men deny racism or if the denial of racism is the more or less common response to accusations of racism. The most obvious insight from readings these stories should be that there are numerous and contentious opinions, and denials of racism are challenged and confronted more often than not. An argument could be made that a much greater percentage of gay men recognize that there is a problem of racism in gay communities that may be greater than in non-gay communities than the percentage of men who are likely to deny such accusations. However, my interest is in exploring *how* gay men deny racism in gay-identified cyberspaces when such denials are made, rather than attempting to outline whether denials are more common than not.

I make no claim that the articles I selected are a representative sample of articles published by gay websites or that the articles I draw on are representative of the type of articles that they publish. Instead, I attempt to address the question of how gay men deny racism by identifying the tactics used by gay white men to deny broad accusations of racism, with a special interest in how they deny sexual racism. In the first chapter, I noted that sexual racism is perhaps the most prevalent form of racism found gay communities. Thus it should not come as any surprise that it is the type of racism that is the most vehemently denied by gay white men and, to some degree, by gay men of color as well.

THAT'S NOT RACIST!

To discount sexual racism as actual racism, readers often resort to defining racism in the narrowest way possible, allowing them to claim that sexual racism isn't actually racism. This comment written by a reader calling themself Lars Eighner in response to the article "Racism or Just Preferences?" published on *LGBTQ Nation* in early 2015 is a good example:

> It is not about who one particular person likes or loves. It is about jobs, education, housing, advancement, finance terms, pricing, law enforcement, red-lining, incarceration rates, and many, many other things. But it isn't about who you, I, or the guy down the street "dates," or tricks with, or marries. Granted, it is much easier to call out an individual for his "dating" preferences than it is to take on the serious, intrenched institutional issues. It is easy because it meaningless.[24]

In their response to the article, Lars Eighner provides some examples of what, to them, constitutes "real" racism to make the argument that sexual racism isn't racism but an individual choice. Not only does Lars Eighner offer a narrow definition of racism that depends on measurable harms, they go even further to minimize sexual racism by suggesting that the real issue of racism gets ignored for something meaningless. In framing their response in this way, Lars Eighner is able to accomplish three goals. First, sexual racism is framed as not being racism. Also, because sexual racism isn't really racism, accusations of such are meaningless. Finally, Lars Eighner's comment belittles those making accusations of sexual racism by painting them as individuals who are not serious about "real" issues of racism and making easy gestures, distracting from real problems, and thus being a problem themselves.

Those who use narrow definitions of racism to discount sexual racism are often particularly confident in their interpretation of what constitutes racism and what does not. Responding to an article titled "Scruff Founders Defend App's Ethnicity Filters: Personal Preference or Casual Racism?," published on *Queerty* in 2016, a reader calling themself willmSF wrote:

> The POV expressed by many lately that everyone should find everyone else sexually attractive is tired, lame and ignorant. It's thrown out by those that simply don't understand the difference between discrimination and sexual attraction. It's easier for people to jump the PC bandwagon than actually stop and think before they write.[25]

From willmSF's perspective, the problem is that those making accusations of sexual racism simply do not know the difference between racism and sexual attraction. When framing sexual racism as being a matter of those who simply do not understand what racism is, willmSF dismisses any possibility that sexual racism can be considered a racist act. Rather, the solution here is for those making accusations of sexual racism to simply learn to "understand the difference."

Another tactic used to argue that racial preferences are not racist is to frame race as simply one of many other traits that might be preferred over another. As a reader calling themself mikenyc352 wrote in response to the article "Is This the Brutal Truth White Gay Men Refuse to Hear?," published on *Queerty* in 2016:

> Although I don't necessarily think any of it is fair or right, how is stating preferences for race any different than people desire for certain ages, body types, heights, eye color, shoe size or the various other characteristics that get some people going while it leaves other people completely uninterested? I personally have no particular sexual preference for or against any race but there are definitely body types and other physical characteristics I am attracted to and

others I just am not. I can no way of changing those any more or less than my strict preference for men and not women.[26]

What mikenyc352 fails to address is that age, body type, height, eye color, shoe size, and any number of other characteristic that some men may prefer over another are characteristics that individuals may possess regardless of race. Members of any racial group may possess such characteristics, and preferring them does not automatically rule out entire groups of people in the way that race does.

Comments similar to those made by mikenyc352 sometimes take a more condescending tone. Shifting the blame to men of color, a poster calling themself Cam wrote in response to a 2009 *Queerty* article, "Is Racism among the Gays the Worst It's Been in Decades?":

> Anytime I hear about anybody feeling uncomfortable in a bar,
> it was never because of what anybody said or did to them, it was
> THIER impression that they weren't welcome in there. To all the
> Black guys, Latin guys, Asian guys, I've got news for you, all the
> white guys in there didn't feel comfortable either. Gay bars can
> be intimidating to single guys looking to meet people. EVERY-
> BODY in there feels like they are being judged. If you didn't feel
> like you were welcome in that bar talk to the tall skinny white guy
> with acne, or the short heavier guy who has gone home alone the
> last 10 times he's been in there. I'm sure they can share some of
> their own feelings.[27]

Here, Cam's comment suggests that race is just another way that gay men discriminate against other gay men based on physical characteristics. At the same time, Cam doesn't seem to be able to see that they equate gay men of color to "undesirable" white men, not all white men. While Cam states that there are white men who also feel uncomfortable at gay bars, they mark these white men with stereotypical physical traits that are perceived to be undesirable. Cam's point is not that all men, even white men, feel rejected, but that men with undesirable traits are rejected. Clearly, the hidden message is that race is just yet another "undesirable" trait.

Even among the men who find problems with explicitly excluding men of another race as potential sexual partners, the issue is about blatantly stating these exclusions rather than having racial preferences in the first place. Consider this response by a reader calling themself Doug regarding an article titled "Grindr Wants Users to Stop Being So Racist and Start Being Kindr: But Is That Even Possible?," published on *Queerty* in 2018:

> It's one thing to have your own preferences, but when you're openly stating on your profile that you don't want specific people based on their race, it's very inconsiderate of how that might make a person who's a minority feel.[28]

Doug's comment reflects the widespread belief among gay men that the issue is not racial preferences, but the ways that such preferences are expressed. The problem is framed as an issue of personal behaviors rather than the hierarchy of racial desire created by the focus and privileging of whiteness within gay communities. The goal becomes one of being nicer and more considerate rather than questioning and challenging racial hierarchies. According to this perspective, explicitly stating racial preferences is a problem, but having racist beliefs that frame men of color as being less worthy than white men of erotic attention is not.

Another tactic of trivializing racism, particularly sexual racism, is to label such accusations as being "PC nonsense," as evident by the comment made by a reader calling themself Plays Well With Others to the article "Sexual Racism on Queer Dating Apps Screws with Your Mental Health," published on *Queerty* in 2019. According to them:

> "Sexual racism" . . . More PC bullthit. Everyone is entitled to have their own sexual preferences. So tired of this nonsense being banded about that if you are not sexually attracted to someone you are a "racist" or a "bigot"

> Stating very clearly whom you are seeking is everyone's right. It also eliminates a lot of back and forth before deciding there is not

a match. As long as you are not spewing hatred nor demeaning persons or a group

To those who deem not being included in the type of person some-one is seeking, you need to put on your big boy pants, move on, find someone where there actually is a chance for a connection and stop pulling out the "racist" or "bigotry" card . . . .[29]

Not only does Plays Well With Others dismiss sexual racism as "PC bullthit [*sic*]," they manage to shift the responsibility back on men of color by suggesting that the problem is their pulling of the alleged race card.

GAY WHITE MEN AS VICTIMS

When confronted, members of dominant groups often rely on the tactic of claiming victimhood to argue that they, not other groups, are the targets of oppression. While this tactic may not specifically address the racist act, it bestows on members of dominant groups the moral authority of the victim, from which they can claim some damage.[30]

While accusations of reverse racism and/or reverse discrimination are common, gay white men's status as sexual minorities offers them a unique opportunity to make specific claims of oppression based on that status. A reader calling themself john_siders wrote in response to the article "Confronting Racism in the Gay Community," published in 2017 on *Queerty*:

Sounds like baiting to me? Every one including gays are tired of the Black community's crying about being picked on by the police and the white man keeping them down blacks are the most pro-tected minority in the US Gays do not have near the protection in jobs or housing blacks do! The 14% that does 76% of the violent crime needs to clean there act up if they want more respect! Chi-cago is a good example Who is killing who !![31]

According to john_siders and many other commentators, the real victims are gay (understood to be white) men who have fewer legal protections and are victims of crimes allegedly committed by Black people.

The sentiment that gay people have less rights and are more oppressed than people of color was widely shared by those who attempted to dismiss racism in gay communities. In responding to the article "Is Racism among the Gays the Worst It's Been in Decades?," published on *Queerty* in 2009, a reader calling themself galefan2004 wrote:

> If you want to start blaming someone for racism then blame the blacks that want to play the victim and use their "oppression" (blacks haven't been legally oppressed since 1964 and aren't even the most oppressed group in the history of this country) as an excuse for their own racism. Blacks today have no clue what it means to be oppressed. The oppression in this generation is towards gays and lesbians. Gays and lesbians can still be denied employment or terminated simply for being gay and lesbian in the majority of states in the country.[32]

According to galefan2004, gays are more oppressed than Black people because they do not have similar legal protections. This belief, earlier echoed by john_siders, that a lack of legal protection, or the existence of legal protections in the case of Black people, is the defining characteristic of being oppressed dismisses any attempt to define oppression beyond that which is blatant and explicit and codified into law. Subtle social oppression that people of color routinely experience—in employment, housing, public accommodations, and any number of other spheres of life—are based on easily observed racial markers that many gay men do not display. By narrowly defining oppression by equating legal protection with a lack of oppression and the lack of legal protection as oppression, gay white men are able to claim victimhood.

Claiming the moral authority of an oppressed minority, gay white men often lob accusations of reverse racism against people of color. After having claimed for gays the role of the "most oppressed group in history," galefan2004 added this comment:

Seriously, I think the tendency in the black community is to throw whitey under the buss. You guys love to bring up slavery and inequality, but you simply overlook abolitionist and white people that fought for racial inequality when you do so. You love to blame the white people for being racist, but the same time you lump all white people together and if a white person dare say or do something you aren't 100% in agreement with you label them as a racist with no questions asked. I'm not saying there are not white radical extreme racist, but there are also black radical extreme racist. Racism is a TWO WAY street.

This idea that racism is a "two way street" is widely shared among the readers of gay media, who are apt to deny that sexual racism is racism. In their view, gays are not only more oppressed than people of color, they are often also victims of racism. The "two way street" argument also reinforces the erroneous belief that anyone can be racist and that racism is an individual act of hatred directed at another individual to which all individuals can be victims.

Accusations of reverse racism also focus on the alleged objectification of white men by men of color. Heywood Jablowme wrote the following in response to the article "Are You An Unwitting Sexual Racist? Find Out," published on *Queerty* in 2017:

> But it's not a one-way street. Almost all the time when black guys have wanted to have sex with me, it was simply racial, they just wanted to f*ck a cute white guy. I didn't instigate anything; in fact 99% of the time I'd have been way too shy to approach them.[33]

Echoing Heywood Jablowme's argument, a reader calling themself Avery Alvarez responded to a 2016 *Queerty* article titled "Asian Man Fed Up with Being Ignored by the White-Painted Gay Community," writing:

> White gay men are fed up, too. They are fed up with all the low self-esteem, narcissistic, entitled non-white gays demanding access 24/7 to their bodies. To put a spin on a Feminist point of view, ones

that's very true—You are NOT entitled to a man's body. He has
100% agency over it, and can deny your for ANY reason, or no reason at all. He doesn't owe you anything. And you can take your
pity party, and cries of "racism" just because someone doesn't want
to be fetishized by you, and head over to your nearest "Safe Space",
have a good cry, and hopefully, get the Fck over yourself.[34]

Not only does Avery Alvarez's comment paint gay white men as victims,
it specifically vilifies men of color by drawing a parallel with a rapist by
suggesting that sexual racism is nothing more than feeling entitled to
white men's bodies. Again, the suggestion is that sexual racism operates
on an individual level only, where the issue isn't about the creation and
maintenance of a racial hierarchy of desire but about individual gay men
of color with low self-esteem who are narcissistic and entitled. The solution, then, is not to address the racial hierarchy but for gay men of color
to "get the Fck over [themselves]."

Even when such statements as "no Blacks, no Asians, no Latinos, etc."
are made, gay white men justify them by redirecting the blame to men of
color. In response to the article "If You Still Don't Understand Why Your
Preferences Are Racist, This Video Might Help Explain," published on
Queerty in 2018, a reader calling themself S.anderson wrote:

> It would be racist and wrong if a profile said "no ***(racial_slur)". I
> am aware many men use strong language in their profiles, but in
> my personal experience this is because many idiots doggedly ignore
> profile interests. What's the point, boys? You think if you take a shot
> at him anyway, you'll win him over to your team? More likely, the
> idiots are doing it to annoy. And, I see this accusation of "racism"
> to be an escalation of the same petulant game.[35]

While acknowledging that using racial slurs would be racist, S.anderson
suggests that the use of such slurs are a reaction to the "idiots" who ignore
profile interests. Of course, there is a logical fallacy to S.anderson's comment in that there would be no way for these "idiots" to be ignoring these
"interests" unless these interests are already blatantly stated. Even as they

address what "would be" racist, the blame is quickly shifted to the targets of racism rather than on the perpetrator. If racism exists, it isn't because the perpetuator is at fault for holding racist beliefs but because he is antagonized to the point of responding in a racist way.

BLACK (AND OTHER PEOPLE OF COLOR) HOMOPHOBIA

The claims of victimhood to neutralize accusations of racism by gay white men are perhaps the most evident in their consistent and constant references to the alleged homophobia in communities of color. In response to a 2016 *LGBTQ Nation* article featuring Michael Sam, the first openly gay NFL player, in which Sam discussed issues of racism in gay communities, a reader calling themself David Hobson commented:

> I've never heard a gay person say, 'I don't accept you because you are black . . . ' I've heard some say they aren't attracted/won't date black people, but that doesn't mean they don't support black rights. Let's not forget it was primarily the str8 black vote that turned out for Obama that torpedoed Prop 8 in California in 2008- so I'd say there's more homophobia in black community than racism in gay community.[36]

Not only does David Hobson deflect the issue of racism in gay communities by attempting to shift the discussion to homophobia in Black communities, they minimize the racism that gay men of color experience by arguing that gay white men who practice sexual racism actively support Black rights, simply that they are not attracted to them.

This tactic of shifting the discussion from racism in gay communities to alleged homophobia in communities of color is widespread. A *Queerty* article titled "Is the Gay Community Racist?" generated numerous allegations of homophobia in communities of color.[37] Clearly, whether Black, Latinx, or Asian communities are homophobic has little to do with the question that was posed by the article. After all, the article was about how a group of gay men treat another group of gay men based on race. We can safely assume that gay men of color are no more homophobic than gay white men, so the question of whether homophobia is a valid response to racism, within this context, is of no consequence. Nonetheless, the poster found no disjuncture in shifting the argument to allegedly homophobic communities of color. In making this connection and implying that homophobia from communities of color justify racism in gay communities *against other gay people*, the poster also lumps gay men of color with non-gay people of color to imply that they are equally culpable of the alleged homophobia.

Ironically, no matter how homophobic white people have been, they are excused of their homophobia in favor of the myth of the minority homophobe. Many posters on the *Queerty* story noted that while Black people may be homophobic, so are many whites. These posters also noted that unlike many whites, Black people who were homophobic did not have the political or economic power to repress gay rights. Several posts down in this discussion, a poster calling themself Citizen wrote:

> I accept that homophobia is a problem in the black community, but I've noticed that its mostly homophobic whites who have the power to dismantle the rights and human dignity of every gay person, regardless of race, class, sex, or gender-identity.

In response to these posts, a poster calling themself Wayne argued:

> I'm not sure I agree with your statement that it's "mostly homophobic whites"; whites as a group actually voted by slim majority against passage of Prop 8.

By focusing on Citizen's post and only on the relatively more socially liberal white people in California, Wayne is able to ignore much of the discussion that led to Citizen's making their observation that homophobic whites were more culpable in denying gay rights across the country.

Earlier posts noted that the majority of the funding for the Pro Prop 8 campaign came from the Mormon Church, hardly a beacon of racial diversity, and that influential white religious leaders like Rick Warren were the most vocal proponents, making numerous television and public appearances in favor of Prop 8 while virtually no Black churches or Black leaders were equally zealous. Newspaper articles demonstrated that most of the advertisements for Prop 8 featuring Black actors were funded by organizations with largely white membership rosters. Citizen's point was that no matter how homophobic Black communities may appeal, it was largely whites who financially and publicly supported the passage of Prop 8 and largely white-led organizations and white religious leaders who actively and consistently promoted Prop 8. Rather than address this point, Wayne simply subsumes all whites under the umbrella of those who "voted by a slim majority against the passage of Prop 8," ignoring all other white people outside of California who voted against gay rights in Southern states in much higher percentages than Black people voted for Prop 8. Instead, gay white men often point to the narrow Prop 8 example to highlight Black homophobia, while completely ignoring the significant percentages of white voters outside of liberal states who voted to deny gay people legal rights. Eight years after the passage of Prop 8, the specter of the homophobic Black voter is revived repeatedly in order to make the point that Black people are homophobic, without any concrete evidence of it, with some even dismissing the evidence that showed that Black voters did not, indeed, torpedo Prop 8.

VICTIM BLAMING

Another prominent tactic is to blame men of color for their own marginalization in gay communities, particularly when it comes to sexual racism. In response to the 2016 *Queerty* article "Asian Man Fed Up with Being Ignored by the White-Painted Gay Community," a reader calling themself stanhope wrote:

> OK this comment won't make me popular here. Thank goodness I don't care. I often marvel at many Asians I see in gay social situations. More often than not they are cajoling and buffooning in front of the gay white men. When they get one they wear the white boyfriend like a Neiman Marcus label. They don't countenance the Latin or Black men. I never see them take a serious sexual look at another Asian.[38]

A reader calling themselves EbonyOnly responded similarly to a 2018 *Queerty* article titled "Grindr Wants Users to Stop Being So Racist and Start Being Kindr: But Is That Even Possible?":

> As a white male, I used to be exclusively Black. Look at my post name. I, however, learned over time that was being racist. I have drastically changed my "taste" due to the fact I'm not interested in having to pay or being asked to "help" a brother out. I'm also not interested in putting myself in possible danger with the high crime in the "at risk" neighborhoods; a term used by the news media. You can't legalize a personal interest in other races or sexual appetites. Everything is not racist as put out by the media.[39]

Given the explicitly racist tone of EbonyOnly's response, one might arrive at the conclusion that they did not actually have any previous attraction to dating Black men. One may even wonder if EbonyOnly has ever met a Black person, let alone dated one.

Nonetheless, EbonyOnly's response represents the racial stereotypes that are deployed to justify excluding men of color as potential sexual partners. Using this tactic, gay white men shift the blame of sexual racism to men of color by arguing that it isn't that they are excluding men of color because of their race but because of their allegedly bad behaviors.

Victim blaming also takes the form of accusing gay men of color of engaging in the same types of racial exclusion as white men. The use of non-white men's preference for white men is often brought up to justify sexual racism. A commenter responding to a 2011 *Queerty* article titled "Has Grindr Turned Gay Men into Racist Homophobic Body Fascists?" wrote:

> I think the real issue comes from the other direction, non-white guys who feel like they will simply die if they don't get a white boyfriend.[40]

In the above commentator's assessment, the "real issue" isn't that white men actively exclude men of color as sexual partners but that men of color desire white men. By this logic, if men of color didn't desire white men, white men's rejection of them would be a nonissue.

For the story "This Is Nelson. He Has Something to Say about Racism in the Gay Community. You Should Listen," published on *Queerty* in 2015, in which Nelson shared his story of being excluded in gay communities and rejected by potential sexual partners because he was Black, a commenter calling themself Ummmm Yeah wrote:

> Well since Nelson only goes for white guys, like most black guys that complain about white guys that are only attracted to white guys, he obviously has the same interests as the first guy. Funny how the white guy is supposed to feel guilty about that, but the black guys gets away with it, isn't it?[41]

According to this logic, if men of color routinely seek white men as sexual partners, why is it wrong for white men to do the same? The problem with sexual racism, however, isn't the race of the person who prefers white men but rather the structural conditions promoted by gay communities and the gay media that leads to white men coming to have more erotic worth than men of color. Given the racial hierarchy of desire, the preference for white men by gay men of color is yet another outcome. This argument also offers an alternative way to promote the "natural" preferences for white men. If preference for white men is not limited to only white men, then it is because white men are "naturally" more desirable than men of color. If that is the case, how can white men be faulted for having the same sexual desires as men of color?

SOME OF MY BEST FRIENDS

Perhaps no other "standard linguistic fare of whites' contemporary color-blind racetalk" is more widely used to counter potential accusations of racism than "some of my best friends are . . . "[42] Gay white men routinely utilized this narrative tactic to establish their nonracist bone fides before attempting to justify their sexual "preference" for only white men. In a comment written in response to the article "Gay Couples More Likely to be Interracial, Multiethnic Than Straights," published on *Queerty* in 2012, a poster calling themself london89 wrote:

> Sorry guys, but why is it always said to be racist when you don't date another ethnicity? I work with people from all over the world, always lived in districts where ethnic minorities are the majority in the neighborhood and try to get to know people from everywhere. That's really great and I like the world becoming more and more open. BUT when it comes to sexual attraction, I can't help myself. I can't force myself to feel attracted to somebody, if I am not. I'm really sorry, but I'm rarely attracted to Asian and black guys. Why? I don't know why![43]

In crafting their response to the article, london89 takes significant care in framing their lack of attraction to men of color as being unrelated to any racialized beliefs. Rather, they go to lengths to discuss how they have lived a life surrounded by people of color and go out of their way to get to "know people from everywhere."

Yet while their "openness" to other people of color in their non-sexual life, such as working and living in places with members of another race, and getting to know others of a different race, are framed as something they work toward and commend themself for, they utterly fail to question their racialized desires as being framed in any way a result of their own actions but rather as something they "can't force [themself]" to feel because they simply do not know why they are not attracted to men of color. In this way, they frame their attractions as internal, unexplainable, and therefore not addressable, unlike working, living, and interacting in the public sphere, for which they deserve high praise for actively working to being open.

Readers go out of their way to demonstrate how not racist they are by pointing out repeatedly that they would gladly be friends with anyone of any race. As one poster calling themself TweetyBird commented to the 2016 *LGBTQ Nation* article "Are Scruff's Ethnicity Filters Racist?":

> For me, I prefer older, white, hairy chest and tall. It's what I like sexually! Personally, I don't care if you're 18–80, white or black,

short or tall, skinny or bear, we can have a drink, watch a game, go to dinner and become great friends but for that "tingle down there" my mind is pretty much set in what it finds hot. If I were to be on a dating app, it would keep it simple to narrow the search field much like "men seeking men" does.[44]

TweetyBird's comment combines two tactics in subtle ways. First, Tweety-Bird goes out of their way to argue that they have "great friends" to provide cover for justifying the exclusion of an entire race of people as potential sexual partners. By noting that they can socialize with non-white people, they attempt to establish themself as being a nonracist so as to minimize their active participation in sexual racism. Second, they paint their attraction to white men as being natural by lumping whiteness with other physical characteristics that are not necessarily raced, such as height and age. In this way, their attraction to whiteness itself is left uninterrogated as simply another trait in a constellation of traits they find attractive.

For the article "Has Grindr Turned Gay Men into Racist Homophobic Body Fascists?," published in 2011 on *Queerty*, a poster calling themself Michael wrote:

> I'm friends with guys of all races. I'm all for people dating and/or fucking whomever they want. I am not, in principle, against fucking black or Asian men MYSELF, but with very rare exception, I am not attracted to them. I like them, I cherish their friendship as much as any of my white, Latin, Indian, or Middle-Eastern friends. I will defend them to the death against anyone who gives them shit, but nine times out of ten, they just don't make my dick hard. And that makes me a racist? I think you need to get a new dictionary.[45]

Here, Michael establishes their antiracist credentials by stating that they aren't "in principle" against dating non-white men, just that they are not attracted to them. This, of course, harkens to similar arguments made regarding those who claim that while they are not opposed to hiring a Black person, qualified ones are rare.

The "some of my best friends" defense sometimes extends to include how an individual treats other people outside of sexual encounters. A commenter calling themself Chris wrote in response to the article "This Is Nelson. He Has Something to Say about Racism in the Gay Community. You Should Listen," published on *Queerty* in 2015:

> I have always tried to be scrupulously fair on social matters and when judging employees' performances, I have always checked myself against what another supervisor says about the same employee. And, I have hired people across a wide range of backgrounds. . . . As far as dating, however, I continue to be more drawn by my own preferences. Just as some people have rejected going out with me for things like my having hair growing out of my ear (it happens to everyone if you get old enough!) or not being dressed in a particular manner or not being tanned enough or being too tanned (yes, both in the same week!) or being overweight or not scruffy enough, I have my own preferences and prejudices. And I freely admit to being a sucker for piercing eyes (of any color) wearing glasses and for someone who is taller than I am. Does that make me "-ist" against shorter people and/or those whose eyes don't make them look like lovable geeks? Well, so be it; tell that to my knees when they get weak.[46]

In Chris's definition, he cannot be a racist, despite his racial exclusion of men of color, because he treats others "scrupulously fair on social matters." Again, racism is defined as deliberate acts of discrimination against others rather than as a larger structural issue that constructs one group as having less worth and value. As long as one treats other *individuals* in a "scrupulously fair" manner, racism isn't an issue.

SEXUAL ATTRACTION AS NATURAL AND BIOLOGICAL

A common method of denying racism, particularly sexual racism, is by claiming that race-based phenomena are natural occurrences.[47] Whites often claim that racial segregation and racial preferences in friends and mates are results of a natural affinity between members of the same group, practiced by all groups, that are biologically driven and innate. In response to the 2016 *Queerty* article "Is This the Brutal Truth White Gay Men Refuse to Hear?," a reader calling themself josh447 wrote.

> Races stick to their own genetic code in general, that's human nature. It's natural selection. Like attracts like. It's not discriminating, but it is discerning. You don't see horses mixing with zebras or hawks mixing w crows in the animal kingdom either. And I hate to break it to you; we are primates and primates are part of the animal kingdom.[48]

By josh447's account, "sticking to your own kind" is simply a matter of biology. Yet what's telling about his comment is that he equates desire for people of a different race with a desire for an entirely different species. It isn't simply that men of color and white men are different by race. It is as if they are an entirely different species.

Similarly, in response to the article "Photographer Hopes to End Sexual Racism with Stunning New Photo Book Celebrating Asian Men," published on *Queerty* in 2019, a reader calling themself astro.dude responded:

> People are attracted to guys of all races seem to have difficulty accepting the fact that most gays and 90% of straights are only attracted to people of their own race. That's the norm. It's the natural thing to be attracted to guys from the same culture and similar background and with the similar physical traits. That's normal. Why do they want to force interracial dating?[49]

Likewise, a reader calling themself ginalex responded to the article "A Gay Dating App Is Relaunching. With a Ban on Sexual Racism," published on *LGBTQ Nation* in 2018, by writing:

> Everyone is born with the DNA to be attracted to a certain type of person. I've never really been attracted to old guys, but does that

make me an agcist? This is a ridiculous argument. The heart wants what the heart wants. It's not racist to not ever be attracted to someone who has a different skin tone than you. Just when I thought we couldn't possibly label anything else racist, here we are saying that people's sexual and romantic preferences are racist. *sigh*. It shouldn't be all that surprising to me and yet it is.[50]

The underlying theme of all of these comments is that sexual attraction to members of the same race are not only natural but also inevitable and something that one does not have any control over. Once veiled in the language of biology and human nature, these arguments become difficult to counter. To suggest the opposite becomes futile because overcoming racial bias is no longer a matter of overcoming beliefs and attitudes or addressing structural inequalities but one of overcoming nature itself.

For gay men, this notion of what is and is not natural is extended by attempts to equate racial preferences to sexuality itself. As one reader calling themself TheAngryFag wrote in response to the article, "Are Scruff's Ethnicity Filters Racist?," published on *LGBTQ Nation* in 2016:

People are attracted to the people they're attracted to. And if we follow the logic that people not attracted to {insert ethnicity group here} is racist, then every gay man is a misogynist because they're filtering out women.[51]

A reader calling themself jay150 responded to the article "Scruff Founder Defends App's Ethnicity Filter: Personal Preference or Casual Racism," published on *Queerty* in 2016, by writing:

Question for the gay men out there: Are you sexually attracted to women? Not do you find some attractive but do you want to jump in the sack and have at it with hot female. Probably not! Why? Because you are attracted to men! You're Gay! So it's just fine for you to discriminate against the majority of people on the planet when choosing a sexual partner because of gender, right? Doesn't that make you a misogynist? . . . No, just a gay man.[52]

The claim that not finding men of color attractive is equivalent to not finding women sexually attractive is repeated in most of the comments on articles that address issues of interracial relationships within gay communities. Because most of these articles discuss gay white men's unwillingness to date men of color, the discussion often delves into justifications from white men as to why they don't date non-white men, with preference being equated with sexuality running rampant.

Explaining sexual preference in biological terms allows the writer to dismiss accusations of racism by framing preference as natural and outside of individual choice, as opposed to racism that, they argue, is a conscious act that involves actively and willfully denying opportunities to people of color. Much like biological models of homosexuality that attempt to argue that gay people are "born this way" and therefore have no control over who they find sexually arousing, biological explanations of sexual attraction absolve individuals from taking responsibility for those attractions, instead allowing them to argue that they are "born this way."

CONCLUSION

Contemporary racism has shifted from blatant exclusion of non-white people from economic, educational, residential, and social institutions to a more colorblind form of racism that actively denies the existence of racism itself. Along with this shift has come strong—at least strongly vocal—condemnation of blatantly racist statements and acts. Because of this, significant energy is expended denying racism and denying that one's actions and statements have racist intent. Similar to the ways that racism is denied outside of gay communities, gay men on internet news sites deny racism using many different maneuvers. Given how common the denial of racism has become, it shouldn't be surprising that gay men utilize familiar tropes to explain away accusations of sexual racism that are directed at them as individuals, at their individual behaviors, or at the gay community in general.

Gay men routinely deny racism by trivializing concerns about race that men of color point out, arguing that they have non-white friends and that they are fair in their dealings with non-whites and turning to veiled accusations of reverse racism, as well as arguing that racial preferences for sexual partners are biological and innate. At the same time, the fact that a man is gay in and of itself offers members of gay communities additional routes of denial, including claiming victimhood based on sexuality and lodging accusations of homophobia against those who accuse them of racism. Because accusations of racism in gay communities often center on the idea of sexual racism, a practice by which gay men of color are either excluded as potential sexual partners or exotified as men of color, the denial of racism takes the shape of defending such actions as individual sexual preferences rather than as acts of racism.

The problem with such denials is that it frames racism as individual acts committed by individual actors against other individuals. This rather limited and limiting definition of racism forecloses on attempts to expand the discussion to address the cause and consequences of sexual racism. When confined to such narrow definitions, we are prevented from arguing that sexual racism exists—that *any* racism exists—since individual beliefs are impossible to deduce. Also, framing racism as something personal, even if it exists, leads to the belief that the solution is for white men to be more considerate in expressing their preferences, or for men of color to get over being marginalized, particularly by getting over their own preferences for white men. Like all methods of denial, the systems that create and maintain structural racism are never challenged, and therefore never confronted.

CHAPTER 5

Don't Trust Any Black Gay Who Has "Teamswirl" in Their Bio

The Politics of Racial Desire

AFTER MONTHS OF PAYING FOR UPGRADED FEATURES, ONLY TO read numerous racist profiles created by gay white men, Sinakhone Keodara had had enough. So in July of 2018, Keodara, founder and CEO of Asian Entertainment Television, announced on Twitter that he was intending to bring a class action lawsuit against the popular gay dating app Grindr. In his announcement, Keodara, who called the dating app a "breeding ground that perpetuates racism against gay Asian men," stated that he was looking for other gay Asian men who have "been offended, humiliated, degraded and dehumanized" by Grindr's allowing gay white men to write comments like "No Asians," "Not interested in Asians," and "I don't find Asians attractive" in their public profiles. Calling these comments "complete bullshit," Keodara added that he would be looking for coplaintiffs across the country to join him.

In this age of fifteen-minute news cycles that pander to the sensationalization of race and sexuality, his announcement was quickly picked up by media outlets, including those that specifically target gay audiences such as the *Advocate* and mainstream media outlets including NBC and the *Guardian*, leading to thousands of Facebook shares of various news stories accompanied by personal stories by men of color about their own experiences of sexual rejection by white men. Yet as Theo Greene noted while discussing the potential lawsuit:

> I also find problematic for gay men of color to weaponize "sexual racism" because of their inability to find a white partner. If you are angry at white men because of their "No Fats, Blacks, or Asians," yet practice the same forms of prejudice and discrimination against other men of color (as many tend to do), you are perpetuating the same system you are attempting to combat. And in that case, my sympathy for you is the size of the world's smallest violin.[1]

The potential class action lawsuit and Greene's comment about the lawsuit represent the long-standing debate among gay men of color regarding what it means to have both interracial and intraracial desires. On the one hand, sexual racism—the rejection of potential sexual partners and/or the fetishization of sexual partners based on race—is perhaps the most rampant form of racism practiced by gay white men and has implications beyond who fucks whom. Sexual racism not only marks men of color as being less sexually desirable than white men, but also creates a racial hierarchy of desire that translates directly to racial worth. At the same time, the focus on and widespread discussion of sexual racism ignores the underlying inconvenient truth that gay men of color themselves overwhelmingly prefer white men as sexual partners.

In a recent study of gay men in San Francisco who utilize the app Jack'd to seek sexual partners, conducted by the website *Angry Homosexual*, gay Asian men were even more likely than even white men themselves to pursue white sexual partners. After examining two hundred randomly selected profiles of Asian men and white men on the mobile platform, the author determined racial preference by counting the reply rate and the racial distribution of those rates, as well as the race of the men that users saved to their list of "favorites." The author discovered that while 40 percent of white men are never interested in Asian men and 29 percent of Asian men are never interested in other Asian men, 57 percent of Asian men specifically preferred only white men, while only 45 percent of white men exclusively preferred other white men.[2] Of course, it is highly likely that white men do not necessarily need to advertise that they are exclusively interested in other white men, given that desire is already equated with whiteness. Thus, the percentage of white men who exclusively prefer other white men is likely to be much higher. Nonetheless, the data make clear that men of color also seem to be highly opposed to dating men of their own race and that they prefer white men.

Also, gay men of color seem to demonstrate a preference for, and seem to be in relationships with, white men in significantly higher percentages than straight men of color.[3] An overwhelming majority of gay Asian men and gay Native American men, a majority of gay Latino men, and a near parity of gay Black men who were in same-sex relationships, were in relationships specifically with white men.[4] Percentages for straight men of color highlight the rather large discrepancy. A recent Pew Research Center survey found that only 26 percent of Latino men, 24 percent of Black men, and 21 percent of Asian men were married interracially.[5]

Because the Pew data do not sort out the percentages of these interracial marriages specifically by race, the actual percentage of men of color married to white women are likely to be lower given that interracial marriages among whites have declined during the time period while marriages between members of different races have increased. My point here is not to argue that these numbers are comparing apples to apples but rather to demonstrate that gay men of color are significantly more likely to be in sexual and romantic relationships with white men than straight men of color are to be in such relationships with white women. Based on the Pew data, it seems that gay men of color are also significantly more likely than even straight women of color to be in sexual and romantic relationships with white men.

So pervasive is this desire for white men that Joseph Beam noted in the introduction to his groundbreaking anthology, *In the Life*, that "Black men loving Black men is the revolutionary act of the eighties."[6] While

Beam may have intended for his famous quote to apply to all the different ways that Black men may love other Black men, including as friends, the fact that it has been largely interpreted to mean Black men loving other Black men romantically is indicative of the underlying sentiment that Black men are not widely perceived to love each other in that way.

Given the racial hierarchy of desire constructed by gay media that is imposed on gay men of color and reinforced through everyday erotic practices among gay men, the fact that gay men of color desire white men should be expected. Remembering his own personal experiences, filmmaker Tony Ayres wrote, "When I first became conscious of being gay, there was not a particular kind of male body I was attracted to. To be honest, anything with a dick would have done. However, as I became a participant in the gay world, I found myself increasingly influenced by the imagery which determined what was desirable."[7]

According to Ayres, desire for white men was a learned response to a racist gay community that presents white men as the only acceptable sexual partner while sexually marginalizing gay men of color. He did not enter the gay world specifically desiring white men but rather came to desire white men within the gay world. He further writes, "The sexually marginalized Asian man who has grown up in the West or is western in his thinking is often invisible in his own fantasies. Our sexual daydreams are populated by handsome Caucasian men with lean, hard Caucasian bodies."[8]

If the default among gay men of all races is to desire white men, why gay men of color desire white men is not hard to understand. Of more interest is how gay men of color manage to find other men of color desirable, despite all social and cultural cues to not do so. While discussions about the impact of sexual rejection and sexual objectification of gay men of color by gay white men are widespread in both the academic and popular press, as is the nature of interracial desire in gay communities, much less is discussed about intraracial desires among members of these groups. At the same time, this lack of discussion in the academic literature regarding intraracial desire is not limited to gay men. Rather, academics seem to have lots to say about interracial relationships, both gay and straight, but much less to say about intraracial ones.

NORMATIVE ASSUMPTIONS ABOUT
INTRARACIAL RELATIONSHIPS

A quick Google Scholar search of "interracial marriage" returns 61,000 results while "intraracial marriage" returns 184. "Interracial dating" returns 5,430 results while "intraracial dating" leads to 34. Also, most of the articles garnered as a result of a search on "intraracial marriage" or "intraracial dating" do not necessarily focus on intraracial desires but bring in intraracial relationships only as a point of comparison to interracial ones. While studies of interracial relationships often focus, for example, on factors that lead to these relationships and the racial politics of such relationships, studies that examine intraracial relationships are likely to focus only on comparing the success of such relationships to interracial ones.

Unlike interracial relationships that need to be examined, explained, and analyzed, intraracial relationships seem to be viewed as unproblematic, natural, and taken for granted, as if it is just the way it's supposed to be. The general consensus among scholars, artists, and commentators who examine desire seems to be that interracial desires need to be explained while intraracial desires do not. Writing about his first sexual encounter with an Asian man, film maker Tony Ayres recalled:

> Touching him was a foreign sensation. I am used to the touch of
> Caucasian skin—hairier. Chinese skin is smooth, yet there is also
> a hardness to it, a polished ivory muscularity. I found myself giving
> way to it, being swept away by a desire which I had never experi-
> ence before. It was desire which had nothing to do with politics.
> He did not want me because I was Chinese. I did not reject him
> because he was Chinese. We just wanted each other. It was simple.
> For a brief moment I felt that for the first time in my life I under-
> stood what desire was about. And in that understanding, there was
> the most exquisite feeling of liberation.[9]

Although Ayres describes touching another Chinese man as a "foreign sensation," he frames sex with another Chinese man as being apolitical and not based on race, therefore not needing analysis or explanation about the racial dynamics of intraracial desires, while the assumption that sex with non-Chinese men is political and based on race, therefore needing analysis. Ayres also presents intraracial desire as a "liberation." But a liberation from what? A clue comes from an earlier part of Ayres's essay in which he states, "Intellectually I know that this inability to feel attracted to other Asian men is a form of internalized racism" while a "separation of desire into racial categories indicates a kind of institutional racism."[10] If the failure to find Asian men desirable represents "internalized racism" and racialized desires are a sign of institutional racism, then isn't desire for another Asian man a liberation from internal racism and a challenge to institutional racism? Yet the assumed naturalness of intraracial desires often leaves such questions unexamined.

However, as Manolo Guzman argued, "An exclusive focus on inter-racial erotic relations in a discussion of sexualized racial ideals prevents us from acknowledging one most important fact: *intraracial erotic relations are, no matter how unremarkable, also racially marked.*"[11] More importantly, "in a society such as ours, rigidly structured in racially hierarchical terms, an erotic preference for members of one's ethnoracial group is, however much fabricated, anything but unusual."[12]

Despite the lack of attention paid to this topic in the academic literature, it has long been a widely and hotly debated issue among gay men of color themselves. In an article published in GLQ, Darieck Scott offered insightful observations regarding the nature of this debate among gay Black men who date interracially and intraracially. As Scott noted, much of the discussion about Black/white gay male couples tends to be framed by "an analytic of suspicion and disapproval," with the Black partner often portrayed as being enamored with whiteness.[13] To demonstrate this tendency, he points to the "raucous division" between "Black gays" and "gay Blacks" evident in a survey published in BLK that reported, "Black gays believe that gay Blacks hate their own race . . . and give their loyalty to the gay rather than to the Black community."[14]

Discussion about interracial coupling among gay men is framed in such a way that the Black partner is assumed to detest his Blackness while being "beguiled and enchanted" by whiteness and therefore "has an exclusive desire for a lover with Nordic features."[15] Moreover, "his political, social, and cultural allegiances are to 'white' gay politics, to white gay men, and to 'white' cultural forms." This sentiment is not unique to Black men. Guzman quotes one Puerto Rican man as stating. "I can't understand how could you not want to be with your own kind. You have to take pride in your kind. It's almost like me saying I'm not proud to be, I don't want to be with a Hispanic because I'm not proud to be Hispanic."[16] Similarly, Philip Tsui explained gay Asian men's desire for white men and rejection of other Asian men as potential sexual partners by arguing, "In an effort to salvage their self-esteem and to maintain their ego integrity, it appears that some gay Asian men adopt a "colonial-slave mentality" with its prominent feature being the identification with the oppressor. They learn to accept the categorization of inferiority, and to externalize their self-denial and self-hate."[17] This sense that men of color who reject members of their own race as potential sexual partners experience ethnic and racial self-hatred is widespread among gay men of color who prefer members of their own race or other men of color.

Even gay men of color who prefer white sexual partners experience a level of dissonance with their own racial preferences. Among gay Asian men, there is a high level of stigmatization of men who date "rice queens," non-Asian men who are almost exclusively attracted to Asian men and who are often stereotyped as being older, less fit, and themselves allegedly less desirable to other white men. Gay Asian men who prefer white men as sexual partners make clear distinctions between themselves and Asian men who date rice queens, with those who only date rice queens perceived as somehow having less worth. While they also prefer white sexual partners, their preference is for white men who don't exclusively date Asian men, and some take great pride in being able to attract white men who are not exclusively attracted to Asian men.[18]

The repulsion that some Asian men have of other Asian men who date rice queens and of rice queens themselves is understandable given the stigmatized position of rice queens in the gay community.[19] But this specific distinction requires unpacking. On the one hand, many gay Asian men prefer only white sexual partners, yet at the same time, they have an aversion to white men who prefer only Asian men. It almost appears as if Asian men themselves come to believe that an exclusive preference for Asian men is a mark of inferiority among white men, making an exclusive desire for Asian men a deviant form of sexual attraction.

A further problem is that accusations of self-hatred based on the internalization of racial inferiority are never lobbed against white men who have sexual preferences for non-white men. Instead, these men are perceived to have sentiments of racial superiority, viewing their whiteness as erotic currency. Gay white men who seek men of color often seek younger sexual partners, and men of color often seek older white men when they seek white partners, leading some to speculate that in the sexual marketplace, white men may be trading race for age while men of color may be trading age for race.[20] For white men, interracial desires are not the result of a feeling of racial inferiority but rather a result of racial superiority by which they can trade the desired racial characteristic for age. In a racialized society, this seeming contradiction is easy to explain. It is because whiteness is seen as having more worth that it comes to be seen as erotic currency. And only because a lack of whiteness is equated with a lack of desirability does one need to trade something else to attain it.

THE POLITICS OF INTRARACIAL DESIRE

The easy dichotomy that surrounds mainstream discussions about such relationships can often blur much more complex examinations about race. Such accusations directed against men of color that they must suffer from internalized self-hatred do little more than create an "imaginary border between political consciousness as an African American gay man [and other men of color] and the lack of such a consciousness."[21] Yet both types of relationships are burdened with the troubled history of race and racism. Often, even men who prefer other men of their own race are accused of engaging in some of the very same racialized practices that white men engage in. As Jeff Baker wrote in an essay published by *The Body Is Not an Apology*:

> Part of the problem is that the typical frame for conversations
> about this subject, especially with regard to internalized racism,
> almost always focuses on commiserating about the tendency for

problematic white gay men to either fetishize or scorn us. While this grievance is valid, an honest dialog about us is long overdue. The fact that many SGL and queer Black men have felt objectified by one another is often the pink elephant in the room. . . . Day in and day out, I observe the same archetypal "thirst traps" glorified: the light-skinned, racially ambiguous, or non-Black "pretty boy," who looks young and fit (or sometimes thick, but rarely plus-sized); or the "trade," who is typically darker-skinned, muscular, tall, and bearded, with ostensibly more passing privilege. These aesthetics seem to infatuate a lot of "us," I am referring to many of the queer Black people—particularly men—who demonstrate a commendable dedication to racial justice.[22]

Similarly, Puerto Rican men who prefer other Puerto Rican men as sexual partners often rely on stereotypes of the Latin lover in justifying and explaining their preferences. While there may be several other reasons for preferring other Latino men as sexual partners, including geopolitical bonds, cultural familiarity, and ease of integrating their romantic partners into their families, some highlighted Latino men's greater sexual ardor. That is, some Puerto Rican men repeatedly emphasized that sexual relationships with other Latino men involved more passion as framed around a Latin lover stereotype, while believing white men to be passionless.[23] Even the earlier description of sex with another Chinese man described by Ayres is embedded with a pseudo-essentialist description of the "differences" between white and Asian men.

It is important to point out, however, that there may be a critical difference when the Latin lover stereotype frames intraracial desire among Latino men. As Manolo Guzman has observed:

When invoked by Latino men in relation to other Latino men, the import and significance of the [Latin lover] stereotype changes diametrically. In the hands of Latino men in the "service" of other Latino men, this racialized erotic ideal is not organized around a desire for that which is different and exotic but a desire for and a love of sameness.[24]

An argument can be made here that while gay men of color do invoke similar racialized sexual stereotypes, invoking such stereotypes in their own intraracial desires is not necessarily an act of self-exotification but one of "strategic essentialism," as discussed by Gayatri Chakravorty Spivak.[25]

Strategic essentialism refers to the strategies that various subaltern groups can mobilize on the basis of a shared identity by temporarily essentializing themselves based on what can be framed as shared characteristics. While Spivak has grown increasingly uncomfortable with the way that the concept of strategic essentialism has been used to promote essentialist arguments, it nonetheless offers a way to understand how gay men of color frame their sexual attraction toward members of their own race.

Strategic essentialism doesn't presume that race is an essence that is shared by all members of any racial group that is bound or fixed. Nor does it negate the multiple different ways that race is experienced by members of these groups. Rather, it allows for the possibility of drawing upon shared cultural, physical, and experiential experiences that make up a group.[26] Quoting Stuart Hall, Katya Azoulay wrote:

> Political identity often requires the need to make conscious commitments. Thus it may be necessary to momentarily abandon the multiplicity of cultural identities for more simple ones around which political lines have been drawn. You need all the folks together, under one hat, carrying one banner, saying we are for this, for the purpose of this fight, we are all the same, just Black and just here.[27]

It would be easy to conclude that gay men of color engage in a distorted form of essentializing of their own race, but it is also possible that in the sexual imagery of men of color themselves, these racial stereotypes have different meanings.

Rather than an exercise in self-fetishizing, the actions of gay men of color can be understood as a way of deploying essentialized notions of race and desirability to frame their own sexual desires for themselves rather than for consumption by white men. While gay white men may deploy these stereotypes to create a sexual other as a means of consuming the other, these same stereotypes in the hands of men of color become a way of de-centering whiteness as the target of sexual desires while simultaneously marking the love of "sameness" as legitimate.[28] Almost like a double negative, a fetish seeking another fetish as the object of desire while simultaneously excluding the fetishizer negates the opportunity of the fetishizer to actively construct a sexual other for their own erotic consumption.

Given the racial logic of desire and the white image that creates this logic, gay men of color who actively seek to pair with other gay men of color and actively use racialized imagery to describe these desires may be engaging in an act of political resistance by defying the hierarchy of racialized desire that the larger society has imposed on them regarding who is and is not desirable and who is and is not deserving of erotic attention.[29] A racial fetish can be transformed from something that is used to trade for whiteness into something that can be enjoyed for its own sake. Thus, racialized ways of being have value outside of what it can do in the service of whiteness. Even terms such as *sticky rice*, which refers to Asian men who engage in intraracial sexual relationships rather than pursuing white men, despite the racialized essentialism of rice, can be understood as a particular type of "world making that contests the primacy of whiteness and the valences of power coalescing around it" and represents a rejection of the dominant group's values, definitions of desirability, and claims of legitimacy.[30] As Kenneth Chan observed, many gay Asian men turn to other Asian men for sexual companionship "because they are tired of the power imbalance and injustices within the 'rice and potato' [Asian and white] relationship."[31] And one way that such imbalance is confronted is through rejection of the dominant norms and beliefs—in this case, transforming an exotic desire for the other that has been imposed from outside to a desire for the same.

While the lack of academic attention paid to intraracial relationships compared to interracial relationships may be the result of seeing intraracial relationships as the default, natural way of paring that need not be explained, for gay men of color, the default seems to be interracial, not intraracial. Despite the dearth of academic literature about intraracial relationships, a growing number of writers have shared their perspectives on the politics of intraracial desire among gay men of color in the popular press. What, then, do these men have to say about this topic?

Even among gay men of color who exclusively date white men, there seems to be a significant level of recognition that white men's desire for men of color is often marked with exotic fetishism of race and that there was a certain "type" of white man who pursued men of color as potential sexual partners. This was a consistent source of irritation and frustration for many. Writing for *Logo*, Lester Brathwaite stated:

> As much as I pursued white boys, they pursued me. Though it was always a specific type of white boy: Ones with the proverbial swirl. I was grateful for this type of boy, but at the same time, wary of, and deeply annoyed by him. . . . These types of boys would be the ones to unfailingly make a point of my Blackness—or my black dick—as if it were another entity, unto itself, in the room. Or they would hold me up to some ideal of black masculinity that I could never hope to achieve, but only passably resemble, before they passed me on entirely.[32]

Brathwaite's acknowledgment that a "certain type" of white man pursues men of color was not unique to him. Rather, it was widely shared by other men of color.

Writing for *Narratively*, Reneysh Vittal, discussing his one and only attempt at trying to date another Indian man, said about the white men that he had previously dated, "Many white exes of mine made little to no effort to understand my background. To some I was a fetish. They found me 'exotic' or 'spicy.' That was reason enough to leave them behind and give this [dating another Indian man] a shot.[33] Likewise, in recalling a white man he dated to describe the difference between appreciation and fetishization, columnist John Paul Brammer wrote on the website *Into*:

> I started to notice things Bradley did when he was around me that raised some concerns. He started using me to practice his *Español* like I was Duo Lingo or something. Never mind that I wasn't raised

with Spanish and learned it in a classroom. Even worse, he would put on this awful, performative, condescending voice when he spoke it to me . . . We were riding on the subway once, and instead of asking me, "are you hungry?" like a normal human being, he said "qūírēs cómídā?" or some hate crime along those lines.[34]

While none of the writers indicated that these experiences prevented them from continuing to pursue white men as sexual partners, with Vittal even concluding that he continues to exclusively date white men, these experiences did give them pause and continued to be a source of concern.

Given this widespread recognition that men of color are fetishized by white men, many gay men of color whose own sexual desire was mostly, or in many cases exclusively, for white men felt a sense of guilt about their own racial preferences. In the *Logo* article discussed above, Brathwaite continued:

The guilt I feel for my attraction to white men is a reflection of my own inner machinations, as well as of the current climate in America. *What kind of Black man am I?*—the militant voice of my conscience asks—*to seek intimacy with my oppressor?* The resolution isn't easy, but comprehensive: decolonize my desire. Stop asking white men to love me and thus I free myself from oppression. My only problem is, I don't feel like I should fucking have to.[35]

Similarly Vittal described his failure to find another Indian man attractive by noting, "All I feel is guilt. I am too ashamed to apologize or make excuses. He'll always think he did something wrong when the fault is really mine. I delete his messages and block his profile. Then I open my saved search filter of local white guys and begin scrolling."

Clearly, many gay men of color recognized that their interracial desires were marked by race and led to some level of self-reflection about their own racialized desires for white men. The question that arises then is, how do these men frame such relationships to alleviate the guilt and concern that they feel?

One of the methods employed by gay men of color was to minimize their own guilt about dating white men by offering specific reasons for not dating men of color, reasons that would, on the surface, seem ludicrous if given by white men for not dating other white men. When asked specifically why he didn't date Black men on *Red Table Talk*, hosted by Jada Pinkett Smith, Don Lemon was quoted by Veronica Wells in *Madamenoire* as replying, "When I'm with the Black men that I've dated, they get it. But you know what? Most of 'em aren't out. Most of them didn't want people to know. I'm not about that life anymore. And I'm not saying you have to live your life that way, that's not the way I want to live my life."[36]

Rather than interrogating his own racial desire, Lemon relies on the trope of the "down low" Black man who is secretive about his sexual behaviors to justify his preferences for white men. According to Lemon, it isn't that he doesn't want to date other Black men but that he's "not about that life," placing the blame on other Black men for failing to live more "authentically." This assertion is problematic for a variety of reasons. While it should be obvious that it is demonstratively not true that gay Black men are more likely to be secretive in their sexual behaviors than white men, the trope Lemon uses to justify his own desire for white men pathologizes other gay Black men by using the language of homonormativity that constructs openly out gay men as being more authentic than others.

Another common trope shared by many men of color who prefer white men is that of homophobia in communities of color. Writing for the *Huffington Post*, author Jeremy Helligar defended his desire for white men in this way:

> Every time I read a critique slamming me because of my white dating history, I flash back to the Black schoolyard bullies who, were they around today, would probably concur. Racism and discrimination against me by white people and by Black people— especially by Black people—defined my formative years. So excuse me if I don't feel a magical connection to Black men just because they're Black.[37]

Yet while arguing that the homophobia he experienced by other Black men shaped his desire for white men, Helligar ignores the racism he claims to have experienced from gay white men and makes no mention of homophobia from straight white people and the growing evidence that people of color are no more homophobic than whites.

Some gay men of color resort to framing intraracial desire as adjacent to incestual relationships to justify their interracial desires. To justify his disinterest in other Black men, bisexual musician Steve Lacy is quoted by Dan Avery in *Logo* as saying:

Growing up around Black males, they were always my competitors, ya know? I never viewed or saw myself doing anything sexual with my neighbors. I literally, like I said, see them as brothers. . . . I'm a n*gga from Compton, I don't dislike Black people, I prefer to live here and be around POC because I love Black people. I'm just not attracted to Black boys, that is it. I still love them and want them to do well in life, we just won't date. Sorry.[38]

[handwritten marginalia: "example of a black man not being attracted to race men?"]

The problem with this explanation is that while it offers cover for a lack of attraction toward members of their own race, it fails to address the larger question of why attraction for "difference" is always pointed toward white men. If the attraction toward white men is guided by a desire for difference, why does that desire for difference only point to white men and not other men of color of a different race?

Some gay men of color who prefer white men go to great lengths to argue that preferences are not rooted in self-hate or internalized racism. Terrence Chappell explained his affinity for white men in *Jet* magazine in this way:

I can't deny it. I have an affinity for white men, and have often thought about whether or not I have issues with self-hatred. I've consistently challenged and charged myself with thinking past sexual preferences to get to the root of my attraction. And I don't have an answer. Real talk, there are Black gay men who exclusively date white men, and all I know is that I'm not one of them. This Black skin is a headache every now and then, but I love the way I look, I love my features and I love the strength and the power that comes with being a Black man in America. Based on my dating history, onlookers will often label my attraction, regardless of its non-exclusivity, as self-hatred. They will even diminish my experiences as a Black person. Although race is a social construct, my Blackness doesn't exist for the sake of people, or anything for that matter. Any ideologies derived from my Blackness aren't countered by dating a white man. Just because a woman marries a man doesn't mean she forfeits her rights and womanhood. It just means she married a man. . . . Self-hatred is the common defense used by fellow Black gay men because it holds historical capital. While it does ring true for some, it is not an absolute. Dating Black doesn't free Black people from self-hatred any more than it absolves white people from racism.[39]

In the above quote, Chappell reaffirms his love of himself while simultaneously noting that some Black men who exclusively date white men may, indeed, feel self-hate. In equating his desire for white men with straight women's desires for men, racial desire becomes naturalized and unexplainable, thus absolving him of having to interrogate his racial preference for white men.

Gay men of color who deny that desire for white men is based on racial self-hatred also attempt to mark their own relationships as being race neutral and their race as being separate from whom they find sexually desirable. In an interview for *Logo*, Justin Simien, creator of the Netflix show *Dear White People*, told journalist Lamar Dawson:

There's this belief that you aren't "down" or you don't understand the struggle if you're dating someone who isn't Black. I honestly think it's a symptom of the larger situation. If Black people didn't feel oppressed, it wouldn't be an issue. People need to see you can be Black as fuck and still date a white guy. Our relationship isn't based on race and I don't think anyone should select their partner based on what other people think you should or shouldn't be doing.[40]

Here, Simien and Chapell are attempting to dispel the belief, common among gay men of color who date men of their own race, that dating a white man is akin to self-hate. Yet by separating these two phenomena and marking interracial relationships as not based on race, both of their arguments allude to sexual desires as being a matter of personal preferences, outside of racial politics and not encumbered by the larger social hierarchies of race. While their desire for white men is explained as being race neutral, why that neutrality is always pointed toward white men is again not explained.

Other men of color justify their desire for white men with the claim of reverse racism (a concept that has been widely dismissed as non-existent) or the claim that white men are not routinely judged in the same way for having interracial desires. In a 2018 article published in *Queerty*, Jeremy Helligar argued that "disapproving" comments about only dating white men made by "resentful gay Black men" who date other Black men were "basically reverse racism disguised as Black pride." He then went on to explain:

> Some of them [gay Black men] conflate having an all-white dating history with making statements like "I'm not attracted to Black people" or "No Asians." That's perfectly plausible. But there's a difference between saying, "I've never been to Spain," and saying, "I'd never go there." One can spend every holiday in London without rejecting Madrid entirely. . . . I already knew that [Black pride is] not contingent on a Black person's number of Black Facebook friends or Black exes. Neither is a white person's level of racial enlightenment. I have Black and white friends who never go Black but are still perfectly woke when it comes to racial matters. I also know white men with Blacks-only sex and dating policies who are absolutely clueless about race and racism.[41]

Helligar's observation that having sexual desires for people of another race doesn't equate with being racially "woke" is widely shared among both public and academic commentators. As Hari Ziyad noted in their article about Milo Yiannopoulos and his Black husband, "John," published in

Afropunk, interracial desires of white people directed toward people of color are yet another type of white supremacy that marks people of color as fetishized objects for consumption.[42] Yet Helligar seems to be using that argument to suggest that since having interracial desires doesn't make you any more racially aware, nor does having intraracial desires, thus equating all types of racial attractions as being the same and ignoring all of the nuance.

Instead of offering a more nuanced discussion about these different racial dynamics that may inform interracial desires of white men toward men of color versus the interracial desires of men of color, Helligar attributes racial attraction to individual preference that is independent of racial politics. Also, because he leaves the possibility of dating a Black man open, despite never having actually dated a Black man, he doesn't consider his desire for white men to be racist. Not surprisingly, accusations of reverse racism are made in several other pieces written by Helligar, who labels dating members of one's own race exclusively as "stick-with-your-own-kind racism."[43]

While easy to dismiss as "stick-with-your-own-kind racism," Helligar ignores a fundamental difference discussed by Donovan Trott in an open letter published in the *Huffington Post*. As Trott points out:

> Every Black and Asian man who grew up on this planet grew up surrounded by positive images of whiteness and white men. Therefore, our desire to date within our own race, when we choose to, is not rooted in any assertion made by society that we're better than anyone else. . . . If your preference for a partner supports an existing racial hierarchy which marginalizes minorities, then your preferences are racist. And yes, that includes rice queens and chocolate chasers too. Fetishizing me is not a compliment, it's propping up harmful sexual stereotypes and, it too, is racist.[44]

Interracial desires are not equally situated within the hierarchy of racial desire. Instead, desires for men of color by white men are a representation of the racial hierarchy whereby white men are free to construct men of color as fetishized sexual objects on whom they can project their own racial fantasies of the other. But gay men of color's preferences for white men are guided by a belief whiteness is more desirable, more valuable, and more worthy of erotic attention. One is a deviation from the norm that is allowed to members of the dominant group, while the other is an aspiration to the norm that is expected from marginalized groups.

INTRARACIAL DESIRE AS PERSONAL JOURNEY
TOWARD RACIAL AWARENESS

Among many gay men of color who prefer men of their own race as sexual partners, there was a widespread sentiment that men of color who prefer white men not only suffer from internalized racism and self-hate but also perpetuate that same racism through their preferences.

Writing for *King of Reads* about a recent viral tweet made by a gay Black man regarding the racism he experienced from two gay white men during a Gay Pride event, Justin James did not focus on the racist actions of the two white men but took the original poster to task by noting that his Twitter profile used a picture of an interracial gay couple as the header and that he wore a T-shirt printed with the phrase "I love white boys" in his profile picture. As James wrote:

> Don't trust any Black gay who has "#TeamSwirl" in their bio and who also has a picture of an interracial couple that isn't them posted as their header. Who does that? Self-loathing coons do. . . . Let's talk about preferences. I say many use that as a disguise. You can try to disguise it as a preference, but it smells and tastes like unseasoned internalized racism to me.[45]

To drive his point home, James also included an image of a tweet posted by the same Black man with a response by another twitter user named Johnathan Gibbs. While many focused on either the shirt or the racism displayed by the white man, far more problematic for Gibbs was the Black man himself asking the white man, "[Is] Black okay?" The problem here, as Gibbs alludes and James makes explicit, is that many Black men, as well as other gay men of color, prefer white men not because of personal preference but because they themselves undervalue men of color, including themselves. For Gibbs and James, the question "Is Black okay?" is indicative of the original poster's lack of self-worth and his own under valuing of his Blackness that he must ask, within this sexual context, if being Black is acceptable to the white man he desires. Sadly, of course, he finds that it is not.

Given the sentiment discussed above, it isn't surprising that many of the personal accounts written by gay men of color who prefer men of their own race follow a narrative pattern that involves loving other men of color as a result of coming to love themselves. In an article titled "Bananas Can Learn," published on the blog site *Gayasianmale.com*, writer Enrico DG described his attraction to Asian men as being the result of a thirty-year struggle with self-love:

> I started experimenting with guys at 15 and had my first relationship at 18 and all the guys I dated were white. The American soldiers that saved my country were white and Jesus Christ was white and since 95% of Filipinos are Catholic, we really were conditioned to worship white guys. My best gay friends were Chinese, Burmese and other Asians but they also dated white guys and I did not find other Asian men attractive at that time. This pattern continued on to my late 20s and I worked through a number of failed relationships not really knowing why I was so unhappy.[46]

This vignette sets up Enrico's narrative in an interesting way by framing his desire for other Asian men as one of gradual progress from one of self-rejection to one of self-acceptance. Discussing his move to Japan that was facilitated by a career move, Enrico wrote:

> Although during my 2 years in Japan I dated other only Expats who happened to be white, but I started noticing Japanese men and the different subtleties of face, hair, height and bodies and started to appreciate the Asian physique. Then I looked into the mirror and saw an attractive Asian man and then started the process of healing I was able to love myself as Asian and understood what was

missing in my earlier relationships with white men. . . . If you do not love yourself as an Asian man first, you cannot begin to love anybody else. It took me almost 30 years to realize this important fact but once I did, I became so much happier and was able to have deeper relationships.[47]

Enrico frames his attraction to white men and his non-attraction to Asian men as an inability to love himself. As Enrico alludes, the inability to find other Asian men sexually desirable is rooted in racial self-hatred that prevents Asian men from loving themselves.

This sentiment is repeated by David Ng in a piece published on the same blog a few months earlier. As Ng notes, interrogating his preference for white men also meant examining his own sense of what it meant to be Asian:

> The struggle is so deep, because racism isn't just an outside force that affects us—it comes from within as well. It's internalized within ourselves, and manifests in many ways: Sometimes through a desire to suppress our own "Asian-ness" and become "more white," or to subject ourselves to a white gaze, or hate our own yellow bodies. . . . Preferences don't just fall from the sky—they are informed by the way we are socialized. I recognize that systems that privilege young, white, masculine, cis, able bodies, inform not only my desires, but also my relationship to my own, yellow, body.[48]

As Ng describes, interracial desires are not merely a matter of personal preferences but are informed by the larger social meanings attached to race. They are neither natural nor inevitable. The biggest damage isn't simply that it leads to desiring white men but to devaluing one's own race and demeaning oneself to fit the white gaze.

In a particularly controversial viral article titled "5 Reasons Gay Asians Should Give Up Potatoes," posted to *Angry Homosexual*, the author noted:

> Many gay Asians have a problematic addiction to potatoes, aka white guys. I was there myself. For years, I always pictured the

"ideal guy" for me to be a dashingly handsome white guy with the perfect features—blue eyes, sandy hair, and a bit taller than me. Lucky for me, I woke up in time to smell the coffee. Many of my fellow gay Asians aren't so fortunate.[49]

While the article continues to provide the list of the five reasons, some of which are tongue-in-cheek, what's telling is the way the author sets up the list in the introductory paragraph cited above. For this particular writer, it isn't simply that he "woke up in time to smell the coffee" but that other gay Asian men who fail to see the problem with exclusively desiring white men "aren't so fortunate." For those men, failure to see that their desire for white men as being problematic is precisely that, a failure.[50]

For some, even finding intraracial love among others is a personal journey. Speaking of his new photo series, *Queer Love in Color*, photographer and digital editor Jamal Jordan of the *New York Times* wrote:

As a child, I thought all gay people were white . . . . Growing up, I had rarely seen queer characters of color in the gay young adult books I read, in episodes of "Queer as Folk," I watched or issues of "XY" or "Out" magazines I stealthily bought at Barnes & Noble. . . . I spent most of my teenage years believing that love between two Black men wasn't even possible. . . . Despite taking the time to learn to love myself, building the courage to drape myself in a body-length rainbow flag and march in the Pride Parade, I still didn't know what it would look like—feel like— to receive love from someone who looks like me. Or, more importantly, how to give it. So, I embarked on an adventure. As a visual journalist, I believe pictures can connect with people in a way that other forms of media can't. To this end, I decided to give a gift to my younger self: the imagery of queer love I've never seen. Queer love in color.[51]

The series, composed entirely of intraracial Black queer couples accompanied by their personal stories, is significant because it is not only a journey of self-discovery but one of actively seeking self-validation among those who are perceived as like-minded people who can offer guidance to others on their own journey of self-discovery.

As alluded to above, personal growth is often coupled with learning to love oneself and radical self-love. For many gay men of color, a move away from exclusively desiring white men is coupled with a growing love of self after a period of self-loathing created by gay media images. As Eliel Cruz wrote in *Out* magazine:

> There isn't a single gay magazine that hasn't made people of color feel ugly. Without fail, the gay men embodying what is attractive are built like a god, masculine to a fault, and almost always white. They don't even have to be into men to be put on a pedestal. Straight white men who play into homoerotic subtext get more notice than actual queer men of color. When I was younger, I would bastardize the pronunciation of my name to make it easier for non-Spanish speakers to pronounce it. I straightened my hair to get the curls out and would avoid aspects of my culture that would paint me as an "other." I wanted to fit in. I wanted to be white. Because being white meant you were desired. The self-loathing came easy. Learning to love myself was harder. Not just accepting who I was, but celebrating myself in all that I am—that took time. It also wasn't a singular moment but an everyday journey. I choose daily to reject a narrative that says I am less beautiful because of my ethnicity.[52]

Continuing on, Cruz attributes his growing self-love to his unwillingness to allow white men to dictate the borders of desire: "I will never let a white man make me feel less than what I am. . . . I, too, am beautiful, and in loving myself I perform a radical act against a culture that tells me otherwise."

A similar sentiment is shared by Chaaz Quigley who wrote on *Hornet*:

> As a Black same gender loving man, I know the struggle of self-love and dating in a community that prizes white bodies above all others. The first gay movie I ever saw was Beautiful Things, a tale

of two English teenaged boys caught up in the midst of a gloriously musical Mama Cass love-affair. It's a seminal teen film about love and at 13, it was my perfect vision of what gay life would be like. The image of those two white boys became my image of what it meant to be gay and the pinnacle achievement of a happy life.[53]

Quigley continues his essay by sharing his eventual coming out and his "nearly a decade chasing one unattainable white guy after another and feeling a sense of bitterness about being rejected by them." Feeling bitterness, Quigley shares how he "started to really look at myself and consider there might be an issue with me. Why was it that my heart was always being broken by some unavailable white boy? I decided that I would no longer pursue white guys to find out what contributed to my pathetic hunger for creamy white dick."[54]

His search for answers eventually led him to porn videos featuring a performer named Ali. According to Quigley, "Ali was burly, hairy-chested, wild bushed, caramel complexioned, Boricua beat-type dude who upon first sight made my dick trip. I'd never seen another chubby Black man who I found so incredibly attractive. . . . Suddenly, I felt desirable and empowered to determine my sexual destiny when I found out how many videos Ali had been featured in." Finding Ali, Quigley was able to shake his "pathetic hunger" for white men and transform the focus of his desire from white men to the "sameness" that Guzman discussed.[55]

Self-love also expanded out to loving other men of one's own race. In an especially poignant and moving essay published in *Logo*, Darnell L. Moore wrote:

I love Black men on purpose because Black men like my dad and Dae [his first lover] loved me out of the haze of lovelessness I learned to wade through; they've loved me back to life by seeing in me parts of themselves. And that is the type of love that costs the giver something, our relinquishing to the fact of our own worth in a society that tries to bankrupt our spirits before deposits of love are made . . . . This is what it means to love radically. Black men loving Black men is, as the deceased Black gay writer Joseph Beam opined in the 1980s, a "revolutionary act" because every moment a Black man is transgressive enough to love what he has been socialized to hate he commits an act of insurgency.[56]

For Cruz, Quigley, and Moore, because of the marginalization that people of color are forced to experience in a racist society, the act of learning to love oneself is itself a radical—and political—act.

DATING AS PROTECTION FROM RACISM

For some men of color, dating other men of their own race is framed as a way of avoiding the racism they experience not only from gay white men but from other white people who inhabit the white man's sphere. In an article published in *Them*, Phillip Henry argued:

> Many LGBTQ+ people of color often date within their own race exclusively. They do it because people of color are beautiful, but they also do it because it can be safer. It can protect them from experiences of racism, abuse, and fetishization in their relationships. . . . Dating within our own race has spared us from the glares of your friends and family when you bring us around, the microaggressions that is your sister asking to touch our hair and your friends asking if we know how to swim the weekend you bring us to your share in Fire Island.[57]

Similarly, in a review published in the *Advocate* of an episode of the TV show *Falling for Angels* that centered on two gay Asian men, Aaron Gettinger framed gay Asian men dating other Asian men as "leaving gay racism behind": "There is much to be said about racist anti-Asian sentiment among gay men—who among us has not seen a Grindr profile bluntly stating, 'No fems, no fats, no Asians'? Even though Gino and Kevin live out their racial heritage differently, this is reality every time an app is opened."[58] In fact, director Steven Liang is quoted as specifically stating that his interest in the script was "because it conveys Asian American men as attractive—not only to other races but to each other."

Part of avoiding racism is also about avoiding fetishization by gay white men that specifically prefer men of color as sexual partners. Writing for *Vice,* André-Naquian Wheeler had this to say after discussing his experiences of being racially fetishized by white men:

> There was a complete absence of white characters in Moonlight, Chiron falling in love with a person of color from the same community and brand of hardships as him. The artistic decision was an understandable one. The sameness of Chiron and Kevin was a refuge, allowing for a common understanding that never had to be spoken. I felt this same comfort with a former Black partner. . . . "You and I will always be queer and POC," they told me once, emphasizing how the two identities would always be intertwined, almost inseparable, for us. "Stop trying to fit in." Maybe Chiron realized this way before I did—knowing that being Black and queer was already hard enough, and that trying to find love and acceptance from a queer white male carried the chance of experiencing a new kind of rejection.[59]

For Wheeler and many other gay men of color, dating a man of their own race allowed them to be more authentic by not forcing them to "fit" a fetishized erotic image expected of them by white men, a concern raised even by men of color who exclusively dated white men.

Dating as a form of protection from racism also involved feeling more comfortable with others to whom one did not have to constantly perform race. As Michael Arceneaux wrote in the *Washington Post*:

> Being Black in this country often requires you to explain yourself in settings where you are the clear minority. Who wants to do that in their personal life? I don't like having to explain why it's okay for me to use "the n-word" and not you, or why you shouldn't touch my friend's hair, no matter how tempted you are. I never want to

have to yell out something like "cuz I'm Black b-!!!!" the way Rihanna once did on Twitter when met with stupid question about "nappy hair."[60]

Arceneaux continued:

> I also think it's important for gay Black men to be seen romantically involved with other gay Black men. I write against the notions that Black people are more homophobic than other groups. I actively speak out on the representation of gay Black men in mass media. I criticize the lack of visibility of Black LGBT couples on television and film. I feel that it's important to counter the caricature-like images of how Black people are presented, so I've gotten a little uneasy about being the Black guy who dates "others."[61]

What's notable about Arceneaux's telling of his personal experiences are that he frames his past history of having only dated Black men as an active choice. For example, while he states that he has "never dated a white man," he did have an unsatisfactory sexual encounter with a white man that led him to avoid them. But Arceneaux is quick to jokingly point out that if Ryan Phillippe drops him a line, he may oblige. Thus, his past history of exclusively dating Black men is not about personal preferences, but an active choice he has made.

This feeling that dating men of the same race was an active choice, discussed earlier by Cruz, Quigley, and Moore, has led many gay men of color to view loving other men of color as a radical, and political, act.

INTRARACIAL DESIRE AS A POLITICAL ACT

Gay men of color who exclusively dated other men of color often recognized that racial desires are rooted in larger social systems of racial domination. As Myles E. Johnson wrote for the *Black Youth Project*, "I know white supremacy doesn't just manifest in public spaces, but can show up in interpersonal, even romantic, experiences. We are all socialized to see whiteness as supreme and Blackness as less than through media and cultural productions. This socialization influences what we think is beautiful and desirable, and this follows us even in dating."[62]

Recognizing that racialized desires are deeply rooted in larger structures of racial hierarchies, many gay men of color come to view intraracial desire as not something that is natural but rather a political decision in response to a racist society that creates such hierarchies of desire. Rather than a default, intraracial desire is something that one consciously develops. Writing for *BDG*, Anthony Williams noted:

> While my personal decision not to date white men is the result of actually dating white men, the decision is rooted less in my experience with the individuals I dated and more in my experience with society. We live in a white supremacist society that promotes a racialized and gendered hierarchy. . . . We live in a world that provides white people with privilege while constantly affirming their whiteness at the cost of Blackness. Living in an anti-Black world, it is easy to internalize these sentiments from a very young age and begin to hate different aspects of ourselves.[63]

In discussing the turning point that led them to fully question their own sexual attraction to white men, they recounted a discussion they had with a friend when they were nineteen. Specifically, they recalled asking their friend, "Do you think he's into Black guys?" As Williams explains:

> That statement didn't stem solely from insecurity or even modesty, but instead from the internalization of anti-Black sentiments I had heard my whole life. . . . These racial microaggressions—which are anything but micro—included: "you're cute for a Black guy" or "you're different from other Black people," and "I don't even think of you as really Black." These comments work on the basis that I am an exception to my race; a part of the talented tenth—or in this case, the attractive tenth—and one of the "good Blacks." I am given white approval by transcending the stereotype of how a Black person looks or behaves, and that is simply wrong on a personal, political, and psychological level. I am a Black man whose

accomplishments are shaped through, and by, my Blackness, not "despite" my Blackness.[64]

While their decision to stop dating white men is clearly couched within the language of racial politics, Williams also delved into the personal as well. For example, they goes on to explain:

> If I am dating a white man, is he fetishizing or exoticizing me
> for my skin, lips, hair or penis? Have I not met his parents because
> of my race or just because of his own internalized homophobia?
> When his friend calls me "Malik or whatever," will he let that
> slide? And finally, when I'm exhausted from the psychological toll
> of racial microaggressions, daily Black Death, and everyday life, do
> I have to educate him on the ways in which he is further dehuman-
> izing me or invalidating my opinions? If so, I'm not interested. This
> also applies to non-Black people of color who aspire to whiteness or
> uphold white supremacist ideals.[65]

Within gay racial desires, the political becomes personal and the personal is also political. Rather than simply a personal preference, intraracial desires become a personal way of confronting white supremacist beliefs about racial worth.

Like the men who equated coming to prefer other gay men of color as sexual and romantic partners framed this change as a matter of personal growth, men who viewed their own desires as a political act also couched it within the narrative of their own past desires for white men. After stating that the "husband" that he imagined in his mind following the US Supreme Court decision in *Obergefell v. Hodges* that legalized gay marriage had a "white man's face," Zach Stafford wrote in the *Guardian*:

> Though the gay community pays lip service to being accepting
> of everyone, we've internalized the feeling that we are not equally
> beautiful or deserving of the same rights. This isn't about me just
> not finding black skin attractive—that's what many people say at
> bars while throwing back drinks. It's because society at large has

decided this. . . . And I am starting to think that this self-reinforcing racism could be part of the higher rates of interracial coupling in our community.[66]

Here, Stafford argues that changing this is a political act, observing, "If we have learned anything during the fight for marriage equality, it's that love is political, no matter what you might think. And our love should actually be used to fight battles that make things better for people like the fight for same-sex marriage just did."[67] While gay men of color's personal experiences led to racial consciousness regarding their own desires, they nonetheless saw their current desires for other men of color as something larger than personal growth that had a greater implication for racial justice than their own sense of well-being.

Men who saw intraracial dating as political acts were likely to be critical not only of the gay men of color who exclusively dated white men, but also of the rationale that those men gave to justify their desire for white men. Some saw the sheer act of complaining about white men not wanting to date men of color as a sign of internalized self-hate. Writing for the *Ashton P. Woods Blog*, Prince Royce Worthington had this to say:

> If I read another rambling think piece or watch another whiny
> YouTube video about some dejected and rejected Black Gay Man
> (or any other ethnicity of gay man for that matter) waxing poetic
> about how racist it is for white Gay Men to rebuke them based on
> solely on race, I am going to smash my head through a wall, seri-
> ously . . . What is wrong with you people? Are you so enamored by
> the white gaze and white supremacy that you will willingly subject
> yourselves to overt racism and constant microaggressions in order
> to be accepted by men who literally view you as a sexual fetish and
> nothing more?[68]

Worthington continues his essay by explaining that racists, by nature, are going to act like racists and notes that "white gay men are still, first and foremost, white men in a society that privileges whiteness and maleness, period." Thus, this group of men behaving in racist ways is nothing worth writing about. Instead, Worthington offers this advice to gay men of color: "So before you write the next maudlin think piece about why racist white men don't want you (easy, it's because they are racist) ask yourself why you don't want yourself. That is the most important inqueery (misspelling intentional. I just thought that was cute)."[69]

In his *Afropunk* article discussed, Hari Ziyad specifically takes aim at others who have argued that exclusively dating white men does not exclude the possibility that one can be racially aware:

> Love is a mixture of personality dispositions and political choices, which is why whom you *decide* to sleep or build a life with says just as much about you as whom you decide to be friends with. In this "post-racial" world that is increasingly showing itself to be anything but, this reality causes very real dissonance within the minds of those who claim to be pro-Black or body positive or anti-ableist, but whose dating practices are anything but. It is much easier to disregard working on the most intimate display of one's politics—love—when the narrative is that love can't be helped. Rather than self-reflecting on the obvious proof of internalized anti-Blackness in not dating other Black people as a Black person, you get to tell the lie that dating has nothing to do with things you need to work on, letting yourself off the hook.[70]

As Ziyad argues, the belief that "you can't help whom you love is a white supremacist bullshit" that is specifically aimed at preventing individuals from evaluating how they can divest from it: "[White supremacy] requires that we believe the way things are now are natural and unchangeable, when they have been affected by centuries of violent social programming. We know white supremacy beauty standards exist, that anti-Black ideas about Black people of all (non)genders exist, but supposedly we can't help whom we love, even though white supremacy has already been helping for ages."[71] For Ziyad, an exclusive preference for white men is not the result of natural or personal preference but instead is reflective of centuries of white supremacist propaganda that has marked whiteness as somehow better, more desirable, and more worthy than Blackness.

For Latino men, there was an added layer of meaning attached to interracial desires. For example, a gay Latino man was quoted by the *San Francisco Weekly* as stating:

> There's this judgmental rampage going on: Who's more Mexican? Who's been whitewashed? To them [Latino men who only date other Latino men] it's like being colonized again if you go out with a white guy. They detest the idea that some Latinos only date white guys in hopes of marrying up.[72]

While the man quoted indicated that he was, at the time, in a relationship with a white man, his statement still demonstrates the rift among gay Latino men regarding the meaning of interracial and intraracial desires and the ways that such desires get framed within a racialized hierarchy. Many gay male writers of color frame intraracial desire as political, yet this sentiment is not without its distractors among other gay men of color who prefer members of their own race. Rather, some find this argument fundamentally problematic.

Responding to another article in which the author with a history of dating white men wrote, "I've become increasingly drawn to the concept of Black love, which celebrates Black couples and affirms Black pride within relationships, and I eventually want to experience this," Avery Ware wrote:

> So you don't want to date a Black man because we're beautiful, creative, resilient, innovative, interesting, and complex; you want to date one of us because you've become "increasingly drawn to the concept" of Black love. You don't want to date a Black man because you love your Blackness and are drawn to others that love theirs and you think y'all can love and empower each other better together than apart. No. You like the idea of Black love. You are drawn to the aesthetics of what you perceive Black love to be. You want the "experience" of Black love just to say you've had the experience, and that's not only extremely problematic, but it's offensive. . . . My point is that Barksdale made Black love out to be

just a concept or a theory and not something that is actually real and legitimate. Black people have, enjoy, and cherish Black love, and that should be recognized.[73]

Unlike other writers who view dating other men of color as a political act, regardless of one's own actual physical attractions (which more often than not also applies to white men), Ware's sentiments more closely align with gay men of color who come to see dating other men of color as a result of coming to love oneself.

Yet even men who frame their own intraracial desires as not being about making political statements come to understand that their relationships do have implications for the ways that racial desire gets constructed. As Efren Bose wrote in *8Asians*:

> After coming out publicly in college, I began to meet other queer Asian men, whose preferences were more toward white men. . . . One guy, who had also dated primarily white men, said in all sincerity, "Wow, that's so cool that your first boyfriend was Vietnamese. That is so, so, revolutionary!" . . . I can see where he was going—that he was going through the now oft-quoted adage (and I'm taking liberties with this) that "Loving Asian men is a revolutionary act," especially if you're another Asian American man who's been taught to believe that white men are the pinnacle of desirability.[74]

Later in his article, Bose shares an experience he had while walking down the street with his Asian partner:

> I remember when my partner and I were first dating, and we would hold hands in the Castro or in Union Square, and people would do double takes seeing two Asian guys together who obviously weren't related. I remember getting the confused stares from fellow Asians with white partners who wondered what we were about—and the creepy, lust-filled looks from white guys trying to imagine us in bed.[75]

Much like Ware, Bose frames his desire for other Asian men as coming naturally to him rather than as an act of racial politics. At the same time, he also recognizes that for many others, seeing two Asian men in a mutually romantic relationship disrupts the expected racial hierarchy of desire, which by its very nature is a radical and revolutionary act.

CONCLUSION

Despite the relative absence of academic work examining intraracial relationships as opposed to the legions of work on interracial relationships, recent years have seen an increasing number of mainstream commentators writing about the politics of intraracial desires, particularly among gay men for whom issues of sexual racism have become a hot topic of discussion.

While sexual racism has come to capture the imagination of both gay and mainstream media and has been the focus of several academic works, attempts to systematically examine the nature of intraracial desire among gay men of color have not been as abundant nor has it become as central in the mainstream press as the much sexier topic of sexual racism.

Yet as discussed in previous chapters, the racial hierarchy of desire constructed in the gay community has led to a situation in which desires for white men have come to be the default, with the majority of all men, regardless of race, indicating a preference for white men. Given this racial hierarchy, it should be obvious why gay men prefer gay white men as sexual partners. The interesting question then is not why gay men of all races come to prefer white men, but why, and how, gay men of color come to prefer other men of color regardless of the rigidly constructed racial hierarchy of desire.

Looking at (mostly) first person essays written by gay men of color about their own racial preferences, there are three primary ways that gay men of color frame their intraracial desires: as a result of their own personal racialized journey of self-acceptance in a racist country; as a way to avoid both the gay community and gay white men, whom they perceived to be racist; and as a political act that disrupts the racial hierarchy of desire and challenges the premises that create such hierarchies. For many of these men, these reasons were not mutually exclusive; more often than not, they intersected and overlapped.

Given these narratives, we can see that sexual desires are not random or simply matters of personal preferences. Nor are members of minority groups blind adherents to dominant narratives. And neither are sexual desires void of political motivations. Rather, sexual desires can be thought of as acts of political resistance to larger structural factors whereby individuals, through personal acts, challenge systems of domination in order to reframe what it means to be racial and sexual minorities.

Conclusion

A Kindr Grindr Is Not the Solution

FOLLOWING PUBLIC ACCUSATIONS THAT SEXUAL RACISM WAS RUN-ning rampant on its platform, and in response to the growing popularity of the website *Douchebags of Grindr* that collects—and collectively mocks—problematic, and in many cases racist, profiles created by white men, Grindr launched a new initiative titled Kindr in September of 2018 using the tag line "Kindness is our preference." Included in the launch were a series of videos, posted to its website and to YouTube, featuring individuals discussing their personal experiences with racism, body shaming, transphobia, HIV stigma, and femme shaming within the gay community. The six episode video series ended with one titled "Grindr Users Make Kindness Their Preference."

Whether the initiative was truly well intended or a response to the media coverage of the lawsuit by Sinakhone Keodara (discussed in chapter 5) and the slew of negative stories published on gay websites and blogs, is unclear. However, several media outlets did note the timing of the initiative, coming just two months after Keodara's threatened suit. Regardless of the reason Grindr launched the initiative, one thing was made clear. According to Grindr, racism in the gay community, and on the app, was a personal, rather than a structural, problem. On the newly launched website, kindr.grindr.com, Grindr introduced the initiative:

> At Grindr, we're into diversity, inclusion, and users who treat each other with respect. We're not into racism, bullying, or other forms of toxic behavior. These are our preferences, and we've

updated our Community Guidelines to better reflect them. Same app. New rules.[1]

In continuing, Grindr also declared:

Everyone is entitled to their opinion. Their type. Their tastes. But nobody is entitled to tear someone else down because of their race, size, gender, HIV status, age, or—quite simply—being who they are.

The problem is that in making this public statement to launch their Kindr initiative, Grindr reinforces the idea that racial exclusion and fetishization are matters of personal preferences and not based on structures of racist beliefs that lead to racialized hierarchies of desire.

While the app is "into diversity [and] inclusion," that diversity and inclusion go only as far as treating each other nicely, whatever one's own racist beliefs may be. And there is no mention of any need to address larger issues of structural racism within gay communities. According to Grindr, the problem isn't that gay white men are racist or that the very structure of gay communities reinforces whiteness at every turn; after all, "everyone is entitled to their opinion." The problem is that they act out their racism publicly. Thus, the alluded solution to racism is to simply be "kindr."

To be fair, some of the commentary by the participants in the various videos do address larger social and structural issues. However, the episodes in the series created by Grindr to allegedly combat sexual racism and other forms of discrimination and marginalization focus heavily on the personal experiences of those who are mocked and ridiculed and urge those who are doing the mocking and ridiculing to be kinder to save the feelings of other users while simultaneously constructing acts of racism, transphobia, and sexism as the actions of few bad seeds rather than a reflection of larger structural issues. However, kindness is not the answer to racism or racial inequality that is structurally rooted. An argument can be made that being polite and kind is another tactic to deny racist beliefs and attitudes that lurk under the surface by covering it with a smile. What Grindr and many gay men themselves believe are personal preferences are actually deeply rooted in larger systems of racial inequalities that construct a racial hierarchy of desire that being kinder is not going to address.

Addressing the structural issues that lead to sexual racism requires that we examine some hard realities about gay communities. If we examine sexual racism and the ways racial desire is constructed, maintained, and performed, we learn that racial preferences are not natural, innate, or unexplainable outcomes of internal lusts. Rather than personal preferences, racialized hierarchies of desire are actively constructed and maintained specifically for the benefit of gay white men. This benefit goes far beyond being perceived simply as more desirable. Instead, the racial hierarchy of desire creates a hierarchy of worth according to which white men are granted more privileges and value inside and outside of sexual exchange, with the hierarchy itself dependent on presenting gay white men as the "good" gay and deserving of empathy and gay men of color as deviant and deserving of mistreatment.

In determining who has worth and who does not, sexual racism also dictates who belongs and who does not. Sexual racism thus creates two barriers, one cultural and one structural, where gay men of color are excluded both as sexual partners by gay white men and from gay social spaces. And once constructed as having no worth, it becomes easy to ignore issues that disproportionately impact gay men of color and, by extension, all queer people of color, regardless of their gender. When we think about all the ways that sexual racism negatively impacts the lives of gay men of color, being sexually excluded seems like a minor inconvenience. Yet it is through sexual exclusion that other types of discriminatory acts come to be justified.

MEDIA IMAGES AND THE CONSTRUCTION OF RACIAL DESIRE

Media images of gay men, whether they appear in specifically gay targeted media or more mainstream media, work to construct the borders of desire for all gay men. These representations shape how we come to see ourselves and others because the way we see the world comes from "within, not outside, representations."[2] As Richard Dyer notes:

How social groups are treated in cultural representation is part
and parcel of how they are treated in life. . . . How a group is
represented, presented over again in cultural forms, how an image
of a member of a group is taken as representative of that group,
how that group is represented in the sense of spoken for and on
behalf of (whether they represent, speak for themselves or not),
these all have to do with how members of a group see themselves
and others like themselves, how they see their place in society. . . .
How we are seen determines in part how we are treated; how we
treat others is based on how we see them; such seeing comes from
representations.[3]

Media images of gay men are a representation of them in a world where
heteronormative images may rob them of the mirror they need to construct themselves. For this reason, gay media images have profound influences on gay men's sense of self, their values, their beliefs, the way they
see themselves and others, and as their place inside and outside of erotic
desires.

Yet gay media images are an unrelenting celebratory parade and praise
of whiteness. Media images of white men populate the pages of gay magazines, cisgender white men make up the majority of gay male characters
on television shows and in movies, and even when non-white men are
portrayed, whether in print or on screen, they are often portrayed as a
deviation from what makes gay men normal and a problematic challenge
to homonormative claims.

Not only are cisgender white men presented as normative, they are also
presented as having little in common with non-cis gender and/or non-
white men. The movie *Love, Simon*, for example, which opened to widespread critical acclaim particularly for its "revolutionary normalcy," begins
with a montage by the protagonist Simon, played by Nick Robinson,
explaining the myriad of ways that he is normal:[4]

I'm just like you. For the most part, my life is totally normal. My
dad is the annoyingly handsome quarterback who married the hot

valedictorian. And no, they didn't peak in high school. I have a sister I actually like. Not that I'd ever tell her that. And last year, after 200 episodes of Chopped ago, she decided she wanted to be a chef. Which means we're pretty much all her test subjects now. And then there's my friends. Two of them, I've known pretty much since the beginning of time, or at least Kindergarten. One of them, I just met a few months ago, but it feels like I've known her forever. We do everything friends do. We drink way too much iced coffee, watch bad 90s movies and hang out at Waffle House dreaming of college and gorging on carbs. So, like I said. I'm just like you. I have a totally, perfectly normal life. Except I have one huge-ass secret.[5]

After having established Simon's "revolutionary normalcy," the audience is taken on a tissue-worthy emotional ride as Simon seeks out a secret online crush. Yet Simon's "revolutionary normalcy" depends on offering a polar opposite that helps define just how normal Simon is.

In one telling scene toward the end of the movie after Simon is outed, he becomes involved in a fight in the cafeteria when he and Ethan, the only other openly gay character in the movie, played by openly gay actor Clark Moore, is mocked by two straight classmates. Following the altercation, Simon and Ethan are sent to the principal's office. While waiting to meet with the principal, Ethan asks Simon why he never told him that he was gay, to which Simon simply responds, "I didn't think we had much in common."

While Simon's sexuality is a "huge-ass secret," it neither marks him nor impacts his identity in any way. Nor does it provide any sense of shared commonality with other gay men. By marking Simon as a normal high school kid who is just like everyone else but with one "huge-ass secret," the movie also presents him as the "good gay," the kind of gay who does not push his sexuality in other people's faces, while Ethan is marked as the "bad gay," who, by simply existing as he is, constantly reminds others of his difference. While Simon's love interest does turn out to be a young Black man during the last few minutes of the movie, he is also presented as being homonormative and racially assimilative.

The whiteness in gay media constructs gay white men as not only normative but also more desirable than men of color. White men, gay or straight, are routinely described in media profiles as desirable and are presented in visual copy posing in seductive and masculine poses while men of color are rarely afforded such erotic praise. And even when they are, they are portrayed in ways that present them as erotic delights meant for white male consumption as an exception rather than the norm. Given this framing of racial desire, it isn't surprising that the majority of gay men of color report preferences for white men. Yet despite the growing public interest in racialized desires within and outside gay communities, the question of desire has remained the elephant in the room whose presence few sociologists have acknowledged. Thus, discussions that center desire, particularly racial desire, are desperately needed to shed new light on how racial desire is created and maintained and what racial desires can teach us about the creation and maintenance of racial hierarchies in general.

NEGATIVE IMPACTS ON MEN OF COLOR

The sad consequence of the relentless equating of whiteness with desirability is the negative impact it has on gay men of color. As Patricia Hill Collins reminds us, "controlling images" such as those found within gay media aren't simply stereotypes to be brushed off.[6] Rather, they often determine how members of marginalized groups come to be seen and come to see themselves and how members of those groups come to embody those images. Controlling images are often used to justify social inequalities and social injustices as being natural and normal. The racialized sexual stereotypes that are now rampant in gay communities—that Black men are sexually aggressive, Latino men are hypersexual, and Asian men are sexually submissive—are nothing new, and they are readily traced to larger racial projects. Much like earlier reiterations of these images that helped mark white men and women as sexually normative while simultaneously marking the alleged sexual behaviors of non-white people as sexually deviant, these images are recycled and redeployed within the gay sexual imagination to construct the normative gay (white) man and the deviant (non-white) gay man.[7] When gay men of color internalize these images, they come to see other men of color as less desirable than white men, and they frame their own sexual worth within the hierarchy of desire. Rather than directing their sexual desires toward other men of color, they themselves come to believe in the racial hierarchy of desire, directing their own sexual longings toward white men and performing racialized roles in the pursuit of pleasure.

More consequentially, gay men of color come to see themselves from the standpoint of white men and frame their own sexual worth according to what they can offer white men. In the erotic marketplace, gay men of color advertise themselves by highlighting the sexual stereotypes associated with members of their group. One can argue that the denying of sexual worth to men of color, which creates a racial imbalance within the gay sexual marketplace, coupled with a desire for white men, lead men of color to take on racialized roles during sexual encounters.[8]

Gay Black men advertise themselves as hypermasculine and overtly sexual, gay Asian men advertise themselves as being sexually submissive, and Latino men often resort to stereotypes of "hombres" and "Latin lovers" popular in the Western imagination. When they do, they are rewarded in the sexual marketplace of desire. When they do not, they are punished. Similarly, white men seek partners of different races based largely on racial stereotypes of what each race offers for white male consumption. These contradictory stereotypes deployed by both men of color and by white men simultaneously work to create the boundaries of the appropriate and normative gay desire. Gay white men are the normative targets of such desires with normative sexual lives, while erotic desires for men of color are a deviation from that norm that adds spice.[9]

Gay men of color report feeling unwelcome, both in sexually charged spaces such as bars and in visibly identifiable gay neighborhoods. There is ample evidence that what they are feeling is not simply their own perceptions but a logical reaction to actively being unwelcomed in those spaces. Gay bars, citing the alleged sexual desires of their clientele, exclude gay men of color in several ways, rendering them invisible in promotional materials and preventing entrance through dubious restrictions based on clothing and forms of identification.

Gay bars are both social anchors and sexual marketplaces within gay communities. Few would deny the centrality of gay bars to the social, political, and community lives of gay men and women. Yet because gay bars are also heavily sexualized spaces, an individual's sexual worth determines their value, which in turn determines their eligibility for entrance. The exclusion of gay men of color from these spaces is more than simply a social act of discrimination. It is also a political act. In effect, the inferior sexual worth that is assigned by gay white men to gay men of color denies gay men of color access to the safe space in a heterosexist world—the gay bar—where they can "be themselves," an access granted to—and largely controlled by—white men.

Marked as having less worth, gay men of color, as well as all queers of color, are ignored and actively excluded from gay spaces beyond just bars. Well-funded national organizations that allege to advocate for gay causes and issues largely ignore issues and concerns that disproportionately impact queers of color, such as asylum seeking, police brutality, and homelessness, in favor of middle-class white issues. Efforts at improving the health of LGBTQ communities continue to focus largely on the needs of gay white men. In some cases, gay neighborhoods themselves become actively hostile to those who are not white, gender conforming, and male. Thus, the true danger of sexual racism isn't that gay white men don't find men of color sexually desirable, but that the hierarchy that it creates affects many other arenas of life for gay men of color, even those who have virtually no sexual or romantic interest in white men.

THE POLITICS OF DESIRE

Gay white men often deny both the existence of racism in the gay community and their own racist racial preferences. They use several tactics to achieve this goal. In terms of racial preferences, gay white men equate preferences with sexuality itself. Rather than question where racial desires are framed, how they are maintained, and how they impact their own sexual desires, gay men, both white and non-white, frame their sexual desires as innate and, much like sexuality itself, unchangeable. White men's defenses of racial sexual preferences are also coupled with a list of imagined nonracist bona fides, including having non-white friends and supporting diversity and equality in work, education, and housing—all areas of life whose private and intimate spaces are already well defended from access by non-whites.

Despite the racial hierarchy of desire, it would be a mistake to assume that gay men of color wholeheartedly embrace, or even accept, the narrative of desire for whiteness. Rather, these narratives are actively challenged and confronted. While one method is to directly challenge racial sexual stereotypes, the biggest challenge to the narratives of white desirability are found among gay men of color who actively seek other men of color for sexual companionship.

In examining the reasons gay men of color gave for their own intraracial sexual desires, I found several patterns, including seeing their intraracial desires as a personal journey of their own racial acceptance and the need to avoid the racism they encountered in the gay community. Yet most interestingly, many gay men of color saw their intraracial sexual preferences as a way to directly challenge the racial hierarchy of desire itself. In framing intraracial rather than interracial desires, gay men of color offer a counternarrative that directly challenges the narrative of gay desires. Yet these narratives are also contested.

THEORETICAL AND SUBSTANTIVE CONTRIBUTIONS

Despite the widespread recognition in the popular press of sexual racism, few scholarly studies have systematically examined the phenomenon. One reason for this gap in scholarship is that gay men of color are rarely the focus of much academic inquiry. According to sociologist Anthony C. Ocampo:

First, in both historical and contemporary times, gay people of color were excluded from mainstream gay social networks and movements, which have provided the basis for most empirical studies on sexual minorities. A second related factor is that researchers have a difficult time locating gay communities of color to study. On the other hand, the under-representation of people for color in academia means that many researchers lack the networks with access to and knowledge of minority communities, let alone gay minority communities. In addition, most gay people of color revolve their lives around their ethnic and racial communities, not mainstream gay communities. Third, although coming out of the closet is the idealized choice among white, middle-class gays, it is not always the norm for gay people of color.[10]

Yet despite these barriers, there have been several studies within the past few decades that have helped bring attention to the lives of gay men of color and provide some insights for new avenues of exploration.

These studies have found that gay men of color experience high levels of racism in gay communities, with several studies indicating that gay men of color report more racism from gay white men than from the larger society.[11] However, these studies have largely taken racism as a given, focusing on the personal experiences of gay men of color with racism or examining how racism impacts a number of outcome variables, including rates of unsafe sex, willingness to "come out," and self-esteem. Using a taken-for-granted definition of racism leaves largely unexamined questions about how and why racism develops and the purpose that it serves.

On a different thread, sociological studies about sexuality and sexual behaviors have tended to ignore the tricky concept of desire, let alone racial desire. A primary reason for this hesitation may be the continuing belief among sociologists that desire is a subconscious, biological phenomenon whose appropriate area of investigation is psychoanalysis, not sociology. Yet the reluctance of sociologists to examine desire has left sociology with a lack of a framework for understanding how larger social structures create, maintain, and shapes erotic desires.[12] Given such a lack of a framework for understanding desire as a structural process, studies of interracial relationships often focus on the factors that are likely to lead people to enter interracial relationships or to compare interracial relationships and intraracial ones based on their relative levels of success or satisfaction. Missing from these discussions are the racial politics of desire and how those racialized sexual desires are societally shaped and maintained. Yet more recent scholarship in interracial relationships points to a clear pattern of racialized hierarchies of desire, particularly among gay men, pointing to the strong possibility that structural factors, rather than personal factors, lead to racialized sexual preferences.

Finally, queer theory has not only ignored race but has actively attempted to erase race from analysis in an effort to present a universalized queer experience focused on the experiences of white, Western, upper-class gay men. In response to the erasure of race from queer analysis, queer of color critique (QOC) attempts both to address the absence of race in queer theorizing and to challenge the universalizing narrative of contemporary queer theory.

Scholars working from the QOC perspective have recently demonstrated that racialized processes cannot be separated from the ways that (homo)sexuality and queer subjectivity have been constructed. As Jasbir Puar has argued, the ability to displace sexual perversity normally associated with gay men onto brown (Muslim) bodies gave rise to "homonationalism" and allowed Western white gays to claim "normality."[13] Sexual racism is part and parcel of a lager project of racial erasing that conflates gayness with whiteness. The constructed desires for white men as normative and the displacement of deviant sexuality onto men of color by presenting racial desires as either exceptions or sexual fetishes allow gay white men to make claims to normality. Exploring sexual racism among gay men demonstrates that constructions of racialized desires among gay men cannot be separated from the larger project of constructing the "good" gay.

At the same time, it would be a mistake to simply view queers of color as victims. Gay men of color actively confront and challenge the larger narrative of racial desires. While I've already discussed the active process of challenging the larger narratives above, their challenges to the narratives about racialized desires can be understood as instances of disidentification. Disidentification involves taking dominant narratives about what it means to be both raced and sexualized and transforming those narratives for different purposes.[14] While gay men of color often do directly challenge narratives of race and sex, they also take existing narratives and utilize them for their own purpose. They also frame their sexual desires around racialized sexual stereotypes. However, when used to construct their own racial desires for members of their own race, racialized sexual stereotypes move from being a way of objectifying the other to centering alleged otherness as the focus of desire rather than a fetish. In this way, gay men of color do not simply respond to white racial sexual fantasies but coopt them for their own use while simultaneously locking white men out of their own sexual fantasies. In the hands of men of color, in service of other men of color, these racial stereotypes get redeployed and reimagined, creating a familiar but also different way of seeing "race" and perceiving racial desire where the desire for same (and different from "white") displaces the desire for the other.

CLOSING

I want to take a moment to reflect back on Patricia Hill Collin's ground-breaking work, *Black Feminist Thought*, specifically her discussion on the importance of self-definition.[15] Perhaps the most important area of potential inquiry is a careful examination of media products created by gay men of color themselves. Despite the lack of widespread coverage, gay men of color have been active for decades in creating and disseminating their own images and narratives. These media products are a rich source of information and reflection on the ways that gay men of color actively challenge racism in the gay community and attempt to create a different gay narrative regarding what it means to be both raced and sexualized. Academic inquiries of these media products are growing robustly in the humanities but have yet to make a dent in the social sciences. I suspect that focusing on those products would produce a much more optimistic view than I have offered here. Much like the personal narratives about intraracial desires that mark other men of color as sexually desirable and actively challenge the narrative of racial desirability, such products will demonstrate that gay men of color are not passive recipients of media messages blindly accepting the narratives offered to them but are actively confronting them through their own media creations.

It would also be useful to dig more deeply into actual intraracial relationships between gay men of color and relationships between men of color of different races. What are the contours of such relationships? How are they differently raced, and how does the logic of racial desire get either embedded or dismantled in such relationships, if indeed it does so at all? Asking such questions will necessarily shift the center of analysis and offer us a rich insight into the ways gay men of color resist and challenge sexual racism. Shifting the analysis to how gay men of color construct other non-white men as potential sexual partners will give us much needed insight into the process of racialization within a multiracial society. How much of the dominant racial narratives are maintained? How much of the racial narratives of non-coracial "other" is challenged? How does one's own racial position within the hierarchy of race impact how one comes to see non-white men of a different race? Answers to such questions would add much needed nuance and widen the discussion of how race is constructed away from the usual "dominant group vs. subordinate group" dichotomy and help add to the literature on race and ethnicity as well as sexuality.

Although this book focused on the experiences of cisgender gay men, one theme that emerges from the analysis is that gender is central to the ways racialized desires are constructed. Within racialized gay desires, Black men are hypermasculinized, and Asian men are feminized. From the perspective of cisgender men seeking other cisgender men for sexual encounters, this "gender non-conformity" is often a detriment. Yet it is likely that the ways that gender and race intersect in sexual desire would look different if we focused on the sexual lives of people other than cisgender gay men. How might gender play into the sexual lives of those who are not gender conforming or simply, not men? How might queer women, genderqueer folks, gender fluid folks, straight people regardless of their gender identity, etc. navigate race and gender in sexual desires? While these questions were beyond the scope of *this* book, making gender more central to a racialized analysis of desire will offer us further insights into the ways that systems of gender, sexuality and race work together.

Finally, in writing a book about desire, I have largely ignored the question of pleasure. When we shift the focus from desire to pleasure, we accomplish two things. First, we shift the focus of our inquiry from the structural to the personal, which allows us to better understand how sexual lives are actually lived. For example, while the data in chapter 3 allow me to examine how desire is constructed and performed, they do not allow me to make any meaningful inquiries into how these men frame pleasure and how seeking pleasure influences the ways they perform desire. Second, shifting the focus to pleasure will also allow us to reimagine how controlling images are negotiated and manipulated in the pursuit of personal pleasure. This question is of importance given that there are indications that such controlling images that have historically hindered racial progress for people of color can be harnessed and utilized in the service of people they once attempted to control.[16]

As should be obvious, this book does not address all the possible questions or hold all the possible insights that the topic of sexual racism might bring up. Instead, by focusing on cisgender gay men and racialized desires, it offers just a glimpse of those questions and those insights. By doing so, I hope that it has raised more questions, more curiosity, and more interest in the topic for future discussions.

NOTES

INTRODUCTION

1 George Lipsitz, *The Possessive Investment in Whiteness: How White People Profit from Identity Politics* (Philadelphia: Temple University Press, 1998).

2 Allan Bérubé, "How Gay Stays White and What Kind of White It Stays," in *The Making and Unmaking of Whiteness*, ed. Birgit B. Rasmussen, Eric Klinenberg, Irene J. Nexica, and Matt Wray (Durham, NC: Duke University Press, 2001), 246.

3 Bérubé, "How Gay Stays White," 235.

4 Niels Teunis, "Sexual Objectification and the Construction of Whiteness in the Gay Male Community," *Culture, Health & Sexuality* 9, no. 3 (2007): 263–75.

5 Dwight A. McBride, "Why I Hate That I Loved Brokeback Mountain," *GLQ: A Journal of Lesbian and Gay Studies* 13, no. 1 (2007): 97.

6 Charles H. Stember, *Sexual Racism: The Emotional Barrier to an Integrated Society* (New York: Elsevier, 1976).

7 Denton Callander, Martin Holt, and Christy E. Newman, "'Not Everyone's Gonna Like Me': Accounting for Race and Racism in Sex and Dating Web Services for Gay and Bisexual Men," *Ethnicities* 16, no. 1 (2016): 3–21.

8 Tony Ayres, "China Doll: The Experience of Being a Gay Chinese Australian," *Journal of Homosexuality* 36, no. 3/4 (1999): 80.

9 Sandra Lee Bartky, *Femininity and Domination: Studies in the Phenomenology of Oppression* (New York: Routledge, 1990).

10 bell hooks, *Black Looks: Race and Representation* (Boston: South End Books, 1992), 21.

11 Sonu Bedi, "Sexual Racism: Intimacy as a Matter of Justice," *Journal of Politics* 77, no. 4 (2015): 998.

12 Brandon Robinson, "'Personal Preference' as the New Racism: Gay Desire and Racial Cleansing in Cyberspace," *Sociology of Race and Ethnicity* 1, no. 2 (2015): 317–30. See also Denton Callander, Martin Holt, and Christy E. Newman, "Just a Preference: Racialised Language in the Sex-Seeking Profiles of Gay and Bisexual Men," *Culture, Health & Sexuality* 14, no. 9 (2012): 1049–63.

13 Peter A. Jackson, "That's What Rice Queens Study! White Gay Desire and Representing Asian Homosexualities," *Journal of Australian Studies* 24, no. 65 (2000): 184.

14 *Tongues Untied*, directed by Marlon Riggs (1989; San Francisco: Frameline and California Newsreel, 2008), DVD.

15 Elena Kiesling, "The Missing Colors of the Rainbow: Black Queer Resistance," *European Journal of American Studies* 11, no. 3 (2017): 1–21.

16 Siobhan B. Somerville, *Queering the Color Line: Race and the Invention of Homosexuality in American Culture* (Durham, NC: Duke University Press, 2000), 8.

17 Rae Rosenberg, "The Whiteness of Gay Urban Belonging: Criminalizing LGBTQ Youths of Color in Queer Spaces of Care," *Urban Geography* 38, no. 1 (2017): 137–48.

18 Anthony C. Ocampo, "Making Masculinity: Negotiations of Gender Presentation among Latino Gay Men," *Latino Studies* 10, no. 4 (2012): 448–72.

19 Dinoa Duazo, "Looking Back in Homage," *Lavender Godzilla*, April 1999.

20 Michael Thai, "Sexual Racism Is Associated with Lower Self-Esteem and Life Satisfaction in Men Who Have Sex with Men," *Archives of Sexual Behavior* 49 (2020): 347–53.

21 H. Fisher Raymond and Willi McFarland, "Racial Mixing and HIV Risk among Men Who Have Sex with Men," *AIDS and Behavior* 13, no. 4 (2009): 630–37. See also Chong-suk Han, "A Qualitative Exploration of the Relationship between Racism and Unsafe Sex among Asian Pacific Islander Gay Men," *Archives of Sexual Behavior* 37, no. 5 (2008): 827–37.

22 Keith Boykin, "No Blacks Allowed," *Temenos*, 2002, www.temenos.net/articles /12-23-04.shtml.

23 Kent Chuang, "Using Chopsticks to Eat Steak," *Journal of Homosexuality* 36, no. 3/4 (1999): 33.

24 Chong-suk Han, "They Don't Want to Cruise You're Type: Gay Men of Color and the Racial Politics of Exclusion," *Social Identities* 13, no. 1 (2007): 60.

25 Horacio N. Roque Ramirez, "That's My Place!: Negotiating Racial, Sexual, and Gender Politics in San Francisco's Gay Latino Alliance, 1975–1983," *Journal of the History of Sexuality* 12, no. 2 (2003): 229.

26 Roderick A. Ferguson, *Aberrations in Black: Toward a Queer of Color Critique* (Minneapolis: University of Minnesota Press, 2003), 40.

27 David L. Eng, *Racial Castration: Making Masculinity in Asian America* (Durham, NC: Duke University Press, 2001).

28 Scott Lauria Morgensen, *Spaces between Us: Queer Settler Colonialism and Indigenous Decolonization* (Minneapolis: University of Minnesota Press, 2011).

29 Jasbir K. Puar, *Terrorist Assemblages: Homonationalism in Queer Times* (Durham, NC: Duke University Press, 2007).

30 Noah Berlatsky, *Gays in the Military* (Detroit: Greenhaven, 2011). See also Suzanna D. Walters, *The Tolerance Trap: How God, Genes, and Good Intentions Are Sabotaging Gay Equality* (New York: New York University Press, 2014).

31 Patricia Hill Collins, *Black Feminist Thought* (New York: Routledge, 1990).

32 Jesús Gregorio Smith, "The Crime of Black Male Sexuality: Tiger Mandingo and Black Male Vulnerability," in *Home and Community for Queer Men of Color*, ed. Jesús Gregorio Smith and C. Winter Han (Lanham, MD: Lexington Books, 2020), 149–72.

33 Carol L. Gallently and Zita Lazzarini, "Charges for Criminal Exposure to HIV and Aggravated Prostitution Filed in the Nashville, Tennessee Prosecutorial Region 2000–2010," *AIDS and Behavior* 17, no. 8: 2624–36.

34 Adam I. Green, "Erotic Habitus: Towards a Sociology of Desire," *Theory and Society* 37, no. 6 (2008), 597.

35 Barbara Risman and Pepper Schwartz, "Sociological Research on Male and Female Homosexuality," *Annual Review of Sociology* 14 (1988): 125–47.

36 Green, "Erotic Habitus."

37 Lisa M. Diamond, "What Does Sexual Orientation Orient? A Biobehavioral Model Distinguishing Romantic Love and Sexual Desire," *Psychological Review* 110, no. 1 (2003): 173–92.

38 Green, "Erotic Habitus," 598.

39 Green, "Erotic Habitus."

40 Douglas E. Allen and Paul F. Anderson, "Consumption and Social Stratification: Bourdieu's Distinction," *Advances in Consumer Research* 21, no. 1 (1994), 70.

41 Emerich Daroya, "Potatoes and Rice: Exploring the Racial Politics of Gay Men's Desire and Desirability" (master's thesis, Carleton University, 2011), 59.

42 Rockney Jacobsen, "Desire, Sexual," in *Sex From Plato to Pagalia: A Philosophical Encyclopedia*, ed. Alan Soble (Westport: Greenwood, 2006), 222–28. See also Rockney Jacobsen, "Arousal and the End of Desire," *Philosophy and Phenomenological Research* 53, no. 3 (1993): 617–32; and Carol Vance, "Social Construction Theory: Problems in the History of Sexuality," in *Sexualities: Making a Sociology of Sexualities*, ed. Kenneth Plummer (London: Routledge, 2001), 356–71.

43 Wilhelm Hofman, Hiroki P. Kotabe, Kathleen D. Vohs, and Roy F. Baumeister, "Desire and Desire Regulation," in *The Psychology of Desire*, ed. Wilhelm Hofman and Loran F. Nordgren (New York: Guilford, 2015), 61–81.

44 Elena Faccio, Claudia Cassini, and Sabrina Cipolletta, "Forbidden Games: The Construction of Sexuality and Sexual Pleasure by BDSM 'Players,'" *Culture, Health & Sexuality* 16, no. 7 (2014): 1–13.

45 Nandita Chaudhary, *Listening to Culture: Constructing Reality from Everyday Talk* (Thousand Oaks: Sage, 2004).

46 Douglas Mason-Schrock, "Transsexuals' Narrative Construction of the 'True Self,'" *Social Psychology Quarterly* 59, no. 3 (1996): 176–92.

47 Kenneth J. Gergen and Mary M. Gergen, "Narrative of the Self," in *Studies in Social Identity*, ed. Theodore R. Sarbin and Karl E. Scheibe (New York: Praeger, 1983), 254–73.

48 Adalberto Aguirre, "Academic Storytelling: A Critical Race Theory Story of Affirmative Action," *Sociological Perspectives* 43, no. 2 (2000), 322.

49 Kevin A. Clarke and David M. Primo, "Overcoming 'Physics Envy,'" *New York Times*, March 20, 2012; See also Kevin A. Clarke and David M. Primo, A *Model Discipline: Political Science and the Logic of Representations* (London: Oxford University Press, 2012).

50 Cited in Marion Fourcade-Gourinchas, "Paul Krugman: The Wicked Economist?" ASA, *Footnotes*, May/June 2004, www.asanet.org/sites/default/files /savvy/footnotes/mayjun04/index.html.

51 Fourcade-Gourinchas, "Paul Krugman."

52 Clarke and Primo, "Overcoming 'Physics Envy.'"

53 Norman Fairclough, *Critical Discourse Analysis: The Critical Study of Language* (London: Routledge, 2010).

54 Phillip B. Harper, "The Evidence of Felt Intuition: Minority Experience, Everyday Life, and Critical Speculative Knowledge," *GLQ: A Journal of Lesbian and Gay Studies* 6, no. 1 (2000): 641–57.

55 Harper, "The Evidence of Felt Intuition," 649.

56 Harper, "The Evidence of Felt Intuition," 654.

57 Matt Brim and Amin Ghaziani, "Introduction: Queer Methods," *Women's Studies Quarterly* 44, no. 3/4 (2016), 16.

58 Yoosun Park, "Culture as Deficit: A Critical Discourse Analysis of the Concept of Culture in Contemporary Social Work Discourse," *Journal of Sociology and Social Welfare* 32, no. 2 (2005), 15.

59 Theo Van Leeuwen, "Genre and Field in Critical Discourse Analysis: A Synopsis," *Discourse & Society* 4, no. 2 (1993), 193.

60 Susa Ainsworth and Cynthia Hardy, "Critical Discourse Analysis and Identity: Why Bother?" *Critical Discourse Studies* 1, no. 2 (2004), 236.

61 Thomas Huckin, "Critical Discourse Analysis," in *Functional Approaches to Written Text: Classroom Applications*, ed. Tom Miller (Washington, DC: United States Information Agency, 1997), 78–92.

62 Chelsea Reynolds, "'I Am Super Straight and I Prefer You Be Too': Constructions of Heterosexual Masculinity in Online Personal Ads for 'Straight' Men Seeking Sex with Men," *Journal of Communication Inquiry* 39, no. 3 (2015): 213–31.

63 Judith Butler, *Bodies That Matter: On the Discursive Limits of Sex* (New York: Routledge, 1993).

64 José Esteban Muñoz, *Disidentifications: Queers of Color and the Performance of Politics* (Minneapolis: University of Minnesota Press, 1999), 31.

1 Chong-suk Han, "One Gay Asian Body: A Personal Narrative for Examining Human Behavior in the Social Environment," *Journal of Human Behavior in the Social Environment* 20, no. 1 (2010), 80.

2 Manisha Krishnan, "So Many Gay Dudes are Openly Racist on Dating Apps: It's Like Another World," *Vice*, January 21, 2016, www.vice.com/en_ca/article/bnpavv/so-many-gay-dudes-are-depressingly-racist-on-dating-apps.

3 Elizabeth Armstrong, *Forging Gay Identities: Organizing Sexuality in San Francisco, 1950-1994* (Chicago: University of Chicago Press, 2002). See also Dwight McBride, *Why I Hate Abercrombie and Fitch: Essays on Race and Sexuality* (New York: New York University Press, 2005); and Niels Teunis, "Sexual Objectification and the Construction of Whiteness in the Gay Male Community," *Culture, Health & Sexuality* 9, no. 3 (2007): 263–75.

4 Jesús Gregorio Smith, "Two-Faced Racism in Gay Online Sex," in *Sex in the Digital Age*, ed. Paul G. Nixon and Isabel K. Dusterhoft (New York: Routledge, 2017), 134–46. See also Jennifer H. Lundquist and Ken-Lou Lin, "Is Love (Color) Blind? The Economy of Race among Gay and Straight Daters," *Social Forces* 93, no. 4 (2015): 1423–99; and Matthew H. Rafalow, Cynthia Feliciano, and Belinda Robnett, "Racialized Femininity and Masculinity in the Preference of Online Same-Sex Daters," *Social Currents* 4, no. 4 (2017): 306–21.

5 Denton Callander, Christy E. Newman, and Martin Holt, "Is Sexual Racism Rally Racism? Distinguishing Attitudes toward Sexual Racism and Generic Racism among Gay and Bisexual Men," *Archives of Sexual Behavior* 44, no. 7 (2015): 1991–2000.

6 Adam I. Green, "The Social Organization of Desire: The Sexual Fields Approach," *Sociological Theory* 26, no. 1 (2008), 25.

7 Adam I. Green, "Playing the (Sexual) Field: The Interactional Basis of Systems of Sexual Stratification," *Social Psychology Quarterly* 74, no. 3 (2011), 254.

8 John L. Martin and Matt George, "Theories of Sexual Stratification: Toward an Analytics of the Sexual Field and a Theory of Sexual Capital," *Sociological Theory* 24, no. 2 (2006): 107–32.

9 Stephen Ellingson, Edward O. Laumann, Anthony Paik, and Jenna Mahay, "The Theory of Sex Markets," in *The Sexual Organization of the City*, ed. Edward O. Laumann, Stephen Elllingson, Jenna Mahay, Anthony Paik, and Yoosik Youm (Chicago: University of Chicago Press, 2004), 5.

10 Joan Nagel, *Race, Ethnicity, and Sexuality: Intimate Intersections, Forbidden Frontiers* (New York: Oxford University Press, 2003). See also David K. Whittier and William Simon, "The Fuzzy Matrix of 'My Type' in Intrapsychic Sexual Scripting," *Sexualities* 4, no. 2 (2001): 139–65.

11 Green, "Playing the (Sexual) Field."

12 Allen Bérubé, "How Gay Stays White and What Kind of White It Stays," in the *Making and Unmaking of Whiteness*, ed. Birgit B. Rasmussen, Eric Klinenberg, Irene J. Nexica, and Matt Wray (Durham, NC: Duke University Press, 2001), 234–65. See also Chong-suk Han, "They Don't Want to Cruise Your Type: Gay men of Color and the Racial Politics of Exclusion," *Social Identities* 13, no. 1 (2007).

13 C. Winter Han, *Geisha of a Different Kind: Race and Sexuality in Gaysian America* (New York: New York University Press, 2015), 141.

14 Jason L. Crockett, "Black and White Men Together: The Case of the Disappearing Organizational Narrative of Racial Sexual Orientation," *Making Connections: Interdisciplinary Approaches to Cultural Diversity* 16, no. 2 (2016): 88–116.

15 Han, *Geisha of a Different Kind.*

16 Green, "Playing the (Sexual) Field," 251.

17 Green, "Playing the (Sexual) Field," 244.

18 Jason Orne, *Boystown* (Chicago: University of Chicago Press, 2017), 67.

19 Susan Sontag, "The Double Standard of Aging," *Saturday Review*, September 1972, 38.

20 Rafalow, Feliciano, and Robnett, "Racialized Femininity."

21 Timothy Rawles, "Public Facebook Bear Community Group: 'No Africans, No Asians,'" *SDLGBTN*, June 26, 2018, https://sdlgbtn.com/news/2018/06/26 /public-facebook-bear-community-group-no-africans-no-asians.

22 Sharon Patricia Holland, *The Erotic Life of Racism* (Durham, NC: Duke University Press, 2012).

CHAPTER 2: DO YOU HAVE A HOT WHITE GUY?

1 John Walker, "Straight White Men Get More Mainstream Gay Magazine Covers Than Queer People of Color," *Splinter*, April 4, 2016, https://splinternews.com /straight-white-men-get-more-mainstream-gay-magazine-cov-1793855969.

2 Ben Freeman, "'Call Me By Your Name' and the Problem with Gay Roles Going to Straight Actors," *JUNKEE*, January 24, 2018, https://junkee.com/gay-roles -straight-actors/143890. See also Seamus Kirk, "'Call Me by Your Name' Is the Latest Gay-for-Pay Oscar Bait," *Them*, December 6, 2017, www.them.us/story /call-me-by-your-name-gay-for-pay-oscar-bait.

3 Richard Lawson, "Stonewall Is Terribly Offensive, and Offensively Terrible," *Vanity Fair*, September 22, 2015.

4 Shannon Keating, "Director Roland Emmerich Discusses 'Stonewall' Controversy," *BuzzFeed News*, September 22, 2015, www.buzzfeednews.com/article /shannonkeating/director-roland-emmerich-discusses-stonewall-controversy.

5 Jonathan Bernstein, "Roland Emmerich: 'I'd Like to Say I Was Driven Out of Germany by the Critics,'" *Guardian*, June 18, 2016.

6 George Lipsitz, *The Possessive Investment in Whiteness: How White People Profit from Identity Politics* (Philadelphia: Temple University Press, 1998).

7   Allan Bérubé, "How Gay Stays White and What Kind of White It Stays," in *The Making and Unmaking of Whiteness,* ed. Birgit B. Rasmussen, Eric Klinenberg, Irene J. Nexica, and Matt Wray (Durham, NC: Duke University Press, 2001), 235.

8   Joe R. Feagin, *The White Racial Frame: Centuries of Racial Framing and Counter Framing* (New York: Routledge, 2013).

9   Adam I. Green, "Erotic Habitus: Toward a Sociology of Desire," *Theory and Society* 37, no. 6 (2008), 597.

10 Jennifer Lundquist and Ken-Lou Lin, "Is Love (Color) Blind? The Economy of Race among Gay and Straight Daters," *Social Forces* 93, no. 4 (2015): 1423–99.

11 Green, "Erotic Habitus," 614.

12 Brandon A. Robinson, "'Personal Preference' as the New Racism: Gay Desire and Racial Cleansing in Cyberspace," *Sociology of Race and Ethnicity* 1, no. 2 (2015): 317–30. See also Denton Callander, Martin Holt, and Christy E. Newman, "'Not Everyone's Gonna Like Me': Accounting for Race and Racism in Sex and Dating Web Services for Gay and Bisexual Men," *Ethnicities* 16, no. 1 (2016): 3–21.

13 Green, "Erotic Habitus," 614.

14 Pierre Bourdieu, *Distinction: A Social Critique of the Judgement of Taste* (Cambridge, MA: Harvard University Press, 1984), 12 and 63.

15 Bourdieu, *Distinction,* 164 and 167.

16 Bourdieu, *Distinction,* 182.

17 Bourdieu, *Distinction.*

18 Douglas E. Allen and Paul F. Anderson, "Consumption and Social Stratification: Bourdieu's Distinction," *Advances in Consumer Research* 21, no. 1 (1994), 70.

19 Bourdieu, *Distinction,* 471.

20 Pierre Bourdieu and Loïc J. D. Wacquant, *An Invitation to Reflexive Sociology* (Chicago: University of Chicago Press, 1992), 167.

21 Loïc Wacquant, "Pierre Bourdieu," in *Key Sociological Thinkers,* ed. Rob Stones (London: Macmillan Education, 1998), 221.

22 Emerich Daroya, "Potatoes and Rice: Exploring the Racial Politics of Gay Men's Desire and Desirability" (master's thesis, Carleton University, 2011), 59.

23 Green, "Erotic Habitus," 599.

24 Richard Dyer, "The Matter of Whiteness," in *White Privilege: Essential Readings,* ed. Paula Rothenburg (New York: Worth Publishers, 2005), 9–14.

25 Erik T. Withers, "Whiteness and Culture," *Sociology Compass* 11, no. 4 (2016), 1.

26 Roland Barthes, *Mythologies* (New York: Farrar, Strauss & Giroux, 1972), 116.

27 William A. Gamson, David Croteau, William Hoynes, and Theodore Sasson, "Media Images and the Social Construction of Reality," *Annual Review of Sociology* 18 (1992): 373–93.

28 Stuart Hall, *Representations: Cultural Representations and Signifying Practices* (London: Open University Press, 1996), 4.

29 Andy Towle, "'The Advocate' Beefcakes Up with Jake Shears," *Towleroad,* June 30, 2020, www.towleroad.com/2010/06/the-advocate-beefcakes-up-with-jake-shears.

30 Audre Lorde, *Sister Outsider: Essays and Speeches* (Berkeley: Crossing Press, 1984).

31 Marisa Laudadio, "Lance Bass: 'I'm Gay,'" *People*, August 7, 2006.

32 David M. Halperin, "What is Gay Male Femininity?" in *American Guy: Masculinity in American Law and Literature*, ed. Saul Levmore and Martha C. Nussbaum (New York: Oxford University Press, 2014), 202.

33 Peter Moskowitz, "The Faggy Magic of Adam Rippon," *Splinter*, February 15, 2018, https://splinternews.com/the-faggy-magic-of-adam-rippon-1823028967.

34 Hall, *Representations*.

35 Feagin, *The White Racial Frame*.

36 Martin A. Berger, *Sight Unseen: Whiteness and American Visual Culture* (Berkeley: University of California Press, 2005), 73.

37 Withers, "Whiteness and Culture," 1.

38 Matthew Rodriguez, "D.C. Gay Bar JR's under Fire after Manager Requests 'Hot White Guy' Instead of Black Model on Ad," *Mic*, January 28, 2017, www.mic.com/articles/166954/dc-gay-bar-jrs-under-fire-after-manager-requests-hot-white-guy-instead-of-black-model-on-ad.

39 Steven Seidman, *Contested Knowledge: Social Theory Today* (Malden, MA: Wiley Blackwell, 2017), 237.

40 John Walker, "Straight White Men Get More Mainstream Gay Magazine Covers Than Queer People of Color."

41 Alex E. Jung, "Darren Criss on Playing Serial Killer Andrew Cunanan in ACS: Versace and Passing as White," *Vulture*, March 14, 2018, www.vulture.com/2018/03/darren-criss-american-crime-story-versace-and-race.html.

42 James Berger, *Ways of Seeing* (New York: Penguin Books, 1974).

43 Berger, *Ways of Seeing*, 54.

44 Jon-Michael Poff, "22 NSFW Gay Sex Scenes That Always Get the Blood Flowing," *BuzzFeed*, August 4, 2017, www.buzzfeed.com/jonmichaelpoff/tv-and-movie-gay-sex-scenes-that-turn-you-on.

45 Jon-Michael Poff, "Which TV or Movie Gay Scene Always Turns You the Fuck On?" *BuzzFeed*, July 28, 2017, www.buzzfeed.com/jonmichaelpoff/gay-sex-scene-add-yours?utm_term=.yvKe483NMo#.mwgjMVEYkm.

46 Zachry Zane, "9 Types of Tops You Encounter in the Sack," *Out*, September 10, 2018, www.out.com/photography/2018/9/10/9-types-tops-you-encounter-sack #media-gallery-media-0.

47 Javier Moreno, "21 Gorgeous Asian Men Guaranteed to Make You Thirsty," *BuzzFeed*, December 20, 2014, www.buzzfeed.com/javiermoreno/gorgeous-asian-men-guaranteed-to-make-you-thirsty; Pablo Valdivia, "A Definitive Ranking of Latino Men Who Caused Your Sexual Awakening," *BuzzFeed*, March 8, 2016, www.buzzfeed.com/pablovaldivia/latino-guys-who-sparked-your-sexual-awakening.

48 Kevin J. Nguyen, "Why Aren't Asian Men Sexy?" *BuzzFeed*, May 26, 2017, www.buzzfeed.com/kevinnguyen/why-arent-asian-men-sexy.

49 Dave, "Hot or Not: Shemar Moore," *Adam4Adam Blog*, January 31, 2013, https://adam4adamblogarchives.com/2013/01/hot-or-not-shemar-moore.

50 Dave, "Hot or Not: Daniel Henney," *Adam4Adam Blog*, November 3, 2017, https://adam4adamblog.com/blog/2017/11/hot-not-daniel-henney.

51 Dave, "Hot or Not: Red Heads," *Adam4Adam Blog*, June 8, 2012, https://adam4adamblogarchives.com/2012/06/hot-or-not-red-heads.

52 Richard Dyer, *The Matter of Images: Essays on Representations* (New York: Routledge, 1993), 9.

53 Serge Moscovici, "Forward," in *Health and Illness: A Social Psychological Analysis*, ed. Claudine Herzlich (London: Academic Press, 1973), xi.

54 Dyer, *The Matter of Images*, 10.

55 bell hooks, *Black Looks: Race and Representation* (Boston: South End Press, 1992).

56 Stephen Ellingson, Edward O. Laumann, Anthony Paik, and Jenna Mahay, "The Theory of Sex Markets," in *The Sexual Organization of the City*, ed. Edward O. Laumann, Stephen Ellingson, Jenna Mahay, Anthony Paik, and Yoosik Youm (Chicago: University of Chicago Press, 2004).

57 Peter Jackson, "That's What Rice Queens Study!: White Gay Desire and Representing Asian Homosexualities," *Journal of Australian Studies* 24, no. 65 (2000), 183.

58 Russell K. Robinson, "Structural Dimensions of Romantic Preferences," *Fordham Law Review* 86, no. 6 (2008).

CHAPTER 3: ALL HORNED UP AND LOOKING FOR SOME FUN

1 Dwight McBride, *Why I Hate Abercrombie & Fitch: Essays on Race and Sexuality* (New York: New York University Press, 2005).

2 McBride, *Why I Hate Abercrombie & Fitch*.

3 McBride, *Why I Hate Abercrombie & Fitch*, 103–4.

4 Mike Alvear, "Why Are Whites Always the Bottom in Interracial Porn?" *Huffington Post*, January 23, 2015, www.huffingtonpost.com/mike-alvear/why-are-whites-always-the_b_6503674.html.

5 Jarrett Neal, "Let's Talk about Interracial Porn," *Gay and Lesbian Review Worldwide* 20, no. 4 (2013), 24.

6 Susan Gubar, *Racechanges: White Skin, Black Face in American Culture* (New York: Oxford University Press, 2000).

7 Gubar, *Racechanges*, 175.

8 Patricia Hill Collins, *Black Sexual Politics: African Americans, Gender, and the New Racism* (New York: Routledge, 2004).

9 Gustavo Subero, "Gay Male Pornography and the Re/De/onstruction of Postcolonial Queer Identity in Mexico," *New Cinemas: Journal of Contemporary Film* 8, no. 2 (2010), 119.

10 Richard Fung, "Looking for My Penis: The Eroticized Asian in Gay Video Porn," in *How Do I Look? Queer Film & Video*, ed. Bad Object Choices (Seattle: Bay Press, 1991), 162.

11 Richard Mora, "Abjection and the Cinematic Cholo: The Chicano Gang Stereotype in Sociohistoric Context," *Boyhood Studies* 5, no. 2 (2011): 124–37.

12 Mora, "Abjection and the Cinematic Cholo."

13 Paisley Dalton, "If the Republicans Have a Problem with Diversity, So Does the Gay 'Community,'" *World of Wonder*, August 8, 2016, https://worldofwonder.net /republicans-problem-diversity-gay-community.

14 Victor Rios, *Punished: Policing the Lives of Black and Latino Boys* (New York: New York University Press, 2011). See also Lincoln Quillian and Devah Pager, "Estimating Risk: Stereotype Amplification and the Perceived Risk of Criminal Victimization," *Social Psychology Quarterly* 73, no. 1 (2011): 79–104.

15 Daniel Villarreal, "Gay Porn in the Trump Age Tackles Issues of Race, Some Not So Well," *Hornet*, July 11, 2017, https://hornetapp.com/stories/racist-gay-porn.

16 Trevon D. Logan, "Personal Characteristics, Sexual Behavior, and Male Sex Work: A Quantitative Approach," *American Sociological Review* 75, no. 5 (2010): 679–704.

17 Charles Berg, "Stereotyping in Films in General and of the Hispanic in Particular," *The Howard Journal of Communications* 2, no. 3 (1990), 296.

18 George Hadley-Garcia, *Hispanic Hollywood* (New York: Citadel, 1990).

19 Fung, "Looking for My Penis."

20 Logan, "Personal Characteristics, Sexual Behavior, and Male Sex Work."

21 Fung, "Looking for My Penis."

22 Nguyen Tan Hoang, *A View From the Bottom: Asian American Masculinity and Sexual Representation* (Durham, NC: Duke University Press, 2014).

23 Matthew H. Rafalow, Cynthia Feliciano, and Belinda Robnett, "Racialized Femininity and Masculinity in the Preference of Online Same-Sex Daters," *Social Currents* 4, no. 4 (2017): 306–21.

24 Nayan Shah, "Race-ing Sex," *Frontiers* 35, no. 1 (2014): 27.

25 Patrick A. Wilson, Pamela Valera, Ana Ventuneac, Ivan Balan, Matt Rowe, and Alex Carballo-Diéguez, "Race-Based Sexual Stereotyping and Sexual Partnering among Men Who Use the Internet to Identify Other Men for Bareback Sex," *The Journal of Sex Research* 46, no. 5 (2009): 399–413.

26 Gubar, *Racechanges*, 174.

27 Edward O. Laumann, Stephen Ellingson, Jenna Mahay, and Anthony Paik, eds., *The Sexual Organization of the City* (Chicago: University of Chicago Press, 2004).

28 David J. Lick and Kerri L. Johnson, "Intersecting Race and Gender Cues Are Associated with Perceptions of Gay Men's Preferred Sexual Roles," *Archives of Sexual Behavior* 44, no. 5 (2015): 1471.

29 Winston Husbands, Lydia Makoroka, Rinaldo Walcott, and Sean B. Rourke, "Black Gay Men as Sexual Subjects: Race, Racialization and the Social Relations of Sex among Black Gay Men in Toronto," *Culture, Health & Sexuality* 15, no. 4 (2013): 434–49. See also Chong-suk Han, "A Qualitative Exploration of

the Relationship between Racism and Unsafe Sex among Asian Pacific Islander Gay Men," *Archives of Sexual Behavior* 37, no. 5 (2008): 827–37.

30 Simon B. R. Rosser, Michael Wilerson, Derek J. Smolenski, J. Michael Oaks, Joseph Konstan, Keith J. Horvath, Gunna R. Kilian, David S. Novak, Gene P. Danilenko, and Richard Morgan, "The Future of Internet-Based HIV Prevention: A Report on Key Findings from the Men's INTernet (MINTS-I, II) Sex Studies," *AIDS and Behavior* 15, no. S1 (2011): S89–S100.

31 Tikkanen Ronny and Michael W. Ross, "Technological Tearoom Trade: Characteristics of Swedish Men Visiting Gay Internet Chatroom," *AIDS Education and Prevention* 15, no. 2 (2003): 122–32.

32 Denton Callander, Martin Holt, and Chrissy E. Newman, "'Not Everyone's Gonna Like Me': Accounting for Race and Racism in Sex and Dating Web Services for Gay and Bisexual Men," *Ethnicities* 16, no. 1 (2016): 3–21.

33 Elizabeth M. Morgan, Tamara C. Richards, and Emily M. VanNess, "Comparing Narratives of Personal and Preferred Partner Characteristics in Online Dating Advertisements," *Computers in Human Behavior* 26, no. 5 (2010): 883–88.

34 Elizabeth Jagger, "Is Thirty the New Sixty? Dating, Age and Gender in Postmodern, Consumer Society," *Sociology* 39, no. 1 (2005): 89–106.

35 James D. Ross, "Personal Ads and the Intersection of Race and Same-Sex Male Attraction." In *Racialized Politics of Desire in Personal Ads*, ed. Neal A. Lester and Maureen Daly Goggin (Lanham, MD: Lexington Books, 2008), 97.

36 Neal A. Lester and Maureen Daly Goggin, "In Living Color: Politics of Desire in Heterosexual Interracial Black/White Personal Ads," *Communication and Critical/Cultural Studies* 2, no. 2 (2015): 131.

37 Wilson et. al., "Race-Based Sexual Stereotyping."

38 Voon Chin Phua and Gayle Kaufman, "The Crossroads of Race and Sexuality: Date Selection among Men in Internet 'Personal' Ads," *Journal of Family Issues* 24, no. 8 (2003): 981–94. See also Jennifer H. Lundquist and Ken-Lou Lin, "Is Love (Color) Blind? The Economy of Race among Gay and Straight Daters," *Social Forces* 93, no. 4 (2015): 1423–99.

39 Jay P. Paul, George Ayala, and Kyung-Hee Choi, "Internet Sex Ads for MSM and Partner Selection Criteria: The Potency of Race/Ethnicity Online," *Journal of Sex Research* 47, no. 6 (2010): 528–38.

40 Joel Kovel, *White Racism: A Psychohistory* (New York: Pantheon, 1970).

41 Erica Owens and Brownwyn Beistle, "Eating the Black Body: Interracial Desire, Food Metaphor and White Fear," in *Body/Embodiment: Symbolic Interaction and the Sociology of the Body*, ed. Dennis Waskul and Phillip Vannini (Aldershot, UK: Ashgate, 2006), 203.

42 Lynne Segal, *Slow Motion: Changing Masculinities Changing Men* (New Brunswick, NJ: Rutgers University Press, 1990), 176.

43 Sarah K. Calabrese, Valerie A. Earnshaw, Manya Magnus, Nathan B. Hansen, Douglas S. Krakower, Kristen Underhill, Kenneth H. Mayer, Trace S. Kershaw, Joseph R. Betancourt, and John F. Dovidio, "Sexual Stereotypes Ascribed to

Black Men Who Have Sex with Men: An Intersectional Analysis," *Archives of Sexual Behavior* 47, no. 1 (2017): 143–56.

44 Frantz Fanon, *Black Skin, White Masks* (New York: Grove, 1970), 120.

45 Cornel West, *Race Matters* (New York: Vintage, 1993).

46 Edward Said, *Orientalism* (New York: Pantheon, 1978).

47 Paul, Ayala, and Choi, "Internet Sex Ads."

48 bell hooks, *Black Looks: Race and Representation* (Boston: South End, 1992), 21.

49 Patricia Hill Collins, *Black Feminist Thought* (New York: Routledge, 1990), 69.

50 hook, *Black Looks*, 21.

51 Sharon Patricia Holland, *The Erotic Life of Racism* (Durham, NC: Duke University Press, 2012).

52 Holland, *The Erotic Life of Racism*.

53 C. Winter Han, *Geisha of a Different Kind: Race and Sexuality in Gaysian America* (New York: New York University Press, 2015), 112.

54 Cory J. Cascalheira and Brandt A. Smith, "Hiearchy of Desire: Partner Preferences and Social Identities of Men Who Have Sex with Men on Geosocial Networks," *Sexuality & Culture* 24, no. 3 (2020): 630–48.

55 Jennifer C. Nash, *The Black Body in Ecstasy: Reading Race, Reading Pornography* (Durham, NC: Duke University Press, 2014). See also Mireille Miller-Young, *A Taste for Brown Sugar: Black Women in Pornography* (Durham, NC: Duke University Press, 2014); and Ariane Cruz, *The Color of Kink: Black Women, BDSM, and Pornography* (New York: New York University Press, 2016).

56 José Esteban Muñoz, *Disidentifications: Queers of Color and the Performance of Politics* (Minneapolis: University of Minnesota Press, 1999).

57 Miller-Young, *A Taste for Brown Sugar*, 275.

58 Nash, *The Black Body in Ecstasy*, 3.

59 Nash, *The Black Body in Ecstasy*, 6.

60 Cruz, *The Color of Kink*, 71.

61 Miguel Muñoz-Laboy and Nicolette Severson, "Exploring the Role of Race, Ethnicity, Nationality, and Skin Color in the Sexual Partner Choices of Bisexual Latino Men," *Archives of Sexual Behavior* 47, no. 4 (2017): 1231–39.

CHAPTER 4: DAN SAVAGE WEPT FOR OBAMA

1 Kevin Clarke, "PHOTOS: A History of Hairy Guys," *Queerty*, November 8, 2013, www.queerty.com/photos-a-history-of-hairy-guys-20131108.

2 Lester Fabian Brathwaite, "Chick-fil-A Chief Dan Cathy Receiving Equality Award," *Queerty*, November 15, 2013, www.queerty.com/chick-fil-a-ceo-dan -cathy-receiving-equality-award-20131115.

3 Lawrence Ferber, "Seven LGBT African-Americans Who Changed the Face of the Gay Community," *Queerty*, February 1, 2012, www.queerty.com/seven-lgbt-african -americans-who-changed-the-face-of-the-gay-community-20120201.

4 Rob Smith, "Five Black LGBTQ Blogs You Need to Start Reading ASAP," *Queerty*, March 14, 2016, www.queerty.com/five-black-lgbt-blogs-you-need-to -start-reading-asap-20160314.

5 Mark Joseph Stern, "I'm Grateful to Be Gay—Otherwise I Might Have Been a Horrible Person," *Slate*, November 26, 2014, https.//slate.com/human-Interest /2014/11/im-grateful-to-be-gay-because-otherwise-i-might-have-been-a-horrible -person.html.

6 Mike Alvear, "Are We More Racist Than Straight Men?" *Queerty*, April 8, 2015, www.queerty.com/poll-are-we-more-racist-than-straight-men-20150408.

7 Dan Savage, "Black Homophobia SLOG," *Stranger*, November 5, 2008, http://slog .thestranger.com/2008/11/black_homophobia.

8 Michael Joseph Gross, "Gay Is the New Black?" *Advocate*, November 16, 2018, www.advocate.com/news/2008/11/16/gay-new-black.

9 Eduardo Bonilla-Silva, "The Linguistics of Color Blind Racism: How to Talk Nasty about Blacks without Sounding 'Racist,'" *Critical Sociology* 28, no. 1/2 (2002): 41–64.

10 Christian S. Crandall, Amy Eshleman, and Laurie O'Brien, "Social Norms and the Expression and Suppression of Prejudice: The Struggle for Internalization," *Journal of Personality and Social Psychology* 82, no. 3 (2002): 359–78.

11 Martha Augoustinos and Danielle Every, "Contemporary Racist Discourse: Taboos against Racism and Racist Accusations," in *Language, Discourse and Social Psychology*, ed. Ann Weatherall, Bernadette Watson, and Cindy Gallois (London: Palgrave, 2015), 233–54.

12 Bonilla-Silva, "The Linguistics of Color Blind Racism."

13 Teun van Dijk, "Discourse and the Denial of Racism," Discourse and Society 3, no. 1 (1992), 87.

14 Bonilla-Silva, "The Linguistics of Color Blind Racism," 42.

15 van Dijk, "Discourse and the Denial of Racism."

16 van Dijk, "Discourse and the Denial of Racism."

17 Martha Augoustinos and Danielle Every, "The Language of 'Race' and Prejudice: A Discourse of Denial, Reason, and Liberal-Practical Politics," *Journal of Language and Social Psychology* 26, no. 2 (2007): 123–41.

18 Samuel R. Sommers and Michael I. Norton, "Lay Theories about White Racists: What Constitutes Racism (and What Doesn't)," *Group Processes and Intergroup Relations* 9, no 1 (2006): 117–38.

19 Simon Goodman and Shani Burke, "'Oh You Don't Want Asylum Seekers, Oh You're Just Racist: A Discursive Analysis of Discussions about Whether it's Racist to Oppose Asylum Seeking," *Discourse & Society* 21, no. 3 (2010): 235–340.

20 Clemence Due, "'Aussie Humour' or Racism? Hey Hey It's Saturday and the Denial of Racism in Online Responses to News Media Articles," *PLATFORM: Journal of Media and Communication* 3, no. 1 (2011), 38.

21 Kevin Durrheim, Ross Greener, and Kevin A. Whitehead, "Race Trouble: Attending to Race and Racism in Online Interactions," *British Journal of Social Psychology* 54, no. 1 (2015): 4–99.

22 van Dijk, "Discourse and the Denial of Racism."

23 Damien W. Riggs and Clemence Due, "The Management of Racism in Celebrity Big Brother," *Discourse & Society* 21, no. 3 (2010): 257–71.

24 Nathan Manske, "Racism or Just Preference? 'You're Really Sweet, I'm Just Not into Black Guys,'" *LGBTQ Nation*, January 4, 2015, www.lgbtqnation.com/2015/01/racism-or-just-preference-youre-really-sweet-im-just-not-into-black-guys.

25 Dan Tracer, "Scruff Founders Defend App's Ethnicity Filters—'Personal Preference' or Casual Racism?" *Queerty*, February 10, 2016, www.queerty.com/scruff-founders-defend-apps-ethnicity-filters-personal-preference-or-casual-racism-20160210.

26 Derek de Koff, "Is This the Brutal Truth White Gay Men Refuse to Hear?" *Queerty*, June 1, 2016, www.queerty.com/brutal-truth-white-gay-men-refuse-hear-20160601.

27 *Queerty*, "Is Racism among the Gays the Worst It's Been in Decades?" *Queerty*, August 11, 2009, www.queerty.com/is-racism-among-the-gays-the-worst-its-been-in-decades-20090811.

28 Graham Gremore, "Grindr Wants Users to Stop Being So Racist and Start Being 'Kindr'—But Is That Even Possible?" *Queerty*, July 30, 2018, www.queerty.com/grindr-wants-users-stop-racist-start-kindr-even-possible-20180730.

29 David Hudson, "Sexual Racism on Queer Dating Apps Screws with Your Mental Health," *Queerty*, September 15, 2019, www.queerty.com/sexual-racism-queer-dating-apps-screws-mental-health-20190915#comments.

30 van Dijk, "Discourse and the Denial of Racism."

31 "Confronting Racism in the Gay Community," *Queerty*, January 7, 2017, www.queerty.com/watch-wilson-cruz-alec-mapa-join-conversation-racism-gay-community-20170107.

32 *Queerty*, "Is Racism among the Gays the Worst It's Been in Decades?"

33 Graham Gremore, "Are You an Unwitting Sexual Racist? Find Out," *Queerty*, July 8, 2017, www.queerty.com/unwitting-sexual-racist-find-20170708.

34 Graham Gremore, "Asian Man Fed Up With Being Ignored by the 'White-Painted Gay Community,'" *Queerty*, January 14, 2016, www.queerty.com/asian-man-fed-up-with-being-ignored-by-the-white-painted-gay-community-20160114.

35 Graham Gremore, "If You Still Don't Understand Why Your 'Preferences' Are Racist, This Video Might Help Explain," *Queerty*, February 9, 2018, www.queerty.com/still-dont-understand-preferences-racist-video-might-help-explain-20180209.

36 "Michael Sam: There's More Racism in Gay Community Than Homophobia in Black Community," *LGBTQ Nation*, March 31, 2016, www.lgbtqnation.com/2016/03/michael-sam-theres-more-racism-in-gay-community-than-homophobia-in-black-community.

37 Japhy Grant, "Is the Gay Community Racist?" *Queerty*, January 9, 2009, www
    .queerty.com/friday-forum-is-the-gay-community-racist-20090109.
38 Gremore, "Asian Man Fed Up With Being Ignored."
39 Gremore, "Grindr Wants Users to Stop Being So Racist."
40 Daniel Villarreal, "Has Grindr Turned Gay Men into Racist, Homophobic Body
    Fascists?" *Queerty*, October 17, 2011, www.queerty.com/has-grindr-turned-gay
    -men-into-racist-homophobic-body-facists-20111017.
41 "This Is Nelson. He Has Something to Say about Racism in the Gay Community.
    You Should Listen," *Queerty*, January 1, 2015, www.queerty.com/this-is-nelson
    -he-has-something-to-say-about-racism-in-the-gay-community-you-should
    -listen-20150101.
42 Bonilla-Silva, "The Linguistics of Color Blind Racism," 28.
43 Dan Avery, "Gay Couples More Likely to Be Interracial, Multiethnic Than
    Straights," *Queerty*, April 26, 2012, www.queerty.com/census-gay-couples-more
    -likely-to-be-interracial-multiethnic-than-straights-20120426.
44 "Are Scruff's Ethnicity Filters Racist?" *LGBTQ Nation*, February 11, 2016, www
    .lgbtqnation.com/2016/02/are-scruffs-ethnicity-filters-racist.
45 Villarreal, "Has Grindr Turned Gay men Into Racist?"
46 "This Is Nelson."
47 Bonilla-Silva, "The Linguistics of Color Blind Racism."
48 de Koff, "Is This the Brutal Truth?"
49 Graham Gremore, "Photographer Hopes to End Sexual Racism with Stunning
    New Photo Book Celebrating Asian Men," *Queerty*, May 24, 2019, www.queerty
    .com/photographer-hopes-end-sexual-racism-stunning-new-photo-book
    -celebrating-asian-men-20190524.
50 Gwendolyn Smith, "A Gay Dating App Is Relaunching. With a Ban on Sexual
    Racism," *LGBTQ Nation*, September 12, 2018, www.lgbtqnation.com/2018/09
    /chappy-relaunches-zero-tolerance-stance-abuse/.
51 "Are Scruff's Ethnicity Filters Racist?"
52 Tracer, "Scruff Founders Defend App's Ethnicity Filters."

CHAPTER 5: DON'T TRUST ANY BLACK GAY WHO HAS "TEAMSWIRL"
IN THEIR BIO

1 Theo Greene, "Hmm . . . I'm going to lay this down here," Facebook, July 14, 2018,
   www.facebook.com/theo.greene.75?he_ref=ARRaS60X4Q354cyxMRDFXNU
   v40NY5nUgvGaVBqEzh6MKF_2ei4g-TqiXnrwWwouk_51&fref=nf.
2 "The Jack'd Racism Study: Asians Are as Racists as Whites," *Angry Homosexual*,
   November 15, 2014, https://angryhomosexual.com/jackd-racism-study.
3 Gary Gates, *Demographics of Married and Unmarried Same-Sex Couples: Analysis of
   the 2013 American Community Survey* (Los Angeles: UCLA School of Law, the
   Williams Institute, 2015). See also Gregory Phillips, Michelle Birkett, Sydney
   Hammond, and Brian Mustanski, "Partner Preference among Men Who Have

Sex with Men: Potential Contribution to Spread of HIV within Minority Populations," *LGBT Health* 3, no. 3 (2003): 225–32; and Russell K. Robinson and David M. Frost, "LGBT Equality and Sexual Racism," *Fordham Law Review* 86, no. 6 (2018): 2739–54.

4 Angeliki Kastanis and Bianca D. M. Wilson, *Race/Ethnicity, Gender and Socioeconomic Wellbeing of Individuals in Same-Sex Couples* (Los Angeles: UCLA School of Law, the Williams Institute, 2014).

5 Gretchen Livingston and Anna Brown, "Intermarriage in the U.S. 50 Years after *Loving v. Virginia*," *Pew Research Center*, May 18, 2017, www.pewsocialtrends.org /2017/05/18/intermarriage-in-the-u-s-50-years-after-loving-v-virginia.

6 Joseph Beam, *In the Life: A Black Gay Anthology* (New York: Alyson, 1986), 17.

7 Tony Ayres, "'China Doll: The Experience of Being a Gay Chinese Australian," *Journal of Homosexuality* 36, no. 3/4 (1999): 91.

8 Ayres, "China Doll," 91.

9 Ayres, "China Doll," 96.

10 Ayres, "China Doll," 92.

11 Manolo Guzman, *Gay Hegemony/Latino Homosexualities* (New York: Routledge, 2006), 26.

12 Guzman, *Gay Hegemony/Latino Homosexualities*, 62.

13 Darieck Scott, "Jungle Fever? Black Gay Identity Politics, White Dick, and the Utopian Bedroom," *GLQ: A Journal of Lesbian and Gay Studies* 1, no. 3 (1994), 299.

14 L. Lloyd Jordan, "Black Gay vs. Gay Black," *BLK* 2, no. 6 (1990), as cited in Scott, "Jungle Fever?" 300.

15 Scott, "Jungle Fever?" 300.

16 Guzman, *Gay Hegemony/Latino Homosexualities*, 73.

17 Philip Tsui, "Power and Intimacy: Caucasian/Asian Gay Relationships as an Indicator of Self-Oppression among Gay Asian Males," *Journal of the Asian American Psychological Association* (1986), 59.

18 Maurice K. Poon and Peter T. Ho, "Negotiating Social Stigma among Gay Asian Men," *Sexualities* 11, no. 1/2 (2008): 245–68.

19 Peter A. Jackson, "That's What Rice Queens Study! White Gay Desire and Representing Asian Homosexualities," *Journal of Australian Studies* 24, no. 65 (2000): 181–88.

20 Gayle Kaufman and Voon Chin Phua, "Is Ageism Alive in Dating Selection among Men? Age Requests among Gay and Straight Men in Internet Personal Ads," *Journal of Men's Studies* 11, no. 2 (2003): 225–35.

21 Scott, "Jungle Fever?" 301.

22 Jeff Baker, "Dear Queer Black Activists: An Honest Letter about Desirability Politics among Our Men," *The Body Is Not an Apology*, September 2, 2018 https:// thebodyisnotanapology.com/magazine/dear-queer-black-activists-an-honest -letter-about-desirability-politics-among-our-men.

23 Guzman, *Gay Hegemony/Latino Homosexualities*.

24 Guzman, *Gay Hegemony/Latino Homosexualities*, 77.

25 Gayatri Chakravorty Spivak, "Can the Subaltern Speak?" in *Marxism and the Interpretation of Cultures*, ed. Cary Nelson and Lawrence Greenberg (Chicago: University of Illinois Press, 1988), 271–313.

26 Katya Azoulay, "Experience, Empathy and Strategic Essentialism," *Cultural Studies* 11, no. 1 (1997): 89–110.

27 Azoulay, "Experience, Empathy and Strategic Essentialism," 102.

28 bell hooks, *Black Looks: Race and Representation* (Boston: South End, 1992); Guzman, *Gay Hegemony/Latino Homosexualities*.

29 Charles E. Wilson, "Black Gay Men Seeking Black Gay Men: Cultural and Historical Implications," in *Racialized Politics of Desire in Personal Ads*, ed. Neal A. Lester and Maureen Daly Goggin (New York: Lexington, 2007),434–49.

30 Cynthia Wu, *Sticky Rice: A Politics of Intraracial Desire* (Philadelphia: Temple University Press, 2018), 1.

31 Kenneth Chan, "Rice Sticking Together: Cultural Nationalist Logic and Cinematic Representations of Gay Asian-Caucasian Relationships and Desire," *Discourse* 28, no. 2/3 (2006), 181.

32 Lester Fabian Brathwaite, "White Guilt: Reconciling the Colonization of My Desire," *NewNowNext*, July 20, 2017, http://articles.newnownext-q.mtvi.com/white-guilt-reconciling-the-colonization-of-my-desire/07/2017.

33 Reneysh Vittal, "Why I'll Never Date a Man Whose Skin Looks Like Mine," *Narratively*, June 21, 2016 https://narratively.com/why-ill-never-date-a-man-whose-skin-looks-like-mine.

34 John Paul Brammer, "Is Reverse Racism Real and Affecting My Dating Life?" *Into*, August 16, 2017, www.intomore.com/you/is-reverse-racism-real-and-affecting-my-dating-life.

35 Brammer, "Is Reverse Racism Real." Emphasis in original.

36 Veronica Wells, "'I'm Not about That Life' Don Lemon Says Relationships with Black Men Didn't Work Because They Weren't Out," *Madamenoire*, February 12, 2019, https://madamenoire.com/1060255/im-not-about-that-life-don-lemon-says-relationships-with-black-men-didnt-work-because-they-werent-out.

37 Jeremy Helligar, "Don't Hate Me Because I'm Not Dating Other Black Men," *Huffington Post*, April 18, 2017, www.huffpost.com/entry/dont-hate-me-because-im-not-dating-other-black-men_b_58efocf4e4b0156697224c79.

38 Dan Avery, "Hip-Hop Artist Steve Lacy Says He's Bisexual: But Would Never Date a Black Guy," *NewNowNext*, October 3, 2017, www.newnownext.com/steve-lacy-bisexual-wont-date-black-guys/10/2017.

39 Terrence Chappell, "Yes I Date White Men, No I Don't Hate Myself," *JET*, February 3, 2016, www.jetmag.com/jetlove/yes-i-date-white-men-no-i-dont-hate-myself/#comment-16217.

40 Lamar Dawson, "'Dear White People' Creator Justin Simien: 'You Can Date a White Guy and Still Be Black as F*ck," *NewNowNext*, April 25, 2019, www.newnownext.com/dear-white-people-justin-simien-gay-lionel/04/2018.

41 Jeremy Helligar, "What If I Only Dated Black Men?" *Queerty*, March 25, 2018, www.queerty.com/dated-black-men-20180325.

42 Hari Ziyad, "Neo-Nazi Milo Yiannopoulos's Black Husband Proves 'You Can't Help Whom You Love' Is White Supremacist Bullshit," *Afropunk*, October 2, 2017, https://afropunk.com/2017/10/neo-nazi-milo-yiannopouloss-black-husband -proves-cant-help-love-white-supremacist-bullshit.

43 Jeremy Helligar, "I'm Black and All My Exes Are White. Does That Make Me Racist?" *Good Men Project*, March 5, 2017, https://goodmenproject.com/featured -content/im-black-and-all-my-exes-are-white-does-that-make-me-racist-lbkr.

44 Donovan Trott, "An Open Letter to Gay, White Men: No, You're Not Allowed to Have a Racial Preference," *Huffington Post*, June 19, 2017, www.huffpost.com /entry/an-open-letter-to-gay-white-men-no-youre-not-allowed_b_5947f0ffe4b0 f7875b83e459.

45 Justin James, "Why I'm Not Bothered About C**ning Black Gays Who Experi- ence the Racism They Perpetuate," *King of Reads*, August 24, 2017, www.king ofreads.com/im-not-bothered-cooning-black-gays-experiencing-racism -perpetuate.

46 Enrico DG, "Bananas Can Learn," *GayAsianmale.com*, January 19, 2018, https:// gayasianmale.com/blog/bananas-can-learn.

47 Enrico DG, "Bananas Can Learn."

48 David Ng, "Poking at My Dating Preferences," *GayAsianmale.com*, August 14, 2017, https://gayasianmale.com/blog/poking-dating-preferences.

49 "Five Reasons Gay Asians Should Give Up Potatoes," *Angry Homosexual*, April 11, 2013, https://angryhomosexual.com/5-reasons-gay-asians-should-give-up -potatoes.

50 The five reasons were (1) you need white guys more than they need you; (2) you'll eventually get dumped for a younger, cuter Asian; (3) rice queens don't care about you as an individual; (4) potatoes age faster; and (5) you will end up old and lonely.

51 Jamal Jordan, "Queer Love in Color," *New York Times*, June 21, 2018.

52 Eliel Cruz, "Love in Black and White: Loving Myself Was a Radical Act," *Out*, January 12, 2017, www.out.com/out-exclusives/2017/1/12/love-black-and-white -loving-myself-was-radical-act.

53 Chaaz Quigley, "No White Boys, Just a Preference," *Hornet*, April 1, 2016, https:// hornet.com/stories/no-white-boys-just-a-preference.

54 Quigley, "No White Boys."

55 Quigley, "No White Boys"; Guzman, *Gay Hegemony/Latino Homosexualities*.

56 Darnell L. Moore, "Black Men Loving Black Men Is a Revolutionary Act," *NewNowNext*, May 11, 2017, www.newnownext.com/black-men-loving-black -men-is-a-revolutionary-act/05/2017.

57 Phillip Henry, "Dear White Gay Men, Racism Is Not 'Just a Preference,'" *Them*, January 19, 2018, www.them.us/story/racism-is-not-a-preference.

58 Aaron Gettinger, "Falling for Angels Explores Asian Men Leaving Gay Racism Behind," *Advocate*, December 8, 2017, www.advocate.com/arts-entertainment /2017/12/08/falling-angels-explores-asian-men-leaving-gay-racism-behind.

59 André-Naquian Wheeler, "As a Queer Black Male, I'm Tired of Being Fetishized on Grindr," *Vice i-D*, May 31, 2018, https://i-d.vice.com/en_us/article/pav3vk/as -a-queer-black-male-im-tired-of-being-fetishized-on-grindr.

60 Michael Arceneaux, "I'm a Black Gay Man Learning to Be Okay with Dating People Who Don't Look like Me," *Washington Post*, June 15, 2015.

61 Arceneaux, "I'm a Black Gay Man Learning to be Okay."

62 Myles E. Johnson, "On Being Left for White Men," *Black Youth Project*, July 26, 2017, https://blackyouthproject.com/left-white-men.

63 Anthony Williams, "Why I Stopped Dating White Men," *BGD*, September 15, 2015, www.bgdblog.org/2015/09/why-i-stopped-dating-white-men.

64 Williams, "Why I Stopped Dating White Men."

65 Williams, "Why I Stopped Dating White Men."

66 Zach Stafford, "The Black, Gay Community May Be Out—But It's Not Proud," *Guardian*, July 5, 2015.

67 Stafford, "The Black, Gay Community May Be Out."

68 Prince Royce Worthington, "Dear Gay Men of Color: Stop Begging Racist White Gay Men to Love You," *Ashton P. Woods Blog*, April 23, 2017, www.ashtonpwoods .com/theblog/dear-gay-men-of-color-stop-begging-racist-white-gay-men-to -love-you.

69 Worthington, "Dear Gay Men of Color."

70 Ziyad, "Neo-Nazi Milo Yiannopoulos's Black Husband."

71 Ziyad, "Neo-Nazi Milo Yiannopoulos's Black Husband."

72 SF Weekly Staff, "You Can't Be Gay—You're Latino," *San Francisco Weekly*, April 14, 1999, www.sfweekly.com/news/you-cant-be-gay-youre-latino.

73 Aaron Barksdale, "What It's Like to Be a Gay Black Man Who Has Only Dated White Men," *Refinery29*, March 4, 2016, www.refinery29.com/en-us /race-and-dating; Avery Ware, "To the Black Man Who Only Dates White Men," *Jettison*, March 14, 2016, http://jettisonarchive.com/home/1358/to-the -black-man-who-only-dates-white-men.

74 Efren Bose, "Gay Interracial Relationships: On Being 'Sticky Rice' and Loving Other Asian Men," *8Asians*, June 17, 2008, www.8asians.com/2008/06/17/gay -interracial-relationships-on-being-sticky-rice-and-loving-other-asian-men.

75 Bose, "Gay Interracial Relationships."

CONCLUSION

1 https://www.kindr.grindr.com.

2 Stuart Hall, *Representations: Cultural Representations and Signifying Practices* (London: Open University Press, 1996), 69.

3 Richard Dyer, *The Matter of Images: Essays on Representations* (New York: Routledge, 1993), 1.

4 Michael Waters, "'Love, Simon': What the Critics Are Saying," *Hollywood Reporter*, March 13, 2016, www.hollywoodreporter.com/news/
love-simon-what-critics-are-saying-1094227.

5 *Love, Simon*, directed by Greg Berlanti, written by Isaac Aptaker and Elizabeth Berger (2018, 20th Century Fox).

6 Patricia Hill Collins, *Black Feminist Thought* (New York: Routledge, 1990).

7 David L. Eng, *Racial Castration: Making Masculinity in Asian America* (Durham, NC: Duke University Press, 2001). See also Roderick A. Ferguson, *Aberrations in Black: Toward a Queer of Color Critique* (Minneapolis: University of Minnesota Press, 2003); and Hiram Perez, *A Taste for Brown Bodies: Gay Modernity and Cosmopolitan Desires* (New York: New York University Press).

8 Chong-suk Han, "A Qualitative Exploration of the Relationship between Racism and Unsafe Sex among Asian Pacific Islander Gay Men," *Archives of Sexual Behavior* 37, no. 5 (2008): 827–37.

9 bell hooks, *Black Looks: Race and Representation* (Boston: South End, 1992).

10 Anthony C. Ocampo, "Making Masculinity: Negotiations of Gender Presentation among Latino Gay Men," *Latino Studies* 10, no. 4 (2012), 452.

11 Kyung-Hee Choi, Jay Paul, George Ayala, Ross Boylan, and Steven E. Gregorich, "Experiences of Discrimination and Their Impact on the Mental Health among African American, Asian and Pacific Islander, and Latino Men Who Have Sex with Men," *American Journal of Public Health* 103, no. 5 (2013): 868–74. See also Alain Dang and Mandy Hu, *Asian Pacific American Lesbian, Gay, Bisexual and Transgender People: A Community Portrait* (New York: National Gay and Lesbian Task Force, 2005); and Gladys E. Ibañez, Barbara Van Oss Marin, Stephen A. Flores, Gregorio Millett, and Rafael M. Diaz, "General and Gay-Related Racism Experienced by Latino Gay Men," *Cultural Diversity and Ethnic Minority Psychology* 15, no. 3 (2009): 215–22.

12 Adam I. Green, "The Social Organization of Desire," *Sociological Theory* 26, no. 1 (2008): 25–50.

13 Jasbir K. Puar, *Terrorist Assemblages* (Durham, NC: Duke University Press, 2007).

14 Jose Esteban Muñoz, *Disidentifications: Queers of Color and the Performance of Politics* (Minneapolis: University of Minnesota Press, 1999).

15 Collins, *Black Feminist Thought*.

16 Jennifer C. Nash, *The Black Body in Ecstasy: Reading Race, Reading Pornography* (Durham, NC: Duke University Press, 2014). See also Ariane Cruz, *The Color of Kink: Black Women, BDSM, and Pornography* (New York: New York University Press, 2016); and Mireille Miller-Young, *A Taste for Brown Sugar: Black Women in Pornography* (Durham, NC: Duke University Press, 2014).

BIBLIOGRAPHY

Aguirre, Adalberto. "Academic Storytelling: A Critical Race Theory Story of Affirmative Action." *Sociological Perspectives* 43, no. 2 (2000): 319–39.

Ainsworth, Susan, and Cynthia Hardy. "Critical Discourse Analysis and Identity: Why Bother?" *Critical Discourse Studies* 1, no. 2 (2004): 225–59.

Allen, Douglas E., and Paul F. Anderson. "Consumption and Social Stratification: Bourdieu's Distinction." *Advances in Consumer Research* 21, no. 1 (1994): 70–74.

Armstrong, Elizabeth. *Forging Gay Identities: Organizing Sexuality in San Francisco, 1950–1994.* Chicago: University of Chicago Press, 2002.

Augoustinos, Martha, and Danielle Every. "Contemporary Racist Discourse: Taboos against Racism and Racist Accusations." In *Language, Discourse and Social Psychology*, edited by Ann Weatherall, Bernadette Watson, and Cindy Gallois, 233–54. London: Palgrave, 2015.

———. "The Language of 'Race' and Prejudice: A Discourse of Denial, Reason, and Liberal-Practical Politics." *Journal of Language and Social Psychology* 26, no. 2 (2007): 123–41.

Ayres, Tony. "China Doll: The Experience of Being a Gay Chinese Australian." *Journal of Homosexuality* 36, no. 3/4 (1999): 87–97.

Azoulay, Katya. "Experience, Empathy and Strategic Essentialism." *Cultural Studies* 11, no. 1 (1997): 89–110.

Barthes, Roland. *Mythologies.* New York: Farrar, Strauss & Giroux, 1972.

Bartky, Sandra Lee. *Femininity and Domination: Studies in the Phenomenology of Oppression.* New York: Routledge, 1990.

Beam, Joseph. *In the Life: A Black Gay Anthology.* New York: Alyson, 1986.

Bedi, Sonu. "Sexual Racism: Intimacy as a Matter of Justice." *Journal of Politics* 77, no. 4 (2015): 998–1011.

Berg, Charles R. "Stereotyping in Films in General and of the Hispanic in Particular." *Howard Journal of Communications* 2, no. 3 (1990): 286–300.

Berger, James. *Ways of Seeing.* New York: Penguin, 1974.

Berger, Martin A. *Sight Unseen: Whiteness and American Visual Culture.* Berkeley: University of California Press, 2005.

Berlatsky, Noah. *Gays in the Military.* Detroit: Greenhaven, 2011.

Bérubé, Allan. "How Gay Stays White and What Kind of White It Stays." In *The Making and Unmaking of Whiteness,* edited by Birgit B. Rasmussen, Eric Klinenberg, Irene J. Nexica, and Matt Wray, 234–65. Durham, NC: Duke University Press, 2001.

Bonilla-Silva, Eduardo. "The Linguistics of Color Blind Racism: How to Talk Nasty about Blacks without Sounding 'Racist.'" *Critical Sociology* 28, no. 1/2 (2002): 41–64.

Bourdieu, Pierre. *Distinction: A Social Critique of the Judgement of Taste.* Cambridge, MA: Harvard University Press, 1984.

Brim, Matt, and Amin Ghaziani. "Introduction: Queer Methods." *Women's Studies Quarterly* 44, no. 3/4 (2016): 14–27.

Butler, Judith. *Bodies That Matter: On the Discursive Limits of Sex.* New York: Routledge, 1993.

Calabrese, Sarah K., Valerie A. Earnshaw, Manya Magnus, Nathan B. Hansen, Douglas S. Krakower, Kristen Underhill, Kenneth H. Mayer, Trace S. Kershaw, Joseph R. Betancourt, and John F. Dovidio. "Sexual Stereotypes Ascribed to Black Men Who Have Sex with Men: An Intersectional Analysis." *Archives of Sexual Behavior* 47, no. 1 (2017): 143–56.

Callander, Denton, Martin Holt, and Christy E. Newman. "Just a Preference: Racialised Language in the Sex-Seeking Profiles of Gay and Bisexual Men." *Culture, Health & Sexuality* 14, no. 9 (2012): 1049–63.

———. "'Not Everyone's Gonna Like Me': Accounting for Race and Racism in Sex and Dating Web Services for Gay and Bisexual Men." *Ethnicities* 16, no. 1 (2016): 3–21.

Callander, Denton, Christy E. Newman, and Martin Holt. "Is Sexual Racism Really Racism? Distinguishing Attitudes toward Sexual Racism and Generic Racism among Gay and Bisexual Men." *Archives of Sexual Behavior* 44, no. 7 (2015): 1991–2000.

Cascalheira, Cory J., and Brandt A. Smith. "Hiearchy of Desire: Partner Preferences and Social Identities of Men Who Have Sex with Men on Geosocial Networks." *Sexuality & Culture* 24, no. 3 (2020): 630–48.

Chan, Kenneth. "Rice Sticking Together: Cultural Nationalist Logic and Cinematic Representations of Gay Asian-Caucasian Relationships and Desire." *Discourse* 28, no. 2/3 (2006): 178–96.

Chaudhary, Nandita. *Listening to Culture: Constructing Reality from Everyday Talk*. Thousand Oaks, CA: Sage, 2004.

Choi, Kyung-Hee, Jay Paul, George Ayala, Ross Boylan, and Steven E. Gregorich. "Experiences of Discrimination and Their Impact on the Mental Health among African American, Asian and Pacific Islander, and Latino Men Who Have Sex with Men." *American Journal of Public Health* 103, no. 5 (2013): 868–74.

Chuang, Kent. "Using Chopsticks to Eat Steak." *Journal of Homosexuality* 36, no. 3/4 (1999): 77–92.

Clarke, Kevin A., and David M. Primo. *A Model Discipline: Political Science and the Logic of Representations*. London: Oxford University Press, 2012.

Collins, Patricia Hill. *Black Feminist Thought*. New York: Routledge, 1990.

———. *Black Sexual Politics: African Americans, Gender, and the New Racism*. New York: Routledge, 2005.

Crandall, Christian S., Amy Eshleman, and Laurie O'Brien. "Social Norms and the Expression and Suppression of Prejudice: The Struggle for Internalization." *Journal of Personality and Social Psychology* 82, no. 3 (2002): 359–78.

Crockett, Jason L. "Black and White Men Together: The Case of the Disappearing Organizational Narrative of Racial Sexual Orientation." *Making Connections: Interdisciplinary Approaches to Cultural Diversity* 16, no. 2 (2016): 88–116.

Cruz, Ariane. *The Color of Kink: Black Women, BDSM, and Pornography*. New York: New York University Press, 2016.

Dang, Alain, and Mandy Hu. *Asian Pacific American Lesbian, Gay, Bisexual and Transgender People: A Community Portrait*. New York: National Gay and Lesbian Task Force, 2005.

Daroya, Emerich. "Potatoes and Rice: Exploring the Racial Politics of Gay Men's Desire and Desirability." Master's thesis, Carleton University, 2011.

Diamond, Lisa M. "What Does Sexual Orientation Orient? A Biobehavioral Model Distinguishing Romantic Love and Sexual Desire." *Psychological Review* 110, no. 1 (2003): 173–92.

Due, Clemence. "'Aussie Humour' or Racism? Hey Hey It's Saturday and the Denial of Racism in Online Responses to News Media Articles." *Platform: Journal of Media and Communication* 3, no. 1 (2011): 36–53.

Durrheim, Kevin, Ross Greener, and Kevin A. Whitehead. "Race Trouble: Attending to Race and Racism in Online Interactions." *British Journal of Social Psychology* 54, no. 1 (2015): 84–99.

Dyer, Richard. *The Matter of Images: Essays on Representations*. New York: Routledge, 1993.

———. "The Matter of Whiteness." In *White Privilege: Essential Readings*, edited by Paula Rothenburg, 9–14. New York: Worth Publishers, 2005.

Ellingson, Stephen, Edward O. Laumann, Anthony Paik, and Jenna Mahay. "The Theory of Sex Markets." In *The Sexual Organization of the City*, edited by Edward O. Laumann, Stephen Elllingson, Jenna Mahay, Anthony Paik, and Yoosik Youm, 3–38. Chicago: University of Chicago Press, 2004.

Eng, David L. *Racial Castration: Making Masculinity in Asian America*. Durham, NC: Duke University Press, 2001.

Faccio, Elena, Claudia Cassini, and Sabrina Cipolletta. "Forbidden Games: The Construction of Sexuality and Sexual Pleasure by BDSM 'Players.'" *Culture, Health & Sexuality* 16, no. 7 (2014): 1–13.

Fairclough, Norman. *Critical Discourse Analysis: The Critical Study of Language*. London: Routledge, 2010.

Fanon, Frantz. *Black Skin, White Masks*. New York: Grove, 1970.

Feagin, Joe R. *The White Racial Frame: Centuries of Racial Framing and Counter-Framing*. New York: Routledge, 2009.

Ferguson, Roderick A. *Aberrations in Black: Toward a Queer of Color Critique*. Minneapolis: University of Minnesota Press, 2003.

Fung, Richard. "Looking for My Penis: The Eroticized Asian in Gay Video Porn." In *How Do I Look? Queer Film & Video*, edited by Bad Object Choices, 145–68, Seattle: Bay, 1991.

Gallently, Carol L., and Zita Lazzarini. "Charges for Criminal Exposure to HIV and Aggravated Prostitution Filed in the Nashville, Tennessee Prosecutorial Region 2000–2010. *AIDS and Behavior* 17, no. 8: 2624–36.

Gamson, William A., David Croteau, William Hoynes, and Theodore Sasson. "Media Images and the Social Construction of Reality." *Annual Review of Sociology* 18 (1992): 373–93.

Gates, Gary. *Demographics of Married and Unmarried Same-Sex Couples: Analysis of the 2013 American Community Survey*. Los Angeles: UCLA School of Law, the Williams Institute, 2015.

Gergen, Kenneth J., and Mary M. Gergen. "Narrative of the Self." In *Studies in Social Identity*, edited by Theodore R. Sarbin and Karl E. Scheibe, 254–73. New York: Praeger, 1983.

Goodman, Simon, and Shani Burke. "'Oh You Don't Want Asylum Seekers, Oh You're Just Racist': A Discursive Analysis of Discussions about Whether It's Racist to Oppose Asylum Seeking." *Discourse & Society* 21, no. 3 (2010): 235–340.

Green, Adam I. "Erotic Habitus: Towards a Sociology of Desire." *Theory and Society* 37, no. 6 (2008): 597–626.

———. "Playing the (Sexual) Field: The Interactional Basis of Systems of Sexual Stratification." *Social Psychology Quarterly* 74, no. 3 (2011): 244–66.

———. "The Social Organization of Desire." *Sociological Theory* 26, no. 1 (2008): 25–50.

Gubar, Susan. *Racechanges: White Skin, Black Face in American Culture*. New York: Oxford University Press, 2000.

Guzman, Manolo. *Gay Hegemony/Latino Homosexualities*. New York: Routledge, 2006.

Hadley-Garcia, George. *Hispanic Hollywood*. New York: Citadel, 1990.

Hall, Stuart. *Representations: Cultural Representations and Signifying Practices*. London: Open University Press, 1996.

Halperin, David M. *How to Be Gay*. Cambridge, MA: Harvard University Press, 2012.

———. "What Is Gay Male Femininity?" In *American Guy: Masculinity in American Law and Literature*, edited by Saul Levmore and Martha C. Nussbaum, 202–12. New York: Oxford University Press, 2014.

Han, C. Winter. *Geisha of a Different Kind: Race and Sexuality in Gaysian America*. New York: New York University Press, 2015.

Han, Chong-suk. "A Qualitative Exploration of the Relationship between Racism and Unsafe Sex among Asian Pacific Islander Gay Men." *Archives of Sexual Behavior* 37, no. 5 (2008): 827–37.

———. "One Gay Asian Body: A Personal Narrative for Examining Human Behavior in the Social Environment." *Journal of Human Behavior in the Social Environment* 20, no. 1 (2010): 74–87.

———. "They Don't Want to Cruise Your Type: Gay Men of Color and the Racial Politics of Exclusion." *Social Identities* 13, no. 1 (2007): 51–67.

Harper, Phillip B. "The Evidence of Felt Intuition: Minority Experience, Everyday Life, and Critical Speculative Knowledge." *GLQ: A Journal of Lesbian and Gay Studies* 6, no. 1 (2000): 641–57.

Hofman, Wilhelm, Hiroki P. Kotabe, Kathleen D. Vohs, and Roy F. Baumeister. "Desire and Desire Regulation." In *The Psychology of Desire*, edited by Wilhelm Hofman and Loran F. Nordgren, 61–81, New York: Guilford, 2015.

Holland, Sharon Patricia. *The Erotic Life of Racism*. Durham, NC: Duke University Press, 2012.

hooks, bell. *Black Looks: Race and Representation*. Boston: South End, 1992.

Huckin, Thomas. "Critical Discourse Analysis." In *Functional Approaches to Written Text: Classroom Applications*, edited by Tom Miller, 78–92. Washington, DC: United States Information Agency, 1997.

Husbands, Winston, Lydia Makoroka, Rinaldo Walcott, and Sean B. Rourke. "Black Gay Men as Sexual Subjects: Race, Racialization and the Social Relations of Sex among Black Gay Men in Toronto." *Culture, Health & Sexuality* 15, no. 4 (2013): 434–49.

Ibañez, Gladys E., Barbara Van Oss Marin, Stephen A. Flores, Gregorio Millett, and Rafael M. Diaz. "General and Gay-Related Racism Experienced by Latino

Gay Men." *Cultural Diversity and Ethnic Minority Psychology* 15, no. 3 (2009): 215–22.

Jackson, Peter A. "That's What Rice Queens Study! White Gay Desire and Representing Asian Homosexualities." *Journal of Australian Studies* 24, no. 65 (2000): 181–88.

Jacobsen, Rockney. "Arousal and the End of Desire." *Philosophy and Phenomenological Research* 53, no. 3 (1993): 617–32.

——. "Desire, Sexual." In *Sex from Plato to Pagalia: A Philosophical Encyclopedia*, edited by Alan Soble, 222–28. Westport, CT: Greenwood, 2006.

Jagger, Elizabeth. "Is Thirty the New Sixty? Dating, Age and Gender in Postmodern, Consumer Society." *Sociology* 39, no. 1 (2005): 89–106.

Jordan, L. Lloyd. "Black Gay vs. Gay Black." *BLK* 2, no. 6 (1990): 25–30.

Kastanis, Angeliki, and Bianca D. M. Wilson. *Race/Ethnicity, Gender and Socioeconomic Wellbeing of Individuals in Same-Sex Couples.* Los Angeles: UCLA School of Law, the Williams Institute, 2014.

Kaufman, Gayle, and Voon Chin Phua. "Is Ageism Alive in Dating Selection among Men? Age Requests among Gay and Straight Men in Internet Personal Ads." *Journal of Men's Studies* 11, no. 2 (2003): 225–35.

Kiesling, Elena. "The Missing Colors of the Rainbow: Black Queer Resistance." *European Journal of American Studies* 11, no. 3 (2017): 1–21.

Kovel, Joel. *White Racism: A Psychohistory.* New York: Pantheon, 1970.

Laumann, Edward O., Stephen Ellingson, Jenna Mahay, and Anthony Paik, eds. *The Sexual Organization of the City.* Chicago: University of Chicago Press, 2004.

Lester, Neal A., and Maureen Daly Goggin. "In Living Color: Politics of Desire in Heterosexual Interracial Black/White Personal Ads." *Communication and Critical/Cultural Studies* 2, no. 2 (2015): 130–62.

Lick, David J., and Kerri L. Johnson. "Intersecting Race and Gender Cues Are Associated with Perceptions of Gay Men's Preferred Sexual Roles." *Archives of Sexual Behavior* 44, no. 5 (2015): 1471–81.

Lipsitz, George. *The Possessive Investment in Whiteness: How White People Profit from Identity Politics.* Philadelphia: Temple University Press, 1998.

Livingston, Gretchen, and Anna Brown. "Intermarriage in the U.S. 50 Years after Loving v. Virginia." *Pew Research Center*, May 18, 2017. www.pew socialtrends.org/2017/05/18/intermarriage-in-the-u-s-50-years-after-loving -v-virginia.

Logan, Trevon D. "Personal Characteristics, Sexual Behavior, and Male Sex Work: A Quantitative Approach." *American Sociological Review* 75, no. 5 (2010): 679–704.

Lorde, Audre, *Sister Outsider: Essays and Speeches.* Berkeley: Crossing, 1984.

Lundquist, Jennifer H., and Ken-Lou Lin. "Is Love (Color) Blind? The Economy of Race among Gay and Straight Daters." *Social Forces* 93, no. 4 (2015): 1423–99.

Martin, John L., and Matt George. "Theories of Sexual Stratification: Toward an Analytics of the Sexual Field and a Theory of Sexual Capital." *Sociological Theory* 24, no. 2 (2006): 107–32.

Mason-Schrock, Douglas. "Transsexuals' Narrative Construction of the 'True Self.'" *Social Psychology Quarterly* 59, no. 3 (1996): 176–92.

McBride, Dwight. *Why I Hate Abercrombie & Fitch: Essays on Race and Sexuality.* New York: New York University Press, 2005.

———. "Why I Hate That I Loved Brokeback Mountain." *GLQ: A Journal of Lesbian and Gay Studies* 13, no. 1 (2007): 95–97.

Miller-Young, Mireille. *A Taste for Brown Sugar: Black Women in Pornography.* Durham, NC: Duke University Press, 2014.

Mora, Richard. "Abjection and the Cinematic Cholo: The Chicano Gang Stereotype in Sociohistoric Context." *Boyhood Studies* 5, no. 2 (2011): 124–37.

Morgan, Elizabeth M., Tamara C. Richards, and Emily M. VanNess. "Comparing Narratives of Personal and Preferred Partner Characteristics in Online Dating Advertisements." *Computers in Human Behavior* 26, no. 5 (2010): 883–88.

Morgensen, Scott Lauria. *Spaces between Us: Queer Settler Colonialism and Indigenous Decolonization.* Minneapolis: University of Minnesota Press, 2011.

Moscovici, Serge. "Forward." In *Health and Illness: A Social Psychological Analysis,* edited by Claudine Herzlich, ix–xiv. London: Academic Press, 1973.

Muñoz, José Esteban. *Disidentifications: Queers of Color and the Performance of Politics.* Minneapolis: University of Minnesota Press, 1999.

Muñoz-Laboy, Miguel, and Nicolette Severson. "Exploring the Role of Race, Ethnicity, Nationality, and Skin Color in the Sexual Partner Choices of Bisexual Latino Men." *Archives of Sexual Behavior* 47, no. 4 (2017): 1231–39.

Nagel, Joan. *Race, Ethnicity, and Sexuality: Intimate Intersections, Forbidden Frontiers.* London: Oxford University Press, 2003.

Nash, Jennifer C. *The Black Body in Ecstasy: Reading Race, Reading Pornography.* Durham, NC: Duke University Press, 2014.

Neal, Jarrett. "Let's Talk about Interracial Porn." *Gay and Lesbian Review Worldwide* 20, no. 4 (2013): 23–26.

Nguyen, Tan Hoang. *A View from the Bottom: Asian American Masculinity and Sexual Representation.* Durham, NC: Duke University Press, 2014.

Ocampo, Anthony C. "Making Masculinity: Negotiations of Gender Presentation among Latino Gay Men." *Latino Studies* 10, no. 4 (2012): 448–72.

Orne, Jason. *Boystown.* Chicago: University of Chicago Press, 2017.

Owens, Erica, and Brownwyn Beistle. "Eating the Black Body: Interracial Desire, Food Metaphor and White Fear." In *Body/Embodiment: Symbolic Interaction and the Sociology of the Body*, edited by Dennis Waskul and Phillip Vannini, 201–11. Aldershot, UK: Ashgate, 2006.

Park, Yoosun. "Culture as Deficit: A Critical Discourse Analysis of the Concept of Culture in Contemporary Social Work Discourse." *Journal of Sociology and Social Welfare* 32, no. 2 (2005): 13–34.

Paul, Jay P., George Ayala, and Kyung-Hee Choi. "Internet Sex Ads for MSM and Partner Selection Criteria: The Potency of Race/Ethnicity Online." *Journal of Sex Research* 47, no. 6 (2010): 528–38.

Perez, Hiram. *A Taste for Brown Bodies: Gay Modernity and Cosmopolitan Desires*. New York: New York University Press.

Phillips, Gregory, Michelle Birkett, Sydney Hammond, and Brian Mustanski. "Partner Preference among Men Who Have Sex with Men: Potential Contribution to Spread of HIV within Minority Populations." *LGBT Health* 3, no. 3 (2003): 225–32.

Phua, Voon Chin, and Gayle Kaufman. "The Crossroads of Race and Sexuality: Date Selection among Men in Internet 'Personal' Ads." *Journal of Family Issues* 24, no. 8 (2003): 981–94.

Poon, Maurice K., and Peter T. Ho. "Negotiating Social Stigma among Gay Asian Men." *Sexualities* 11, no. 1/2 (2008); 245–68.

Puar, Jasbir K. *Terrorist Assemblages: Heteronationalism in Queer Times*. Durham, NC: Duke University Press, 2007.

Quillian, Lincoln, and Devah Pager. "Estimating Risk: Stereotype Amplification and the Perceived Risk of Criminal Victimization." *Social Psychology Quarterly* 73, no. 1 (2011): 79–104.

Rafalow, Matthew H., Cynthia Feliciano, and Belinda Robnett. "Racialized Femininity and Masculinity in the Preference of Online Same-Sex Daters." *Social Currents* 4, no. 4 (2017): 306–21.

Raymond, H. Fisher, and Willi McFarland. "Racial Mixing and HIV Risk among Men Who Have Sex with Men." *AIDS and Behavior* 13, no. 4 (2009): 630–37.

Reynolds, Chelsea. "'I Am Super Straight and I Prefer You Be Too': Constructions of Heterosexual Masculinity in Online Personal Ads for 'Straight' Men Seeking Sex with Men." *Journal of Communication Inquiry* 39, no. 3 (2015): 213–31.

Riggs, Damien W., and Clemence Due. "The Management of Racism in Celebrity Big Brother." *Discourse & Society* 21, no. 3 (2010): 257–71.

Riggs, Marlon, dir. *Tongues Untied*. 1989; San Francisco: Frameline and California Newsreel, 2008. DVD.

Rios, Victor. *Punished: Policing the Lives of Black and Latino Boys.* New York: New York University Press, 2011.

Risman, Barbara, and Pepper Schwartz. "Sociological Research on Male and Female Homosexuality." *Annual Review of Sociology* 14 (1988): 125–47.

Robinson, Brandon. "'Personal Preference' As the New Racism: Gay Desire and Racial Cleansing in Cyberspace." *Sociology of Race and Ethnicity* 1, no. 2 (2015): 317–30.

Robinson, Russell K. "Structural Dimensions of Romantic Preferences." *Fordham Law Review* 86, no. 6 (2008): 2787–819.

Robinson, Russell K., and David M. Frost. "LGBT Equality and Sexual Racism." *Fordham Law Review* 86, no. 6 (2018): 2739–54.

Ronny, Tikkanen, and Michael W. Ross. "Technological Tearoom Trade: Characteristics of Swedish Men Visiting Gay Internet Chat Rooms." *AIDS Education and Prevention* 15, no. 2 (2003): 122–32.

Rosenberg, Rae. "The Whiteness of Gay Urban Belonging: Criminalizing LGBTQ Youth of Color in Queer Spaces of Care." *Urban Geography* 38, no. 1 (2017): 137–48.

Ross, James D. "Personal Ads and the Intersection of Race and Same-Sex Male Attraction." In *Racialized Politics of Desire in Personal Ads*, edited by Neal A. Lester and Maureen Daly Goggin, 97–111. Lanham, MD: Lexington, 2008.

Rosser, Simon B. R., Michael Wilerson, Derek J. Smolenski, J. Michael Oaks, Joseph Konstan, Keith J. Horvath, Gunna R. Kilian, David S. Novak, Gene P. Danilenko, and Richard Morgan. "The Future of Internet-Based HIV Prevention: A Report on Key Findings from the Men's INTernet (MINTS-1, II) Sex Studies." *AIDS and Behavior* 15, no. S1 (2011): S89–S100.

Said, Edward. *Orientalism.* New York: Pantheon, 1978.

Scott, Darieck. "Jungle Fever? Black Gay Identity Politics, White Dick, and the Utopian Bedroom." *GLQ: A Journal of Lesbian and Gay Studies* 1, no. 3 (1994): 299–321.

Segal, Lynne. *Slow Motion: Changing Masculinities Changing Men.* New Brunswick, NJ: Rutgers University Press, 1990.

Seidman, Steven. *Contested Knowledge: Social Theory Today.* Malden, MA: Wiley Blackwell, 2017.

Smith, Jesús Gregorio. "The Crime of Black Male Sexuality: Tiger Mandingo and Black Male Vulnerability." In *Home and Community for Queer Men of Color*, edited by Jesús Gregorio Smith and C. Winter Han, 149–72. Lanham, MD: Lexington, 2020.

———. "Two-Faced Racism in Gay Online Sex." In *Sex in the Digital Age*, edited by Paul G. Nixon and Isabel K. Dusterhoft, 134–46, New York: Routledge, 2017.

Somerville, Siobhan B. *Queering the Color Line: Race and the Invention of Homosexuality in American Culture.* Durham, NC: Duke University Press, 2000.

Sommers, Samuel R., and Michael I. Norton. "Lay Theories about White Racists: What Constitutes Racism (and What Doesn't)." *Group Processes and Intergroup Relations* 9, no. 1 (2006): 117–38.

Spivak, Gayatri Chakravorty. "Can the Subaltern Speak?" In *Marxism and the Interpretation of Cultures,* edited by Cary Nelson and Lawrence Greenberg, 271–313. Chicago: University of Illinois Press, 1988.

Stember, Chalres H. *Sexual Racism: The Emotional Barrier to an Integrated Society.* New York: Elsevier, 1976.

Subero, Gustavo. "Gay Male Pornography and the Re/De/construction of Postcolonial Queer Identity in Mexico." *New Cinemas: Journal of Contemporary Film* 8, no. 2 (2010): 119–36.

Teunis, Niels. "Sexual Objectification and the Construction of Whiteness in the Gay Male Community." *Culture, Health & Sexuality* 9, no. 3 (2007): 263–75.

Thai, Michael. "Sexual Racism Is Associated with Lower Self-Esteem and Life Satisfaction in Men Who Have Sex with Men." *Archives of Sexual Behavior* 49 (2020): 347–53.

Tsui, Philip. "Power and Intimacy: Caucasian/Asian Gay Relationships as an Indicator of Self-Oppression among Gay Asian Males." *Journal of the Asian American Psychological Association* (1986): 59–61.

van Dijk, Teun. "Discourse and the Denial of Racism." *Discourse & Society* 3, no. 1 (1992): 87–118.

Van Leeuwen, Theo. "Genre and Field in Critical Discourse Analysis: A Synopsis." *Discourse & Society* 4, no. 2 (1993): 193–223.

Vance, Carol. "Social Construction Theory: Problems in the History of Sexuality." In *Sexualities: Making a Sociology of Sexualities,* edited by Kenneth Plummer, 356–71. London: Routledge, 2001.

Wacquant, Loïc. "Pierre Bourdieu." In *Key Sociological Thinkers,* edited by Rob Stones, 215–29. London: Macmillan Education, 1998.

West, Cornel. *Race Matters.* New York: Vintage, 1993.

Whittier, David K., and William Simon. "The Fuzzy Matrix of 'My Type' in Intrapsychic Sexual Scripting." *Sexualities* 4, no. 2 (2001): 139–65.

Wilson, Charles E. "Black Gay Men Seeking Black Gay Men: Cultural and Historical Implications." In *Racialized Politics of Desire in Personal Ads,* edited by Neal A. Lester and Maureen Daly Goggin, 77–96. New York: Lexington, 2007.

Wilson, Patrick A., Pamela Valera, Ana Ventuneac, Ivan Balan, Matt Rowe, and Alex Carballo-Diéguez. "Race-Based Sexual Stereotyping and Sexual

Partnering among Men Who Use the Internet to Identify Other Men for Bareback Sex." *Journal of Sex Research* 46, no. 5 (2009): 399–413.

Withers, Erik T. "Whiteness and Culture." *Sociology Compass* 11, no. 4 (2016): 1–11.

Wu, Cynthia. *Sticky Rice: A Politics of Intraracial Desire*. Philadelphia: Temple University Press, 2018.

INDEX

Criss, Darren, 70
critical discourse analysis, 24–25
critical race theory, 23
Cruz, Ariane, 106
Cruz, Eliel, 161, 163, 165
cultural products, 63, 64
cultural sexual racism, 39

D'Amico, Antonio, 70
Daroya, Emerich, 20, 63
Dawson, Lamar, 154
Dear White People, 154
denial of racism: in contemporary
    society, 114–15; examples of, 116–18;
    individual kindness as, 175–76; as
    reproduction of racism, 115–16; and
    sexual racism, 119–23; by white gay
    men, 181–82
denial of racism, tactics of: blaming men
    of color, 126–27; claiming victim-
    hood, 123–25; defining racism nar-
    rowly, 119–21; minority homophobe
    myth, 127–28; misogyny comparison,
    136–37; naturalization of sexual attrac-
    tion, 134–37; "PC Bullshit" claim,
    122–23; reverse racism claim, 125;
    "some of my best friends" claim, 131–
    34; victim blaming, 129–31
DePiano, Darryl, 13
desirability: and class, 35; and disidenti-
    fication, 30; and race, 8, 9, 10, 35, 39;
    rejecting dominant definitions of,
    30, 148–49, 171, 182; in sexual fields,
    35–36, 37; and sexual racism, 8; of
    white gay men, 70, 78; of whiteness,
    40–44, 55–56, 77, 179
desire: equation of with whiteness, 5,
    7, 10, 141; naturalization of, 181–82;
    as political resistance, 173; and race,
    39–40; and sexual racism, 55; socio-
    logical studies of, 19–20; structural
    factors contributing to, 19–20, 21, 61,
    78; and whiteness, 7, 24, 60, 68–69

desire/pleasure distinction, 20–21, 106,
    186
deviant sexuality: ascribed to men of
    color, 17, 18, 60; ascribed to non-
    white people, 16
Dijk, Teun van, 116
disidentification, 29–30, 184
Disidentifications (Muñoz), 29
Douchebags of Grindr, 7, 33, 174
down low trope, 152
Dyer, Richard, 64, 77, 177

economic justice, 6, 11
8Asians, 171
Emmerich, Roland, 59, 77
Eng, David, 16–17
erotic capital: characteristics of, 63; and
    class, 20, 34, 63; and erotic habitus,
    20, 63; in gay media, 70, 71; of gay
    men of color, 32, 45; and race, 37; and
    structural factors, 20, 131; of white
    gay men, 60, 69, 70, 131; and white-
    ness, 7–8, 20, 42–43, 63, 67, 146
erotic habitus: definition of, 20, 61; and
    erotic capital, 20, 63; of gay bars, 68–
    69; influence of gay media on, 26, 61,
    64, 79; vs. personal preference, 62
Ethnic Minority Men's Study, 25
Evans, Thom, 72

Falahee, Jack, 74
Falling for Angels, 163
Fanon, Frantz, 91
Ferguson, Roderick, 16
fetishization: of Asian gay men, 50–51,
    52, 70, 72–73, 75–76; of Black gay
    men, 44–45, 47, 73, 80–82; of gay men
    of color, 5, 7, 8–9, 37, 55, 105, 156–57,
    164; in gay pornography, 81–82; in
    intraracial relationships, 148–49; of
    Latino gay men, 46, 83; in online
    personal ads, 90–104; and racialized
    desires, 17–18; resistance to, 149

71; representations of men of color in, 69–70; trivialization of racism in, 109–10. See also *Advocate*; *LGBTQ Nation*; *Queerty*

Geisha of a Different Kind (Han), 36, 106

gender: and interracial desire, 81; intersection of with race, 86; and racialized desires, 186; and representations of men of color, 80–87

gender non-conformity: ascribed to men of color, 17; ascribed to non-white people, 16

Gettinger, Aaron, 163

Gibbs, Jonathan, 157–58

GLAAD. *See* Gay and Lesbian Alliance Against Defamation

GLQ, 144

Gmojiz, 58

Godard, Jean-Luc, 77

"good gay," the: and assimilation, 17, 178; construction of, 184; and gay media, 60; and homonationalism, 16; and racialized desire, 16; and whiteness, 16, 17, 176

Grand, Steve, 71

Grand Central bar, 12

Green, Adam Isaiah, 19, 34, 35, 38, 61–62

Greene, Theo, 140

Grindr: class action lawsuit against, 139–40; denial of racism by, 175; Kindr initiative, 174–75; racist comments on, 7, 33, 139, 163

Gross, Michael Joseph, 114

grounded theory approach, 28

Guardian, 59, 140, 167

Gubar, Susan, 82

Guzman, Manolo, 144, 147, 162

habitus, 61, 62–64

Hall, Stuart, 18

Halperin, David, 67

Harper, Phillip Brian, 23

Haskell, James, 71

Helligar, Jeremy, 152–53, 155–56

Henney, Daniel, 76

Henry, Phillip, 163

heteronormativity, 16, 17, 59, 66, 177

hierarchy of desire: construction of, 20, 26, 29, 142; and erotic capital, 21, 34, 176, 181; and interracial relationships, 156–57, 170; navigation of by men of color, 41–42, 44; negative consequences of, 48–52, 55, 180; normalization of, 105; and norm of whiteness, 122, 176; and preference for white men, 131, 172; resistance to, 29, 149, 172, 182; and sexual expectations, 88; and sexual racism, 140, 34, 126; and sexual rejection, 78–79

HIV: and criminalization, 18; and sexual racism, 13–14

Holland, Sharon Patricia, 56, 105

Hombres Latinos, 6

homonationalism, 16, 184

homonormativity, 60, 152

homophobia: and denial of racism, 138; as justification for racism, 128; minority homophobe myth, 28, 58, 113, 127–29, 152–53

hooks, bell, 8

Hornet, 162

"Hot or Not: Shemar Moore" article, on *Adam4Adam Blog*, 76

How to Bottom Like a Porn Star (Alvear), 81

How to Get Away with Murder, 74

HRC. *See* Human Rights Campaign

Huffington Post, 152, 156

Human Rights Campaign, 36, 58

Hynes, Devonté, 69

images: interpretation of, 64–65, 67; used by gay bars, 69–70; and white privilege, 69

"I'm grateful to be gay" article, on *Slate*, 111–12

role of white gay men in, 114; and sexual racism, 9

racialized desires: creation and maintenance of, 171, 176, 179; and fetishization, 17, 18, and the "good gay," 16; on Grindr, 33; naturalization of, 132–33, 154; in online personal ads, 91–104; vs. personal preference, 9, 16, 78, 154–55, 156; and structural factors, 165–66

racial justice, 168

racism: attributed to gay men of color, 113; as behavioral vs. structural, 117, 134, 136, 137, 174–75; contemporary forms of, 114–16, 137; definitions of, 3, 183; experiences of, 49, 52; in gay spaces, 12–13, 44; on Grindr, 33; and interracial relationships, 90; naturalization of, 18

Red Dragon bar, 6

Red Table Talk, 152

reverse racism, 117–18, 123, 125, 155–56

Ricamora, Conrad, 74

rice queens, 145–46, 156

Riggs, Marlon, 10

Rippon, Adam, 67

Risman, Barbara, 19

Robinson, Nick, 177

RuPaul, 58, 69

Saint John, Jesse, 57

Sam, Michael, 70, 127

San Francisco Entertainment Commission, 11

San Francisco Human Rights Commission, 11

San Francisco Weekly, 170

Savage, Dan, 113–14

Schwartz, Pepper, 19

Scott, Darieck, 144

Segal, Lynne, 90

Sense8, 74

sexual behaviors: and norm of whiteness, 75, 87, 105, 179; in sexual fields, 38;

and sexual stereotypes, 45–47, 88–89; studies of, 27, 183

sexual fields: characteristics valued in, 34–35; definition of, 34; and gay aesthetics, 43–44; interactional processes in, 38; navigation of, 44–47; race in, 35–36, 37; and structural factors, 35, 54–56

sexual racism: definition of, 7–8, 39, 140; denial of, 119–20, 125, 127, 129–30, 131–34; and exclusion of queer people of color, 12, 18; experiences of, 49–50; and gay media, 7, 25; in gay spaces, 12–13; on gay websites, 119; on Grindr, 174–75; and hierarchy of desire, 9, 126, 140; as individual vs. structural, 126; and invisibility, 18; negative impact of, 9, 14, 48–52, 55, 176; and norm of whiteness, 34; vs. personal preference, 9, 120; and preference for white men, 130, 140; and rates of HIV, 13–14; resistance to, 26, 28–29, 52–54; and white supremacy, 9

Sexual Racism (Stember), 7–8

sexual rejection, 7, 8, 140, 142

sexual stereotypes: of Asian gay men, 95–100; of Asian men, 86; of Black gay men, 91–92; of Black men, 86; enactment of as resistance, 30; and intraracial desire, 146–49; and norm of whiteness, 179–80; in online personal ads, 89

sex work, 84, 85

Shah, Nayan, 87

Shears, Jake, 65

Simien, Justin, 154–55

Slate, 111

slavery: and hypersexualization of Black men, 82, 84; and race play, 9

Smith, Jada Pinkett, 152

Smollett, Jussie, 70

sociology: and construction of the Black other, 16; empiricism in, 22–23;

sociology (*continued*)
"structure or agency" debate, 62; studies of sexuality in, 19, 61, 183–84; treatment of narratives in, 22
Sontag, Susan, 39
speculative reasoning, 23–24
Spivak, Gayatri Chakravorty, 148
Splinter, 67
Stafford, Zach, 167–68
Stember, Charles H., 7–8
sticky rice, 149
Stonewall film, 59, 77
Stonewall riots, 59
straight acting trope, 59, 66
straight audiences, 59–60
straight cisgender white men: representation of in gay media, 58–59, 69, 71
strategic essentialism, 148
structural factors: and desire, 61, 173, 183–84; and erotic capital, 131; and personal preference, 62–63; and racism, 115, 117–18, 134, 136, 174–76; in sexual fields, 35, 55
structural racism, 115, 138, 175
structural sexual racism, 39

Tatum, Channing, 71
#TeamSwirl, 157
The Body Is Not an Apology, 146
The L.A. Complex, 74
Them, 163
"The New Queer Black Male" article, in *Out* magazine, 69
The Stranger, 113
Thompson, Rickey, 69
Tiger Mandingo. *See* Johnson, Michael
Tongues United, 10
tops: Black gay men as, 85, 91–95; Latino gay men as, 85, 103–4; white gay men as, 75, 95–98
Towle, Andy, 66
Towlroad, 66

trans women, 11
Trott, Donovan, 156

Urban League of Atlanta, 109, 110

Valentino, Rudolph, 85
Vartian, Aram, 67
Versace, Gianni, 70
Vice, 164
Vittal, Reneysh, 150, 151
Voodoo Lounge bar, 6

Walker, John, 58, 69
Wang, Alexander, 70
Ware, Avery, 170–71, 172
Warren, Rick, 129
Washington Post, 164
Wells, Veronica, 152
West, Cornel, 91
Wheeler, André-Naquian, 164
white gay men: claiming of victimhood by, 123–24, 126, 127; denial of racism by, 109, 111–12, 113–14, 131–34; erotic capital of, 67, 131, 179; fetishization by, 34–35, 81–82, 148–49, 164; and interracial relationships, 150–51; normalization of, 60–61, 73, 75, 78, 80–81, 87; power in bargaining sexual activity, 45–46; preference for white men by, 140–41; racism of, 33, 163, 168–69; representations of in pornography, 77; self-portrayal of, 93–94; sexual racism of, 34, 119, 130, 131, 137; voting patterns of, 114
white gaze, 30, 168
white men: sexual stereotypes about, 86
whiteness: centrality of to gay desire, 7, 68–69; conflation of gayness with, 5, 6–7, 18–19; construction of, 16; desirablity of, 40–41, 60–61, 156–57; as erotic currency, 7, 8, 20, 34, 42–43, 69, 146; and the "good gay," 16, 17;

ABOUT THE AUTHOR

C. Winter Han, also known as Chong-suk Han, is associate professor of sociology at Middlebury College. He is the author of *Geisha of a Different Kind: Race and Sexuality in Gaysian America* (NYU Press, 2015) and coeditor of *Home and Community for Queer Men of Color* (Lexington Books, 2020). Prior to becoming an academic, he was an award-winning journalist and served as the editor of the *International Examiner*, the oldest continuously publishing pan-Asian Pacific American newspaper in the United States.